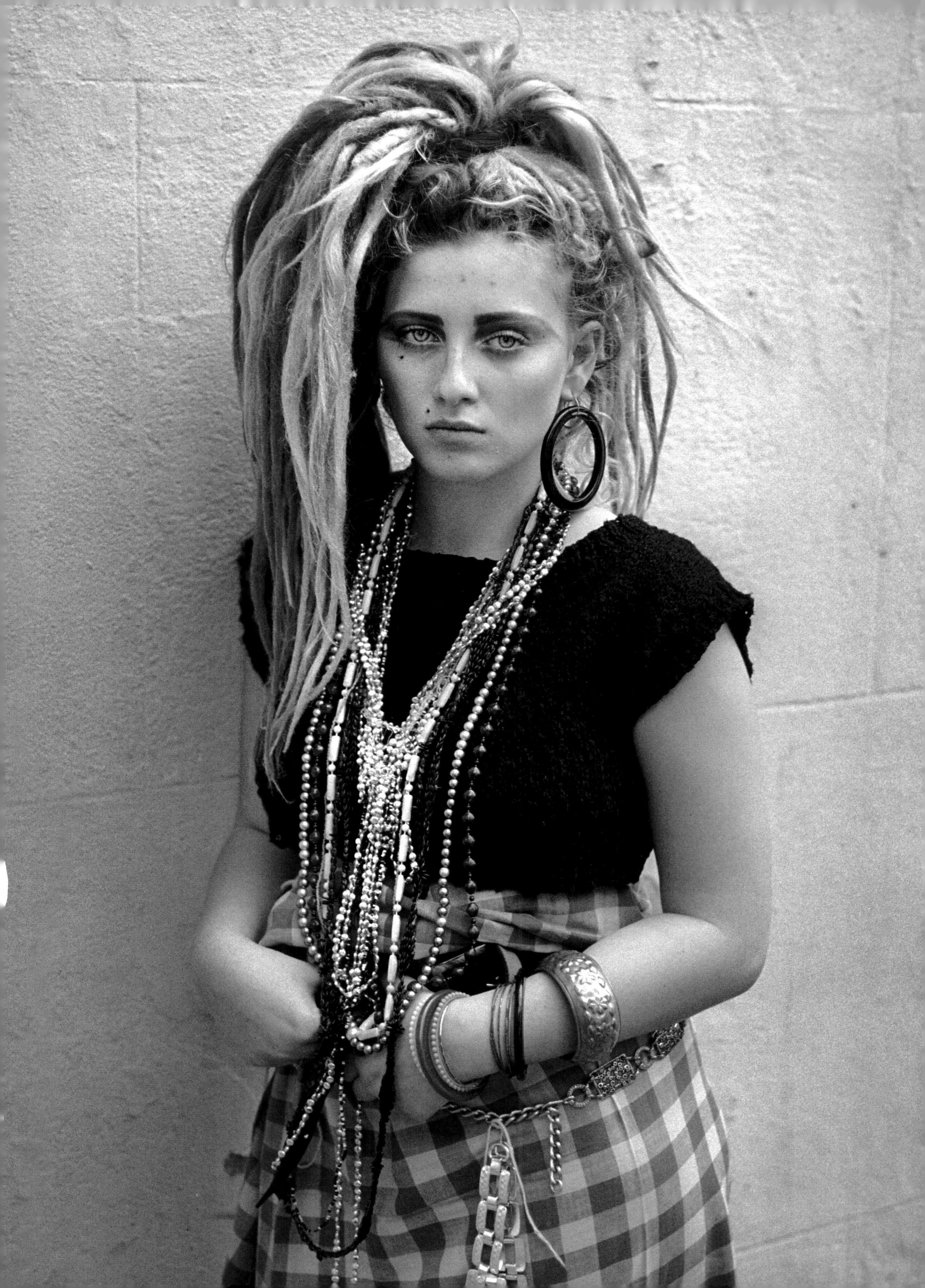

A catalogue record for this book is available from the British Library.

First Edition 2017
First published in Great Britain in 2017 by Carpet Bombing Culture.
An imprint of Pro-actif Communications
www.carpetbombingculture.co.uk
email: books@carpetbombingculture.co.uk

CARPET BOMBING CULTURE

www.carpetbombingculture.co.uk

in the eighties

Portraits from another time
by Derek Ridgers

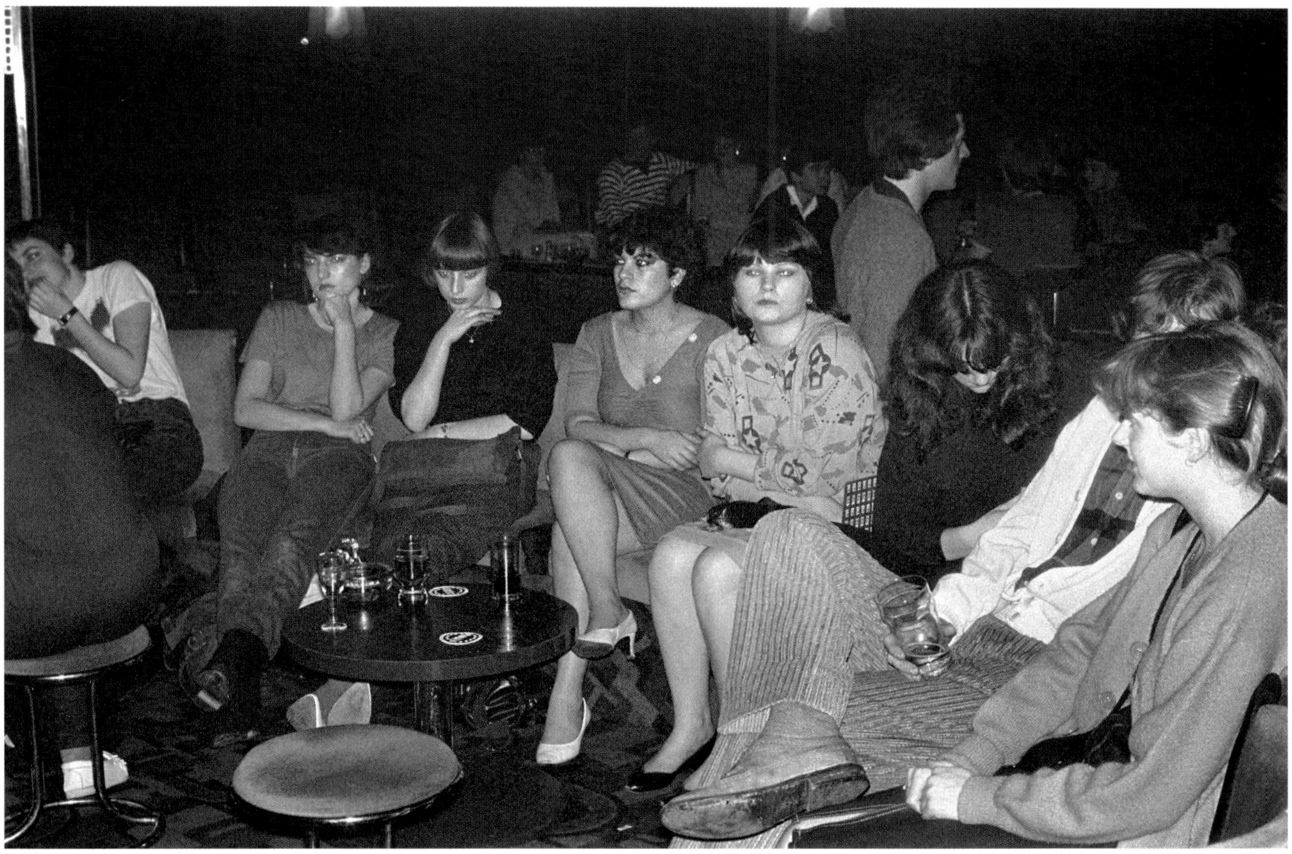

THE LAST DECADE

The 1950s invented the Teenager and Moral Panic. The 1960s brought the Teen Subculture. The 1970s saw youth style tribes diversify. The 1980s saw the youth subculture explode into pieces as pop began to eat itself. By the end of the 1990s Youth Culture was no longer Subculture, it had burned itself like the phoenix to rise again as the whole ideology of western society. Youth became the whole point. Of everything.

SUBCULTURE BECAME CULTURE

The first big subculture in the UK was the Teddy Boys in 1950s London. Their uniquely British response to the explosion of Rock & Roll was to imitate the Edwardian style of dress. They rebelled against post-war austerity by publicly breaking the rules on rationing fabric with their long coats.

In the 1960s the story continued with the Hippies, Mods and the Rockers, big style tribes representing different ideas as well as looks. Then in the 1970s there was Disco, early Hip-Hop and Punk. These were the Big Subcultures but even as they flowered they began to splinter off into different variations.

Then in the 1980s this breaking down into smaller and smaller youth tribes continued even further. Big, solid, boring identities gave way to little, ephemeral, fascinating ones. Youth cultural styles proliferated. Young people finally became scene surfers, eclectic individuals browsing an endless supermarket of street styles.

This collection of photographs captures some of the rich multiplicity of identity games that young people were playing in the UK during the 1980s. It was a different time, perhaps even the precise moment in which our current world was born. In 1980 young people looked forwards towards immense uncertainty, by 1990 it seemed like things could only get better.

After 1990 the idea of decades ceased to be relevant. Why? Because to brutally oversimplify: we chose individual freedom over class struggle.

By 1987 the battle for socialism in the UK was over, although it has taken thirty years to measure the cost of that. The opposing forces in this struggle both appeared to the youth of the day as conservative. Paternal Trade Unionists vs Patriarchal Politicians. No wonder young people chose neither.

As the Berlin Wall fell, all the young people could say is this: 'We don't know what we want but we don't want politics.' The wind of change may have been blowing but they didn't ask where. They talked a lot about freedom, of course. They all wanted to escape from history.

This drama of mass identity versus individual identity played out as much in the youth cultures of the decade as in the miners' strike, the two recessions and the mass transfer of state properties into private hands, known as Thatcherism.

All the style tribes and their myriad sub-groups represented stances and attitudes towards the political backdrop. Even and especially sub-cultures that seem to be purely escapist - tell a rich story about what they were trying to escape. Youth unemployment was high throughout the decade. Teenagers' wages were very low. There was not the 24 hour youth culture machine that there is now. The world then was not made for young people. Young people were still outsiders by virtue of their age bracket alone.

The 1980s was the last political decade. It was certainly the last decade in which young people could pose with a book of Marx and expect to get laid and even then only in Liverpool. Nobody in the 1990s was Political with a capital P. What happened was a disintegration of big political narratives into a plethora of single issue identity struggles.

Without a blueprint for a brave new world the left was left with nothing but snark and opposition. The 1980s was a golden age for political satire in Britain. There was a new sense of freedom to say whatever you like about the powerful, but it had absolutely no affect on their power.

IT'S ALL ABOUT IDENTITY

Journalist Adam Curtis has called the 20th Century 'The Century of Self'. This is not simply a puritanical attack on 'selfishness' whatever that might be - but a look at how the idea of identity changed with the advances of lifestyle marketing. This was intrinsically tied up with the revolutionary subcultures of the 1960s. As Thomas Frank demonstrated in 'Conquest of Cool' corporate culture walked hand in hand with the counter culture right from the start.

In order to sell more stuff two key developments happened in the 1980s. The proliferation of new identities was harnessed to create 'target markets'. The explosion of youth culture was as much driven by this factor as by any DIY subcultural movement. The second big change was the massive extension of credit. People didn't borrow money to go shopping in 1980. In 1990, everybody from 18 up had a credit card. How much of the money spent in youth culture meccas like Camden Market cames from overdrafts, credit cards and student loans?

The more the youth attempted to escape the grim reality of 1980s life through identity games, the more they fed into this new lifestyle marketing machine. At the beginning of the decade Punk was already little more than an off-the-shelf product. The New Romantics, being a group of arty students, were well aware of the relationship between subcultures, the media and capital. Many segued from youth rebellion into lucrative career paths. All this was a far cry from naive hippies who genuinely hoped to live 'outside of society'.

If there is something utopian about this multiplicity of outsider poses, perhaps it is that the desire for a more playful society burgeoned in the 1980s. Times of great conflict are often times of intense creativity. That flourishing of 100 schools of forbidden desires can too easily be dismissed as Thatcherite greed - but wasn't it also a reaching for a society built around pleasure and play?

In a decade characterised by inner city decay, riots, rising poverty, strikes, far right activism, and on the top of it all an all-powerful leader proclaiming that there was no such thing as society and people were poor because they were lazy* - escape into hedonism seems a fair choice.

*Not to mention the Falklands, the IRA, The Yorkshire Ripper, Maradona's 'Hand of God', the Cold War, Clause 48, Hillsborough, Mary Whitehouse, Roland Rat and Mullets.

In 1982 there was a real feeling that society could be torn apart. Britain was intensely divided. In the end it was not torn apart but simply dissolved. All that was solid melted into air. Something about Thatcherite ideology seemed to offer more individual freedom, and we wanted that so much that we were willing to ignore the price tag attached to it. We wanted to be fun, exciting, dynamic people playing out fascinating individual life stories - not grim faced and morally pure revolutionaries proud to be exactly like everybody else in our metaphorical village. We wanted to be flawed adventurers not doomed romantics.

An honest day's work for an honest day's pay? Bollocks. 24 Hour Party People? Yes mate.

And so here we are, in a society where we can dip into any cultural form at any time, flitting from one identity to another as easily as switching social media accounts. Digital technology flattens hierarchies and dissolves space and time. There is nowhere to hide, nowhere that is disconnected and therefore no space for a subculture to be sub.

Yet there is trouble in paradise. The 1980s seems like the last decade because it was the last time we had to have a serious conversation as a nation about who we wanted to be. The argument was settled for thirty years. Now we are equally as divided as we were in 1980. Britain is a face off between the 48% and the 52%.

The hidden costs of Thatcherite economics are beginning to rise up, like mislaid bills demanding to be paid. The kids who were young in the 1980s are about to take the controls - and they can no longer escape the big questions. Do we want there to be such a thing as society? And if we do - what does it mean? Who is invited and who is not?

As for youth culture, it was a case of 'something lost and something found'. The breakdown into smaller and smaller configurations of subculture inevitably gave way to a near infinite tapestry of niche markets. And why confine yourself to one such identity? The loyalty and the sense of tribal identity that the original skinhead may have had gives way to the total freedom of the scene surfer. Why limit yourself?

FADE TO GREY

You can read the 1980s as a decade of escape. There was a huge desire to escape the old world and enter into a new cultural space. The old given identities were stuck and stagnant, people longed for a world in which they could choose their own identity. The young people rehearsed this brave new world in nightclubs, pubs and suburbs.

You could say to the world that you were not a plumber from Handsworth but a Heavy Metal Rocker, a wild and free beast living your own rules. You were not a middle class college kid on your way to becoming a dentist but a bizarre and exotic futurist living out a new androgynous existence at the Blitz.

It was difficult to do these things. Society was still moralistic, patronising and hypocritical. You could still get beaten up for dressing like these kids in the photos. It was hard to find the look and buy the music. You had to go a long way to get the right magazines to read. All this reinforced the tribal camaraderie that makes a true subculture.

At the same time, money too was busy trying to escape the restrictions placed on it by reality. Computers were bringing complex financial products into the market. Heavy industry packed up and fled Britain. We started to believe that only fools and horses work. We were beginning our nationwide obsession with becoming famous.

It's difficult to overestimate the impact of the youth culture movements of the 1980s on the present day. Hip-hop, post-punk, rave, electro, techno, happy hardcore, Balearic house, jungle, dub, two-tone, reggae, northern soul, indie, rockabilly, goth, new wave, R&B, swing, stadium rock, heavy metal and cyberpunk were all fully formed aesthetics of the decade, and this is probably not the full story.

From this technicolour palette comes all the tones and shades of the youth culture spectrum we see today.

Why do the 1980s look so contemporary? Consider that the term 'streetwise' itself came into British vocabulary in the early part of the decade. This now fundamental concept of representing yourself as having 'street credibility' came to dominate in the 1980s.

Youth culture is about dreaming yourself into existence through playing roles. These dreams seem always to alternate between dreams of authenticity and dreams of artifice. Skins dreamt of working class authenticity. Punks rejected authenticity, dreaming instead of artifice, remaking themselves. Middle class kids dreamt of rejecting their privileges to discover a more authentic way of life. Working class kids dreamt of having enough money to look good and show off their earning potential. Both attempted, in the streets and the clubs, to meet each other as human beings and not social classes.

This attempt to escape from mass politics into a world of limitless individuality has defined our culture, at work and at play, for the last thirty years.

THE EIGHTIES WAS THE LAST DECADE

In the eighties the old youth tribes began to break down, along with the whole notion of society, leaving space for a multiplicity of sub-sub-sub cultures to emerge. By the end of the decade, the notion of a common culture defining a ten year period becomes completely untenable. There were no 1990s.

(They stopped trying to name decades after the journalist who coined the noughties died of embarrassment.)

This story is about identity. The one line meaning of the decade is this: We chose self-expression over class struggle. It's not hard to understand why. In a time when the left and the right appeared equally conservative - young people wanted to run from the old world. These images show people trying to escape from something. And perhaps they did, for a few glorious moments, step outside the grim reality of 1980s Britain, into a world of their own making.

'The Decade' is a fantasy. An utterly ridiculous notion by any measure, and yet a powerfully fascinating one. Let's pretend we accept that the 1980s was the last decade. Which was the first? The 1950s of course. There were no 'youths' prior to this. You were a child and then you were an adult. End of story.

(And you will notice in this book, the lingering influence of the 1950s/1960s/1970s. With the invention of decades almost immediately came the notion of retro. Flick through and you'll discover it's fun to play 'which decade should this picture have been taken in?')

What combination of social factors caused the explosion of Rock & Roll to colonise the whole world? It's hard to say. Most bombastically, Youth Culture Saved Capitalism. If you find that hard to swallow, you'll find it easier to admit that 'all culture is now youth culture'. The underground is the mainstream.

But it wasn't. Not quite. Not in the 1980s.

Our 21st century obsession with the 1980s runs deeper than anyone could have predicted. For a long time the 1960s held sway as 'the greatest decade of human history' while the dark days of the eighties were despised and reviled. Yet now it is the 1980s that feels the most relevant decade to obsess over. Why?

Maybe because it was the decade in which we thrashed out the terms of a new settlement. The settlement that we agreed on as a society still holds, just about, today. But it is breaking down. And we know it is. And we're scared. We were scared in the 1980s too. So it all feels doubly relevant.

WHO SAID 'ALL THAT IS SOLID, MELTS INTO AIR?'

Big, solid, boring identities gave way to little, ephemeral, fascinating ones. The rockers you see here would have been fanatically loyal to their subculture and puritanical about the range of music they would deem to be relevant to their identity. By the end of the 1980s kids were already much more likely to be scene surfers. It didn't take a genius to realise that more fun could be had by experiencing a wider range of cultural forms. Why tie yourself down?

In the UK in particular, DJ's like John Peel proselytised a passionate eclecticism that helped make UK youth happy to listen electronica and rock in the same space at the same time without having a nervous fit.

By the late 1990s it would have been ridiculous to compare what the kids were doing to the genuine subcultures of the past. Digital culture does not leave space for anything to be 'outside of society'. Subcultures require lag. They need space in which to exist, germinate and develop before they are published and commodified. The Internet has killed all that. Not necessarily a bad thing but a thing nonetheless.

Patrick Potter

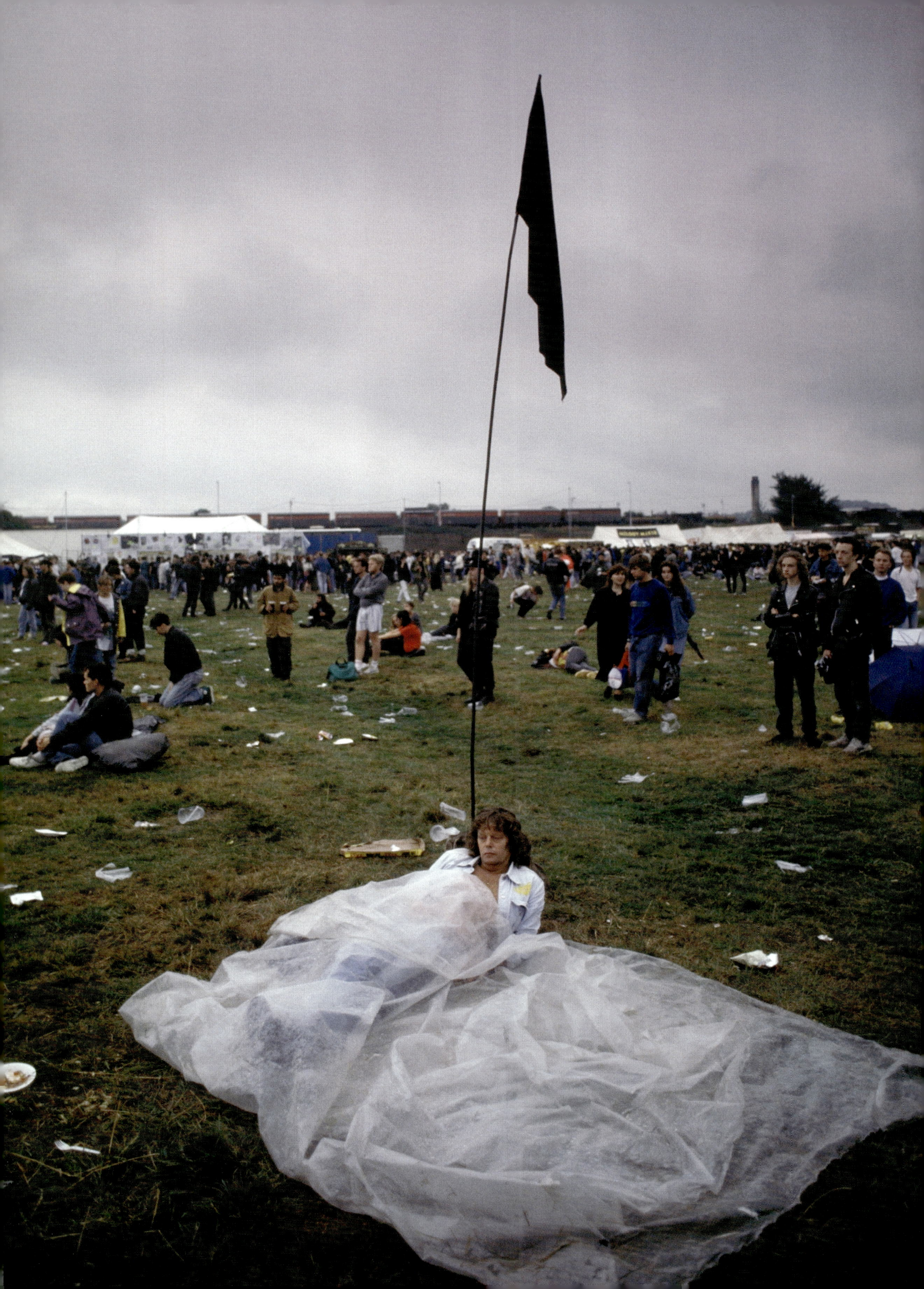

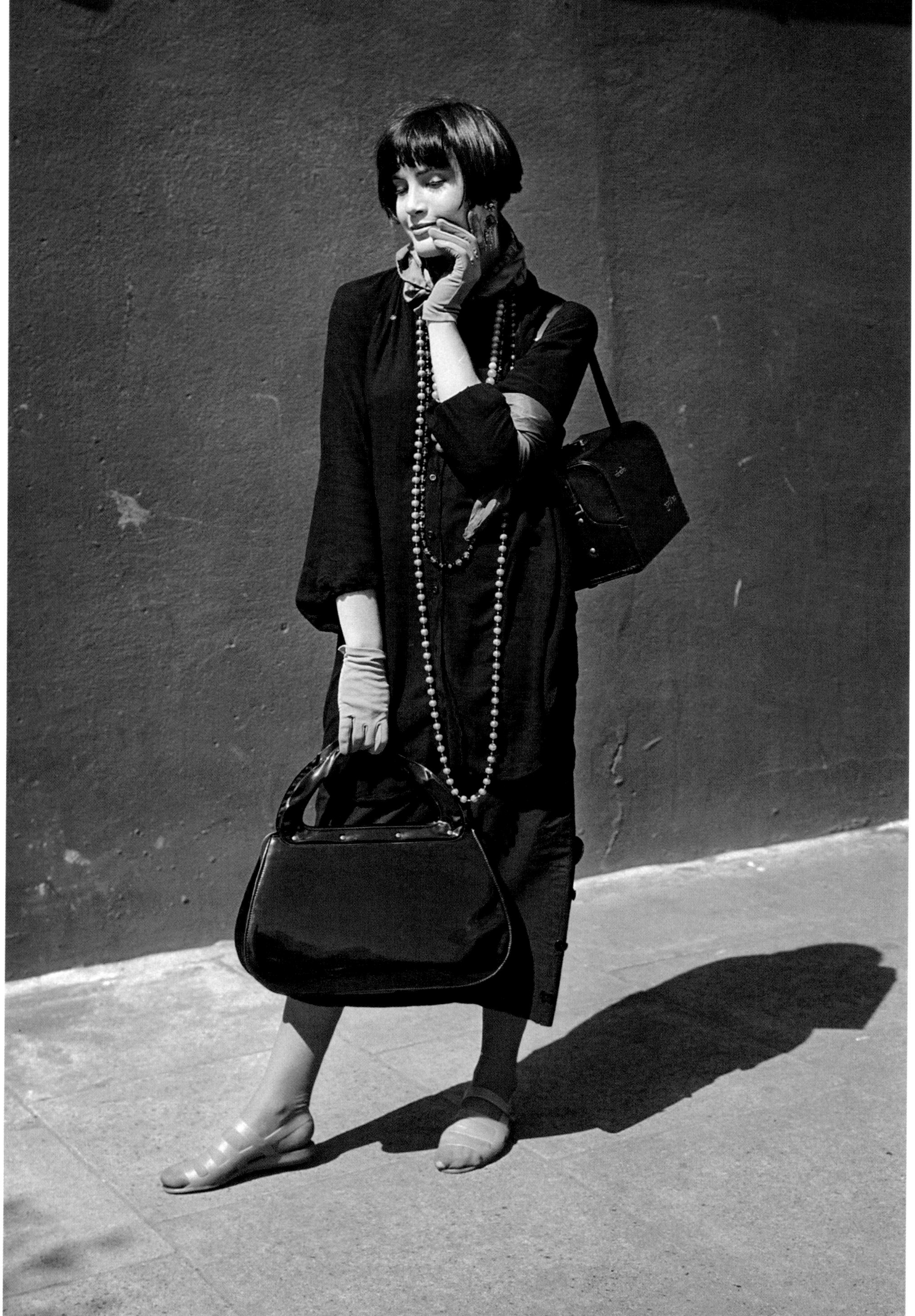

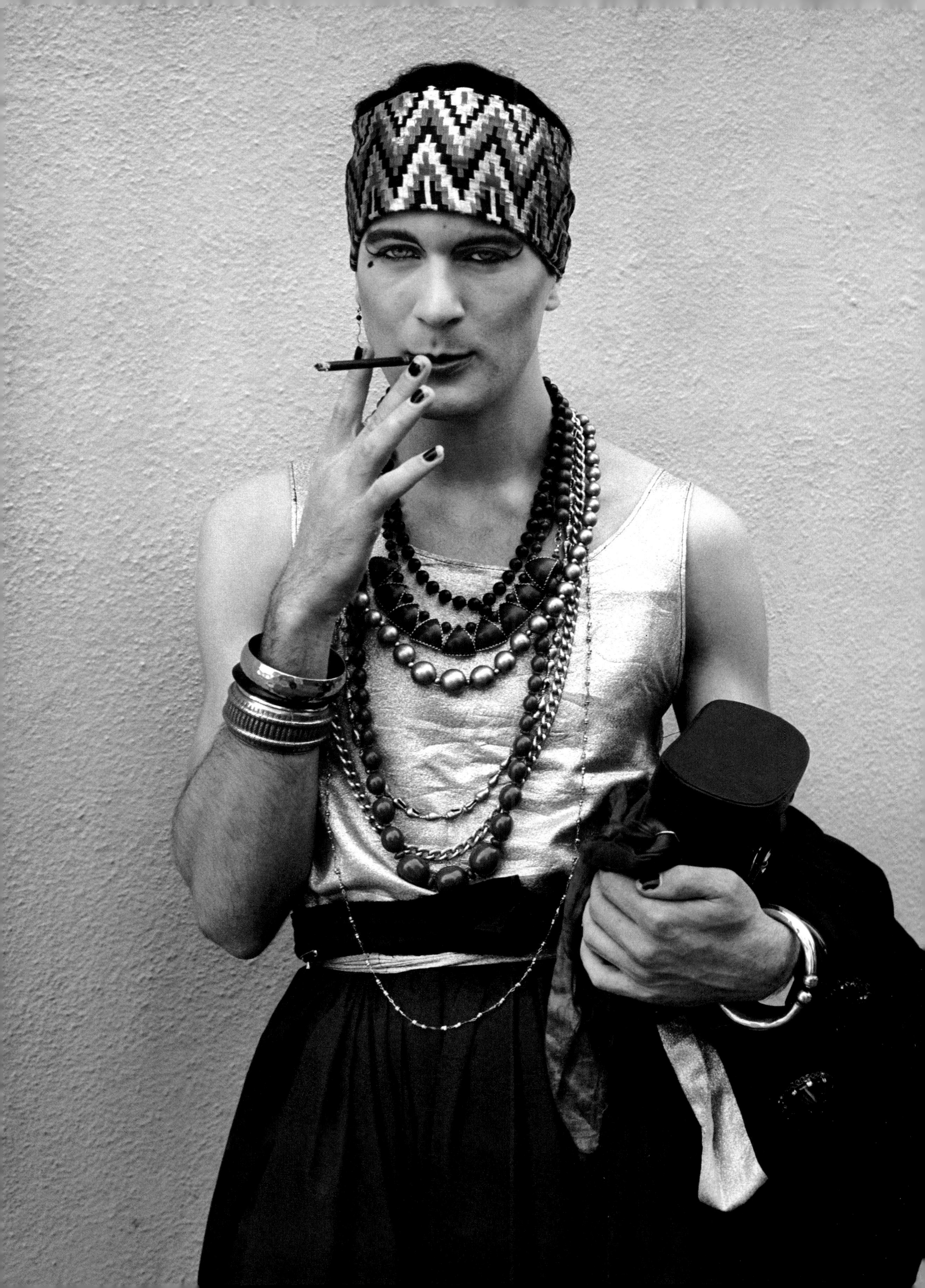

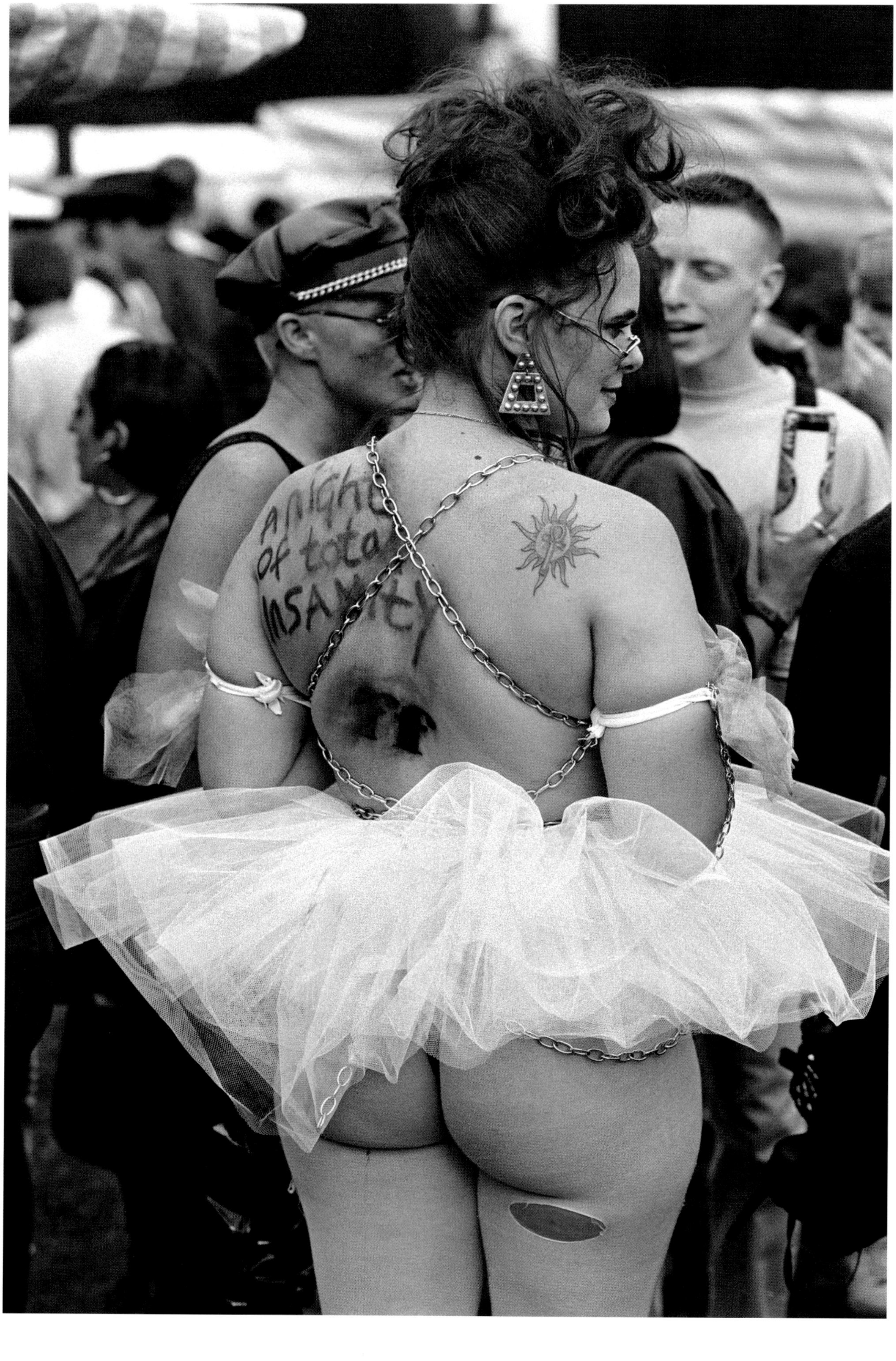

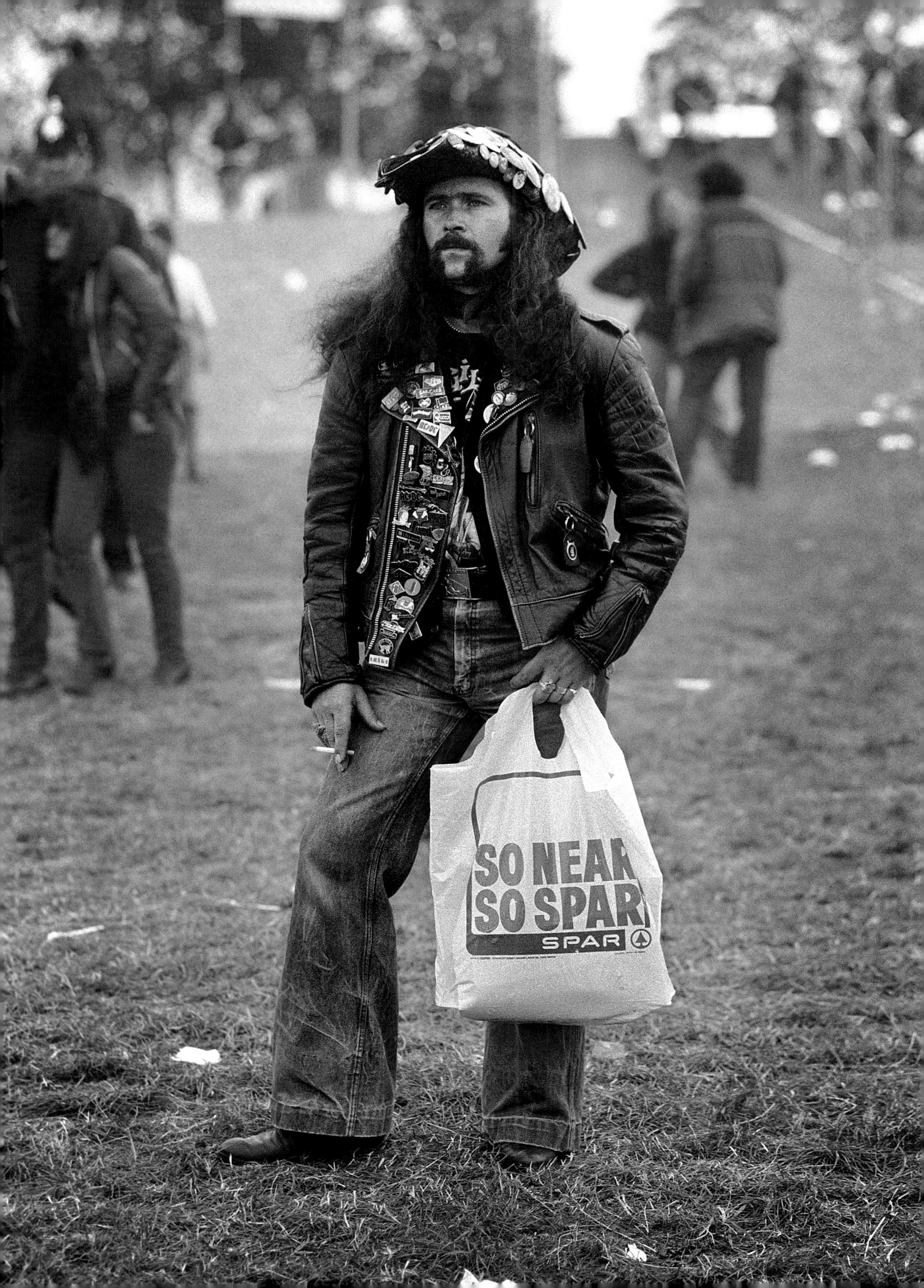
SO NEAR
SO SPAR
SPAR

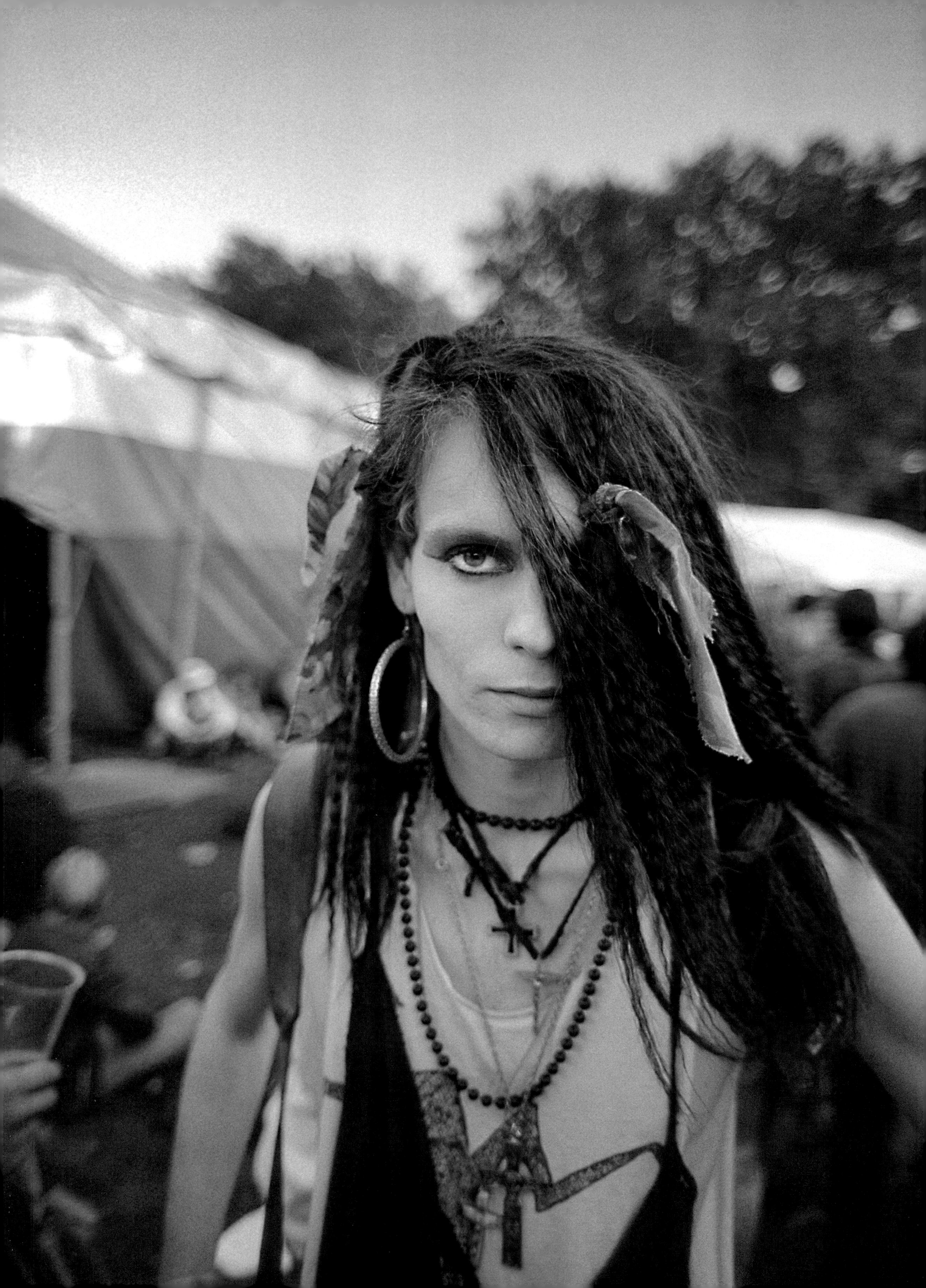

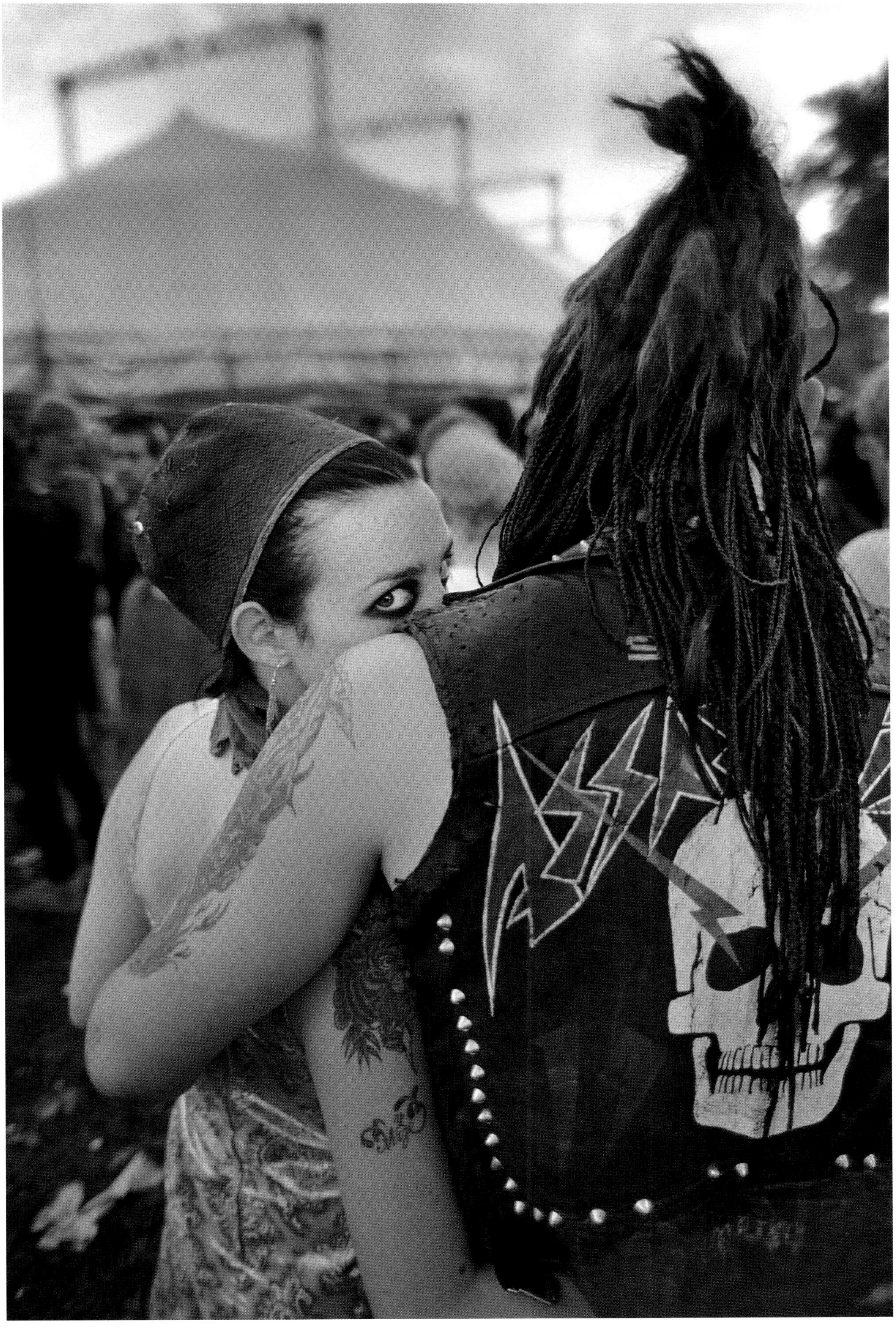

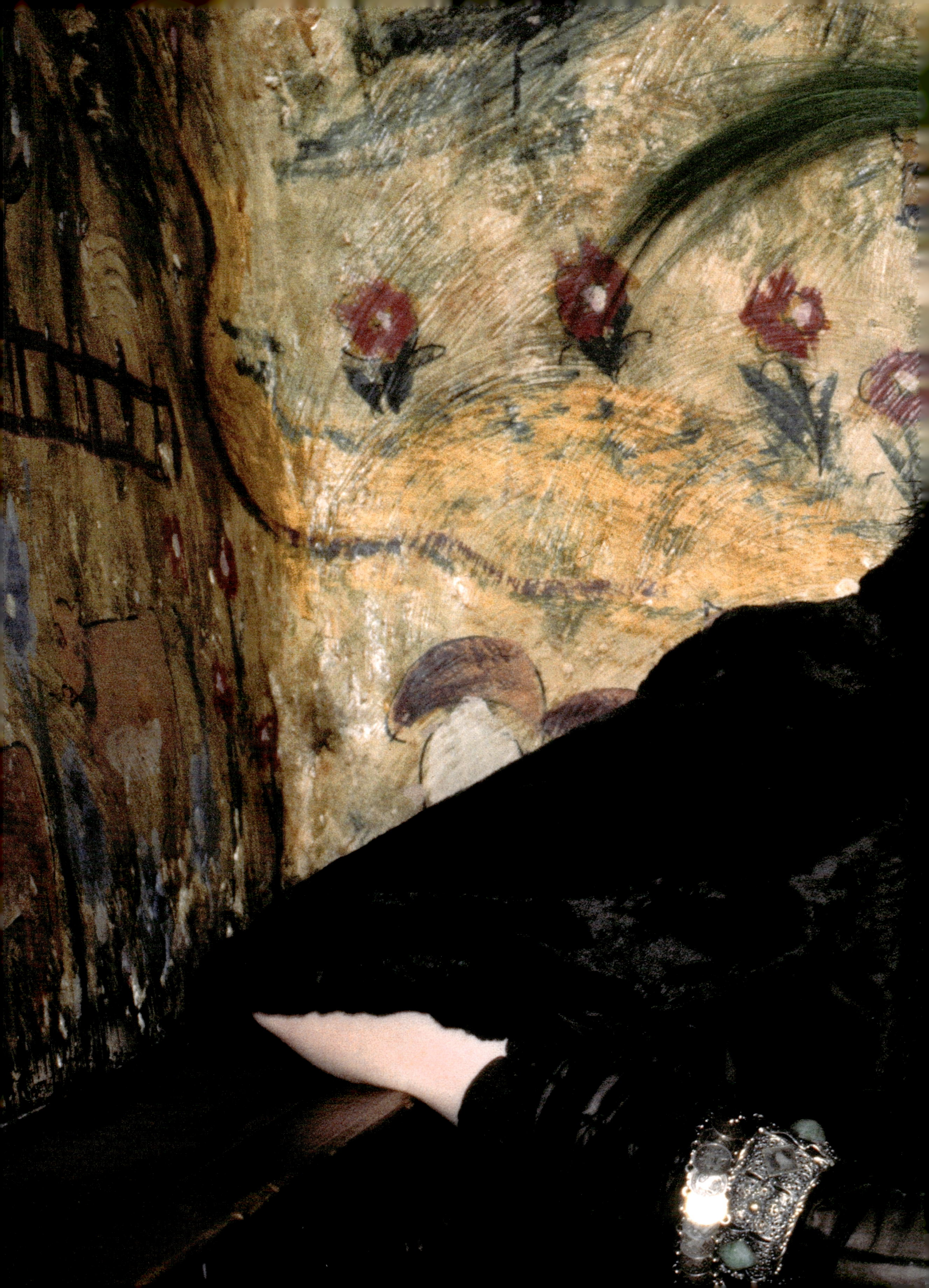

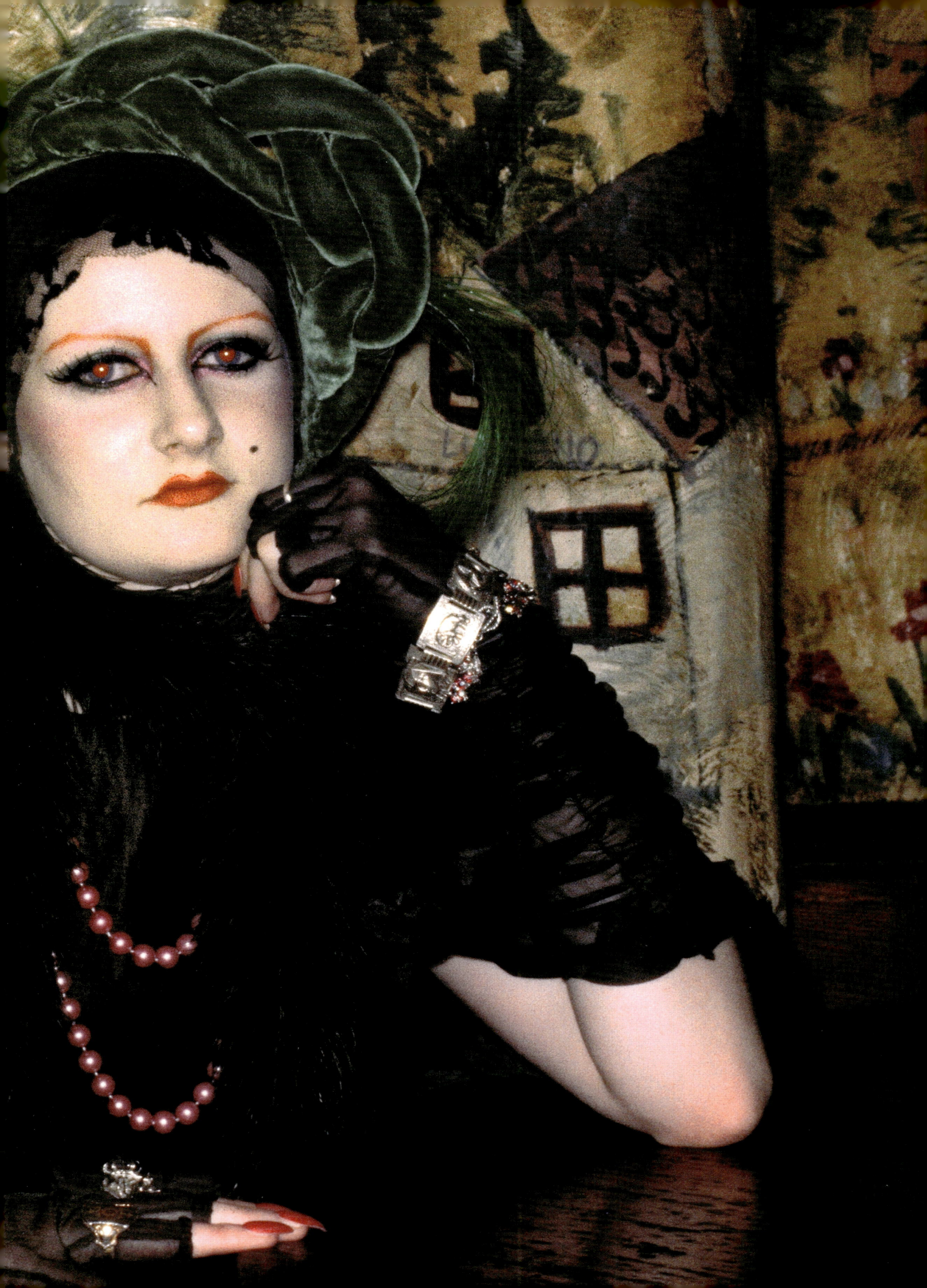

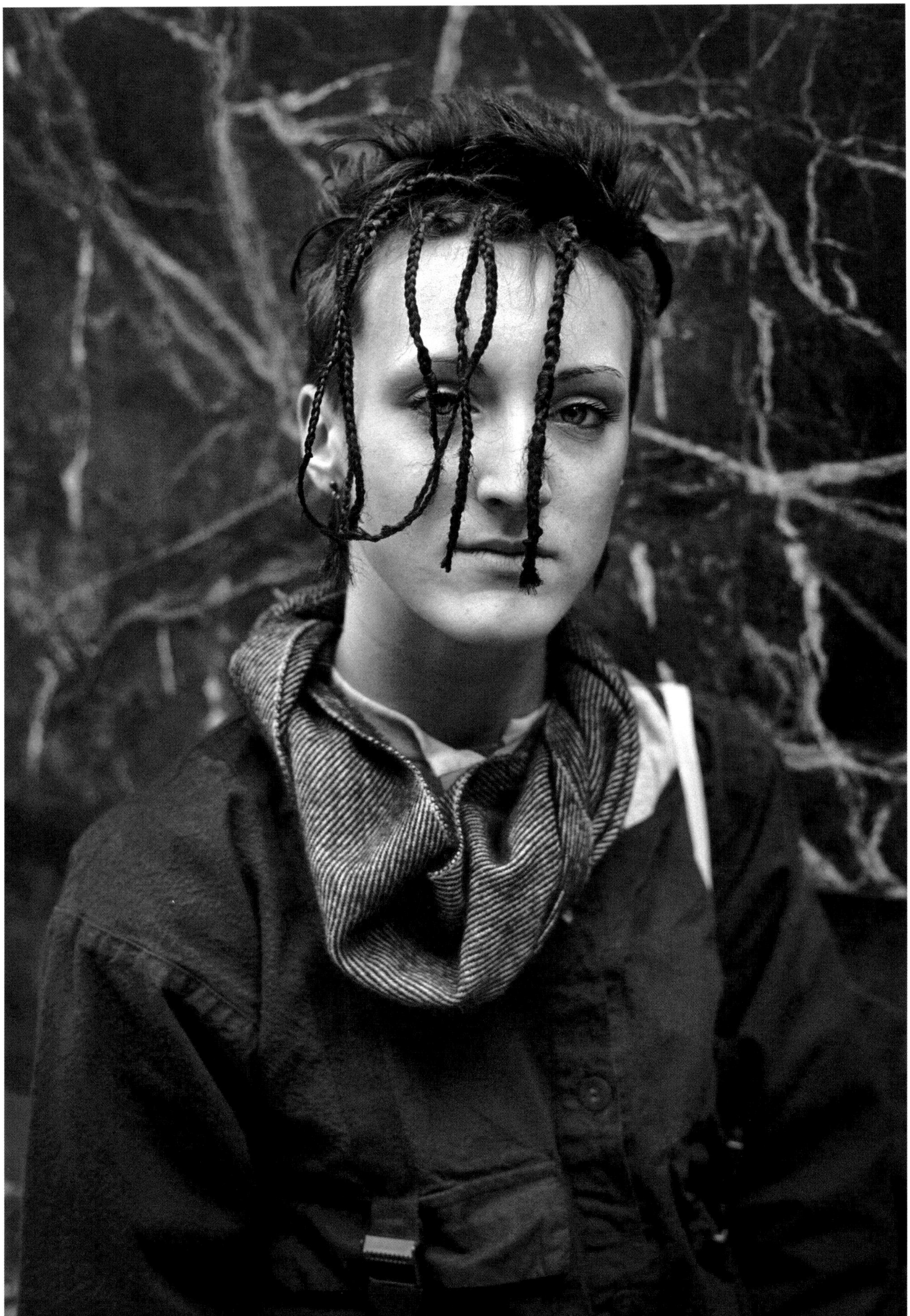

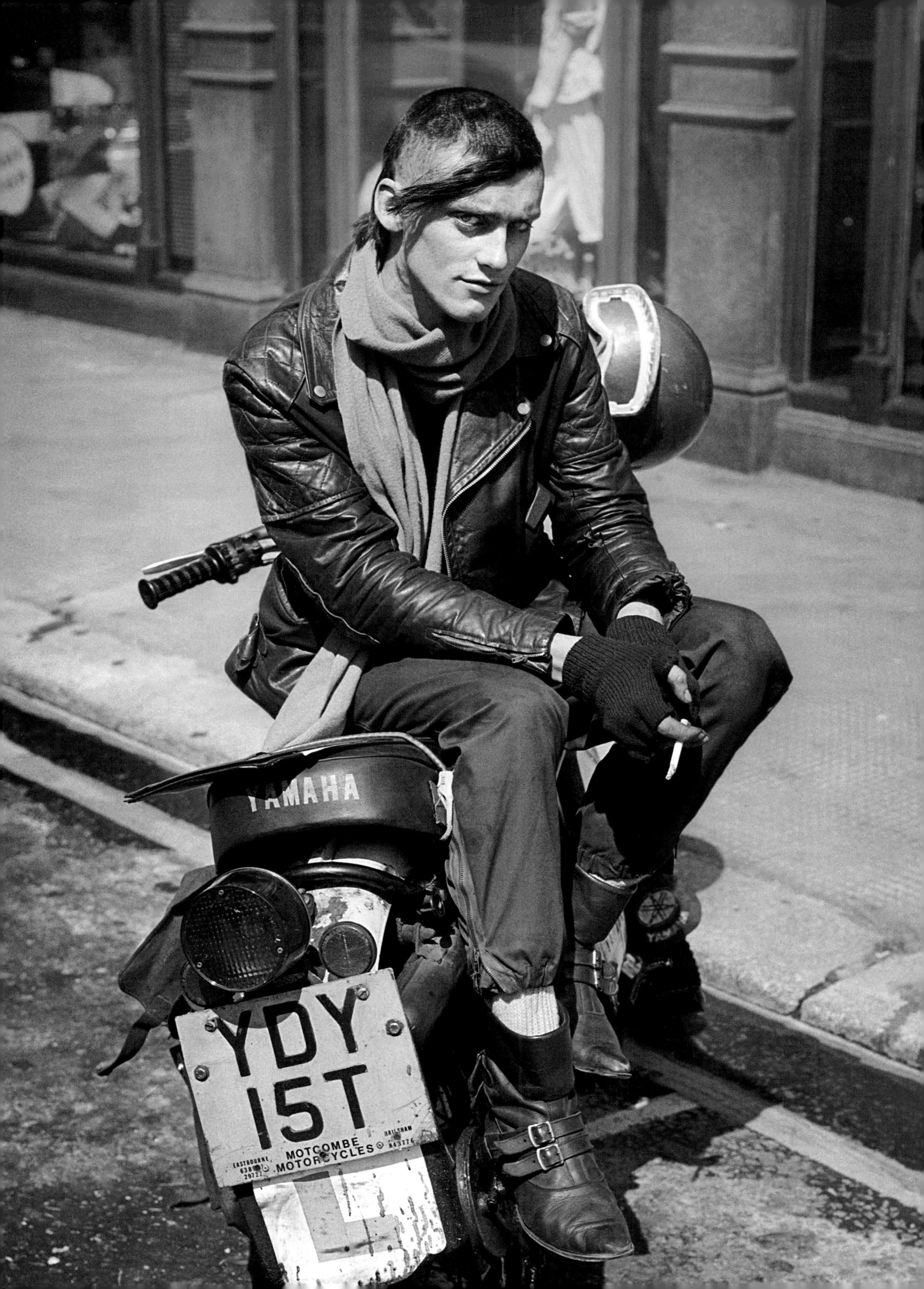
YAMAHA
YDY
15T
MOTCOMBE
MOTORCYCLES
EASTBOURNE
HAILSHAM

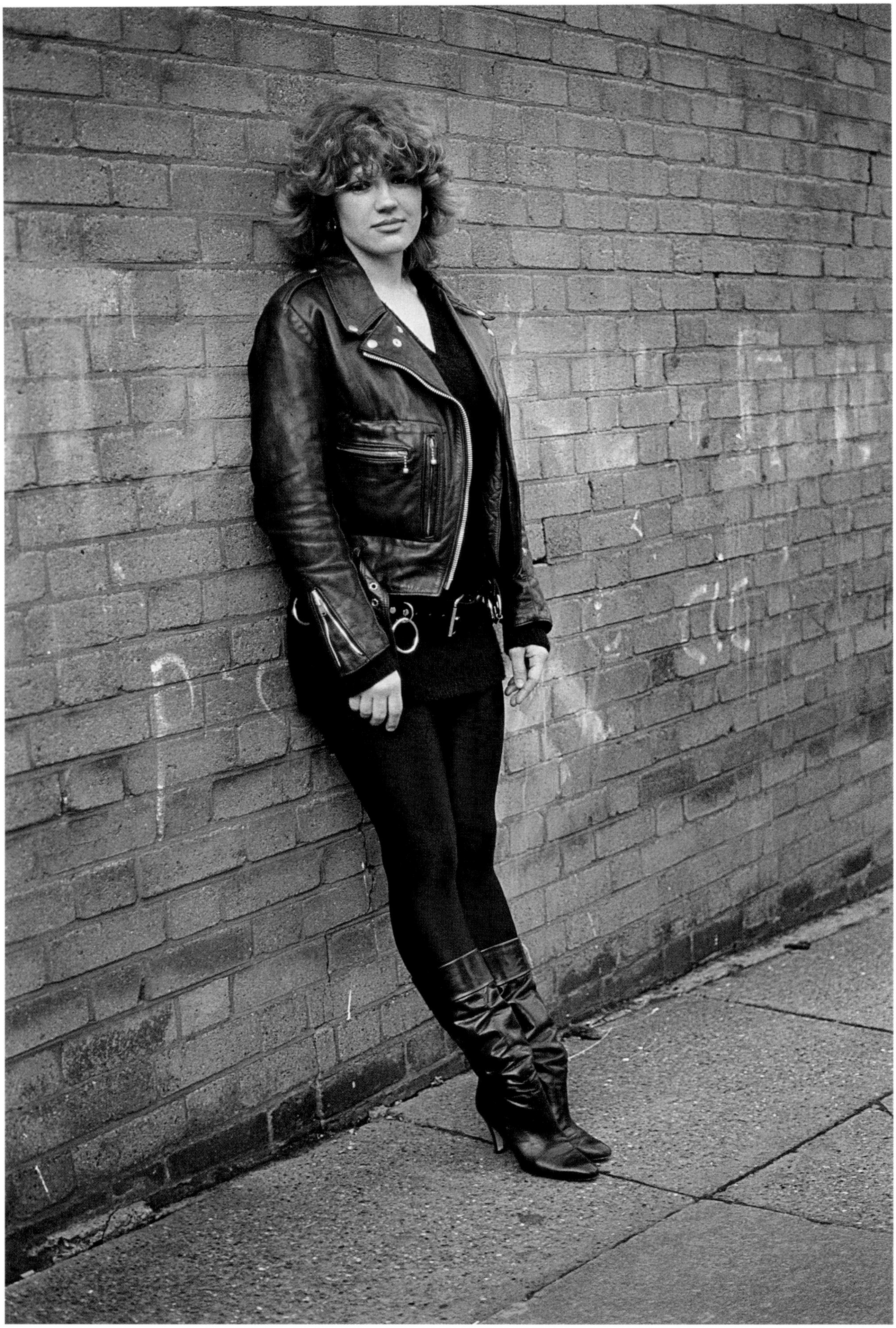

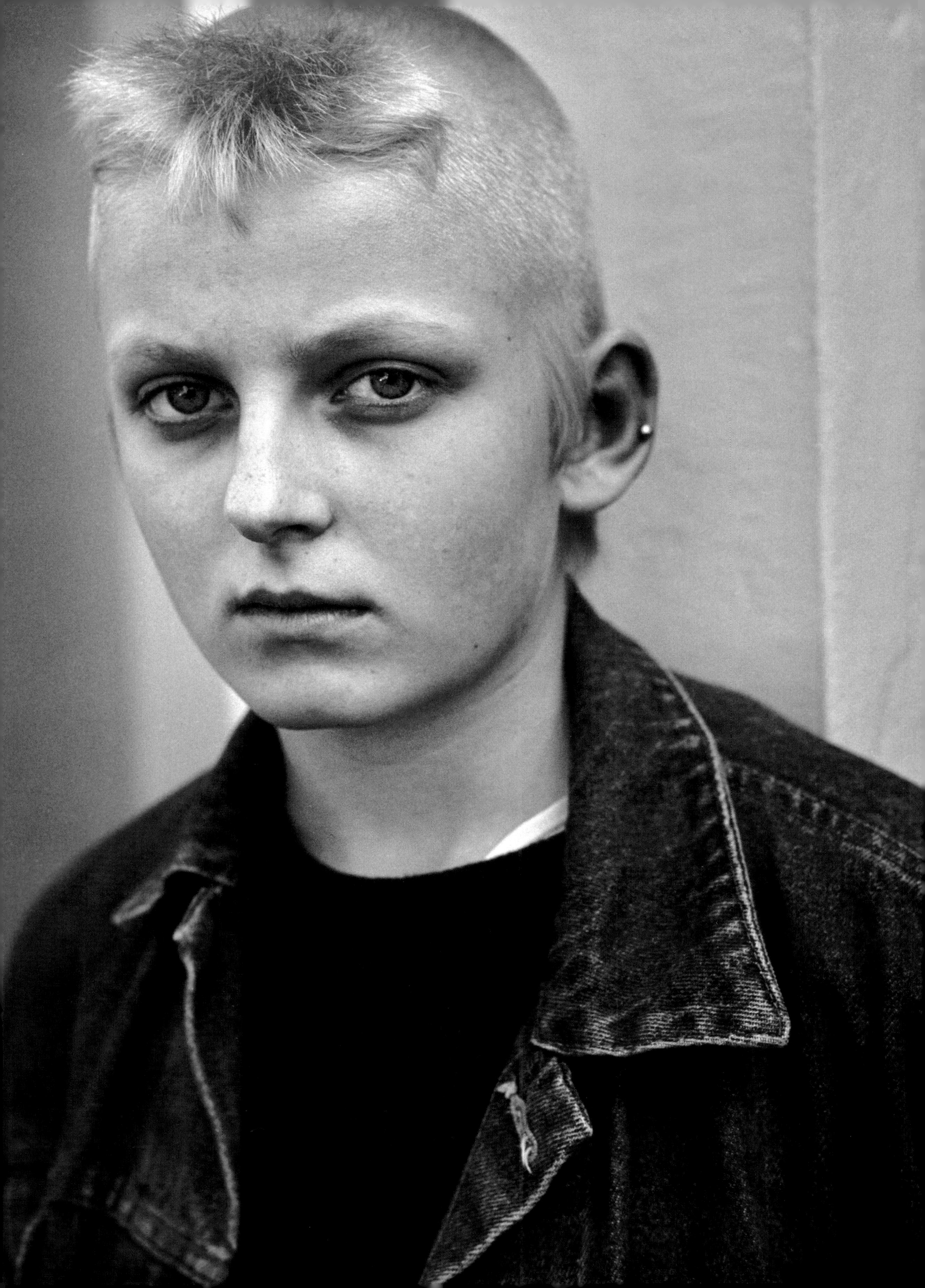

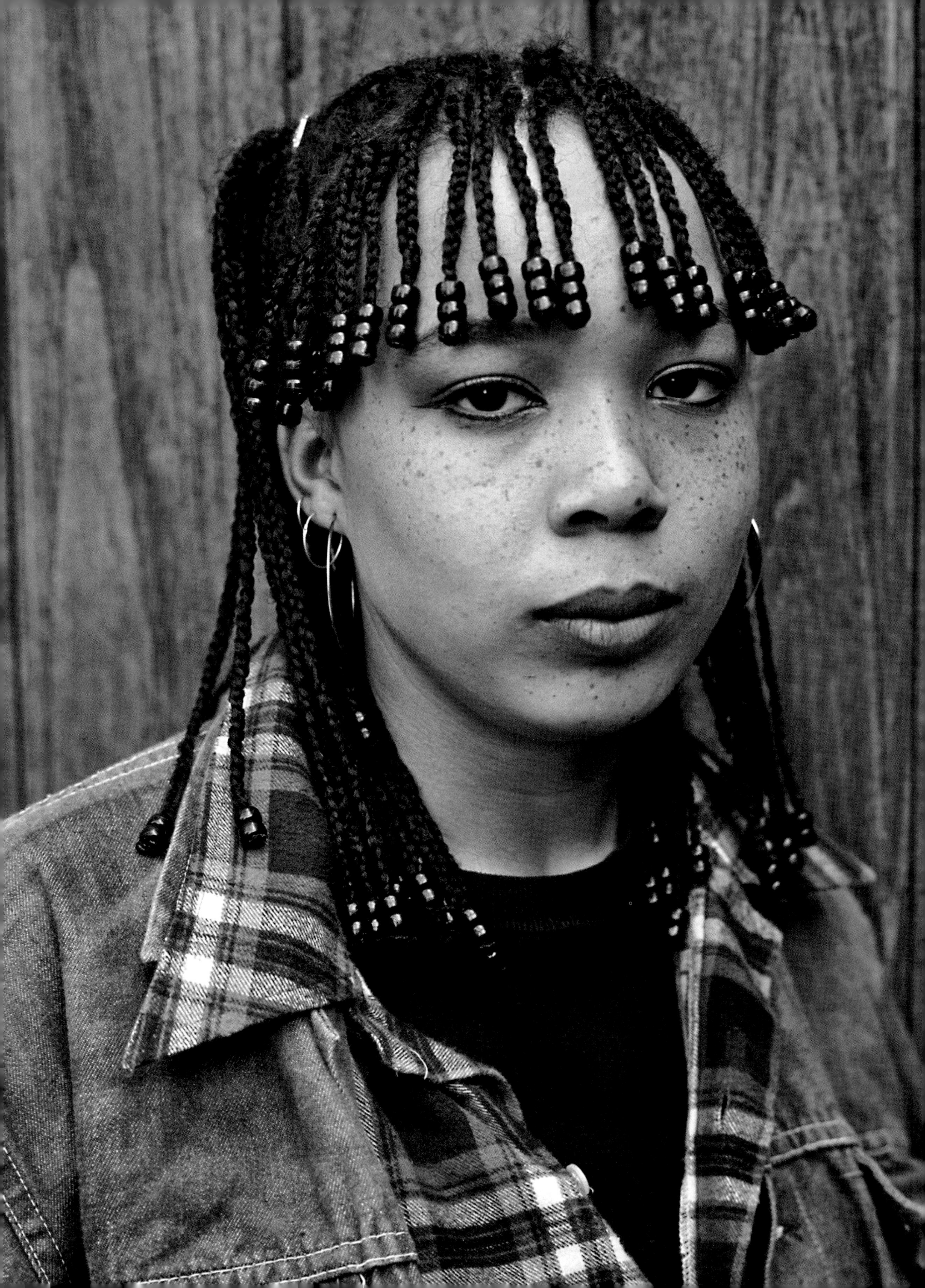

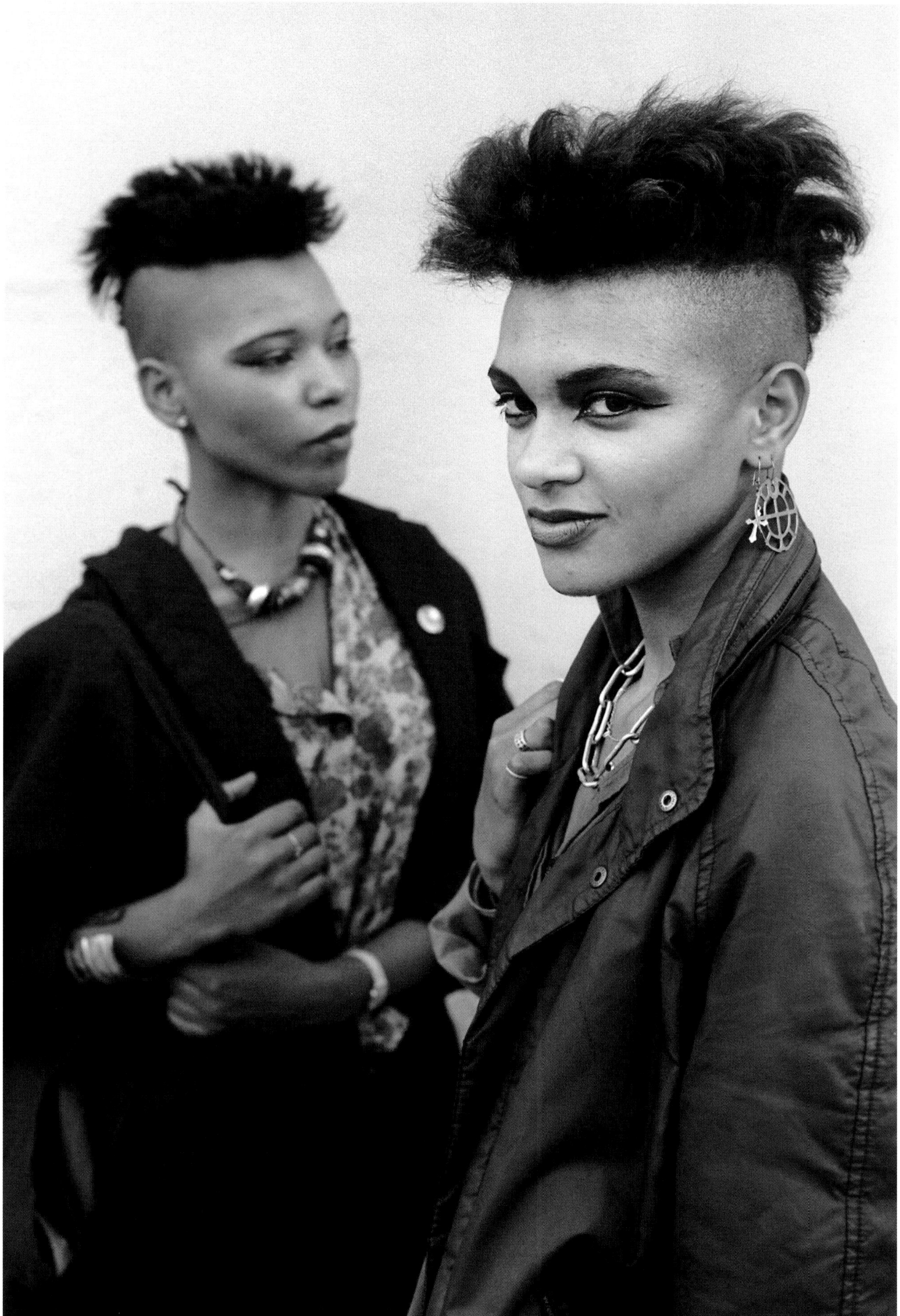

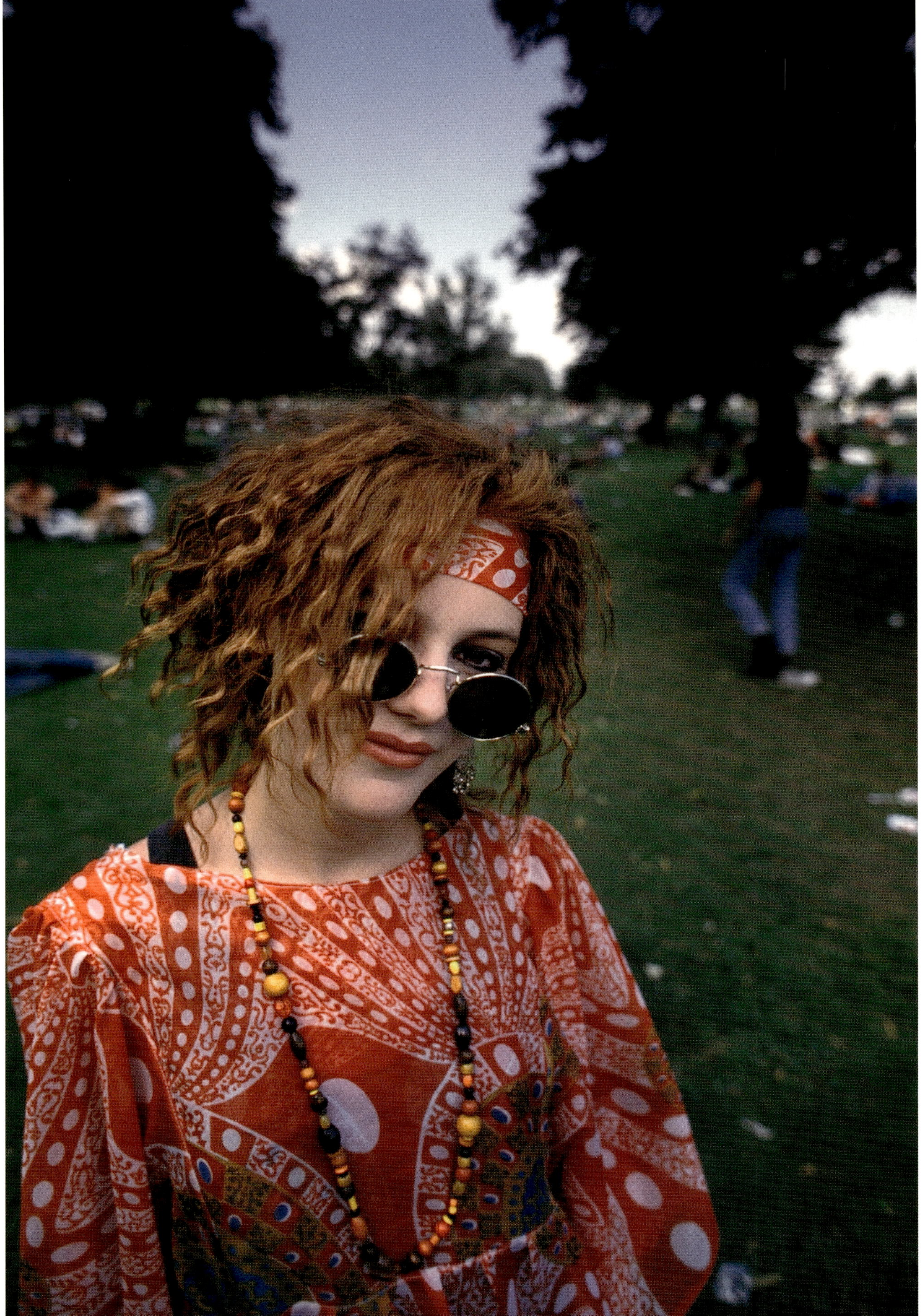

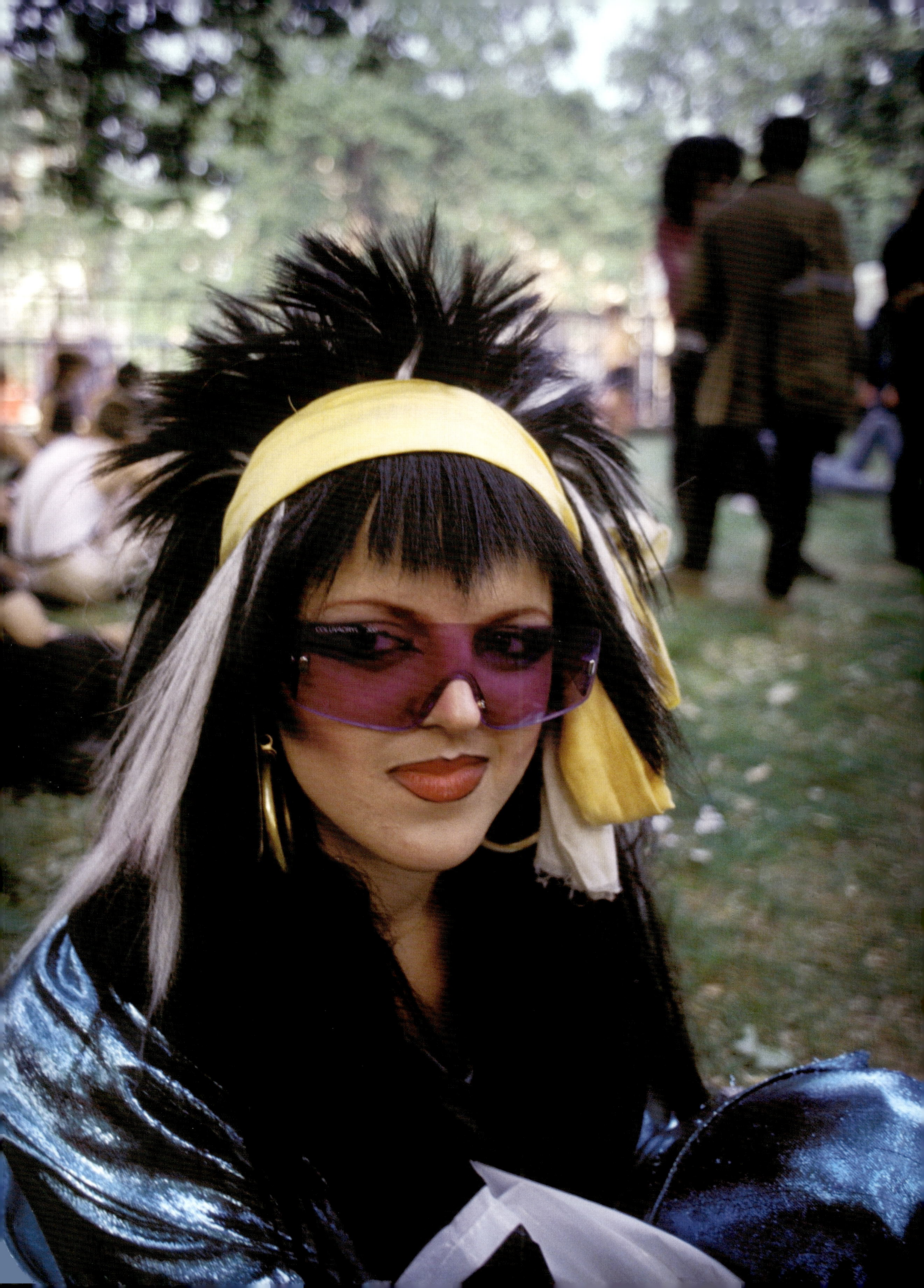

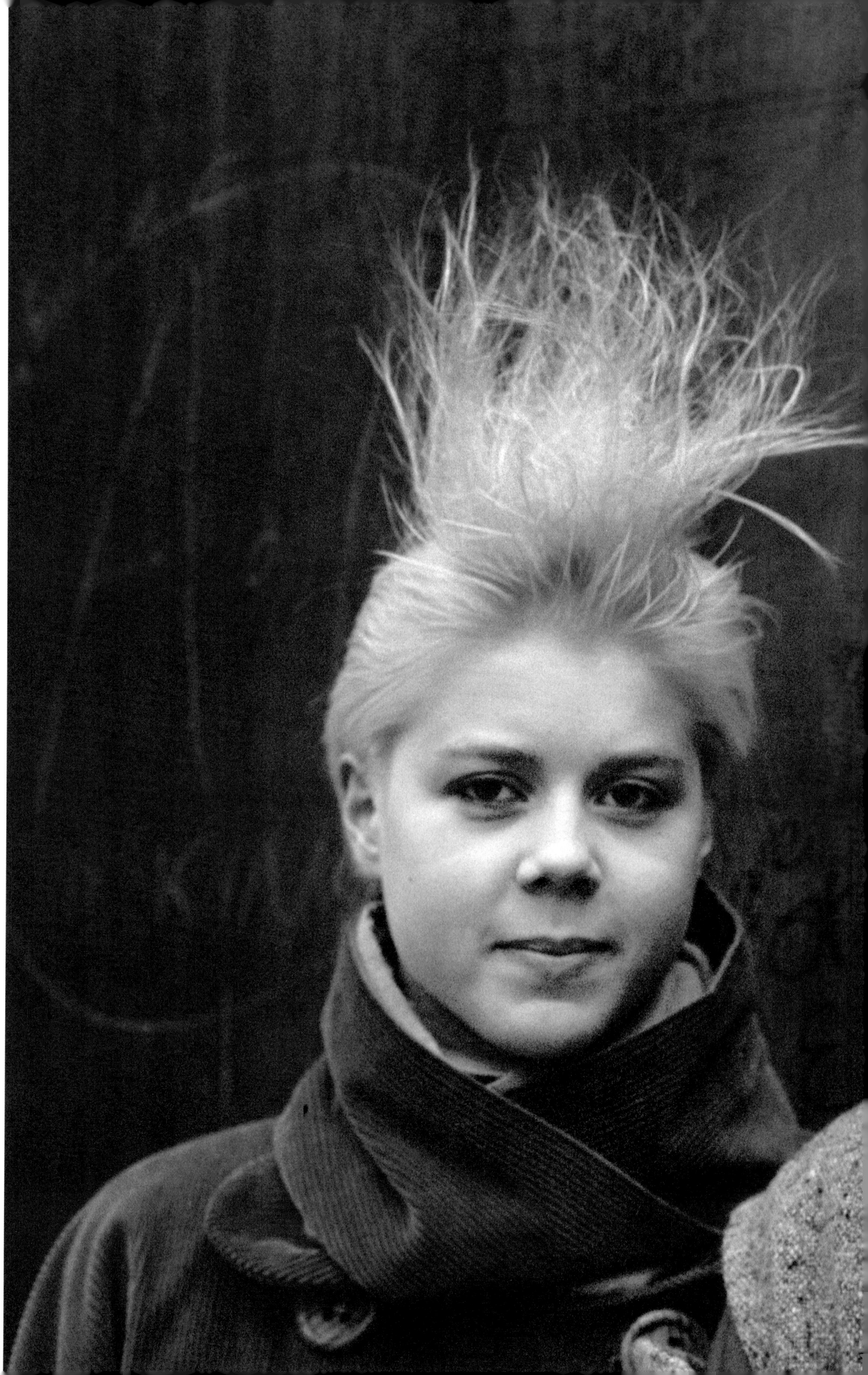

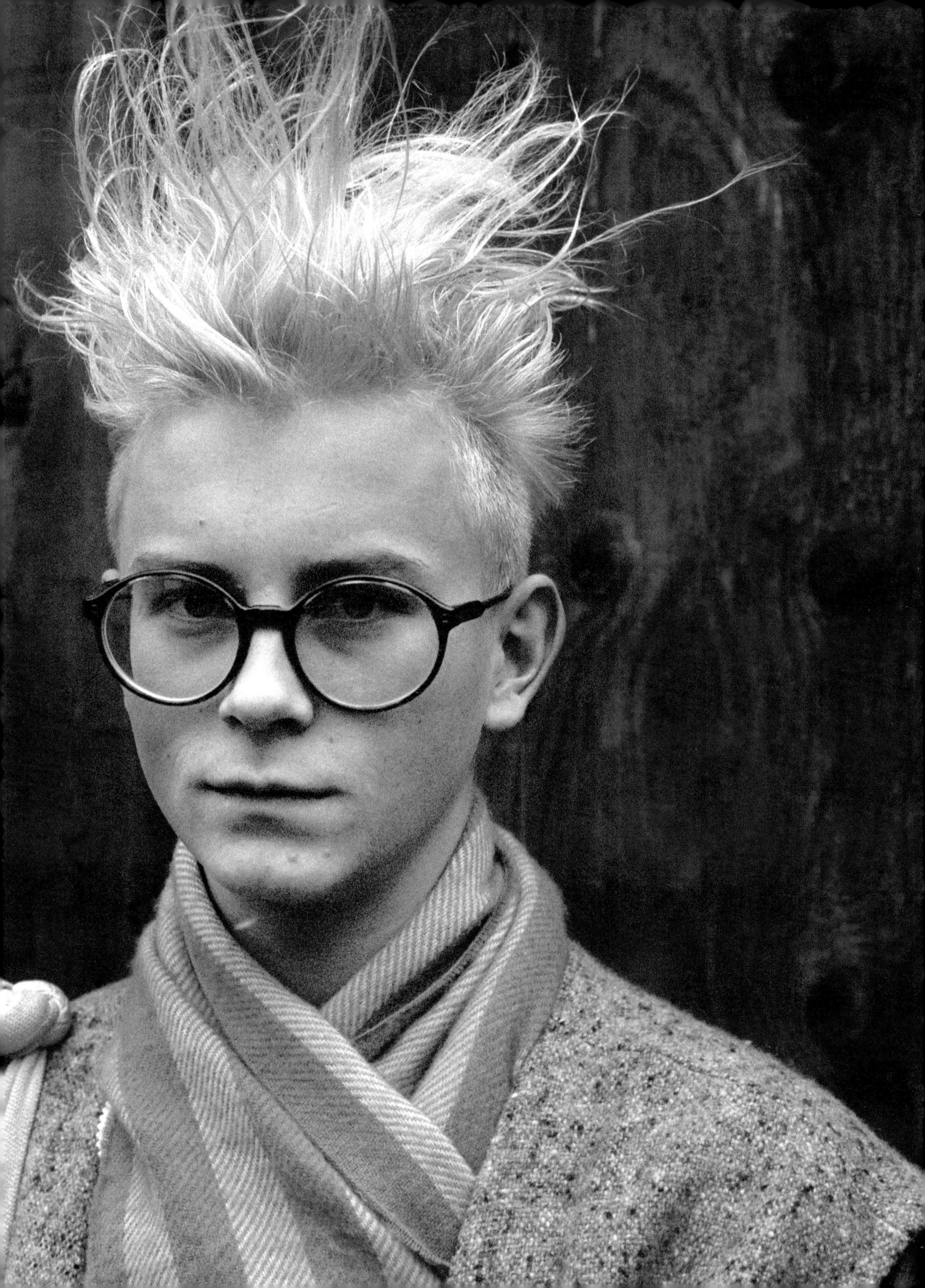

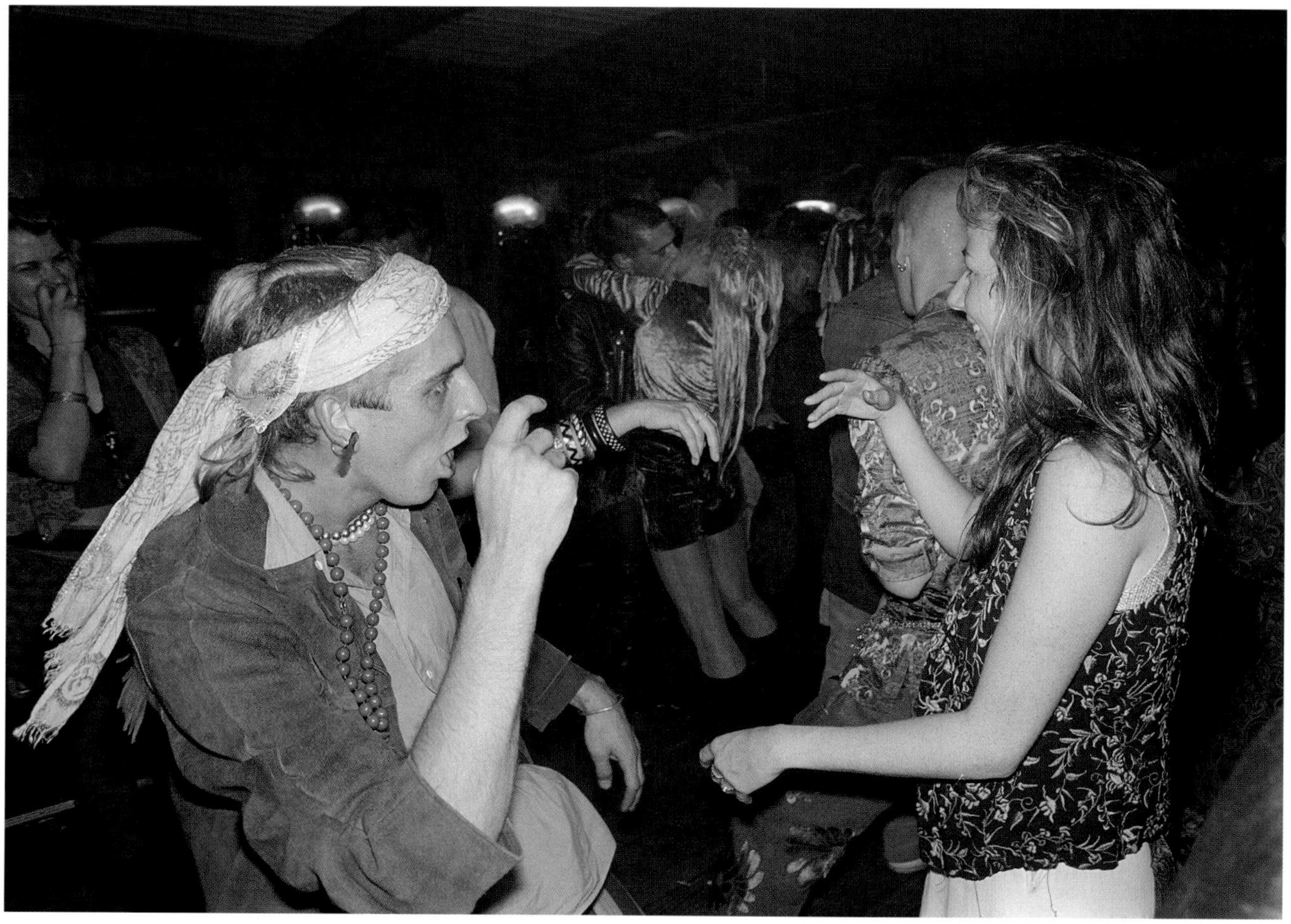

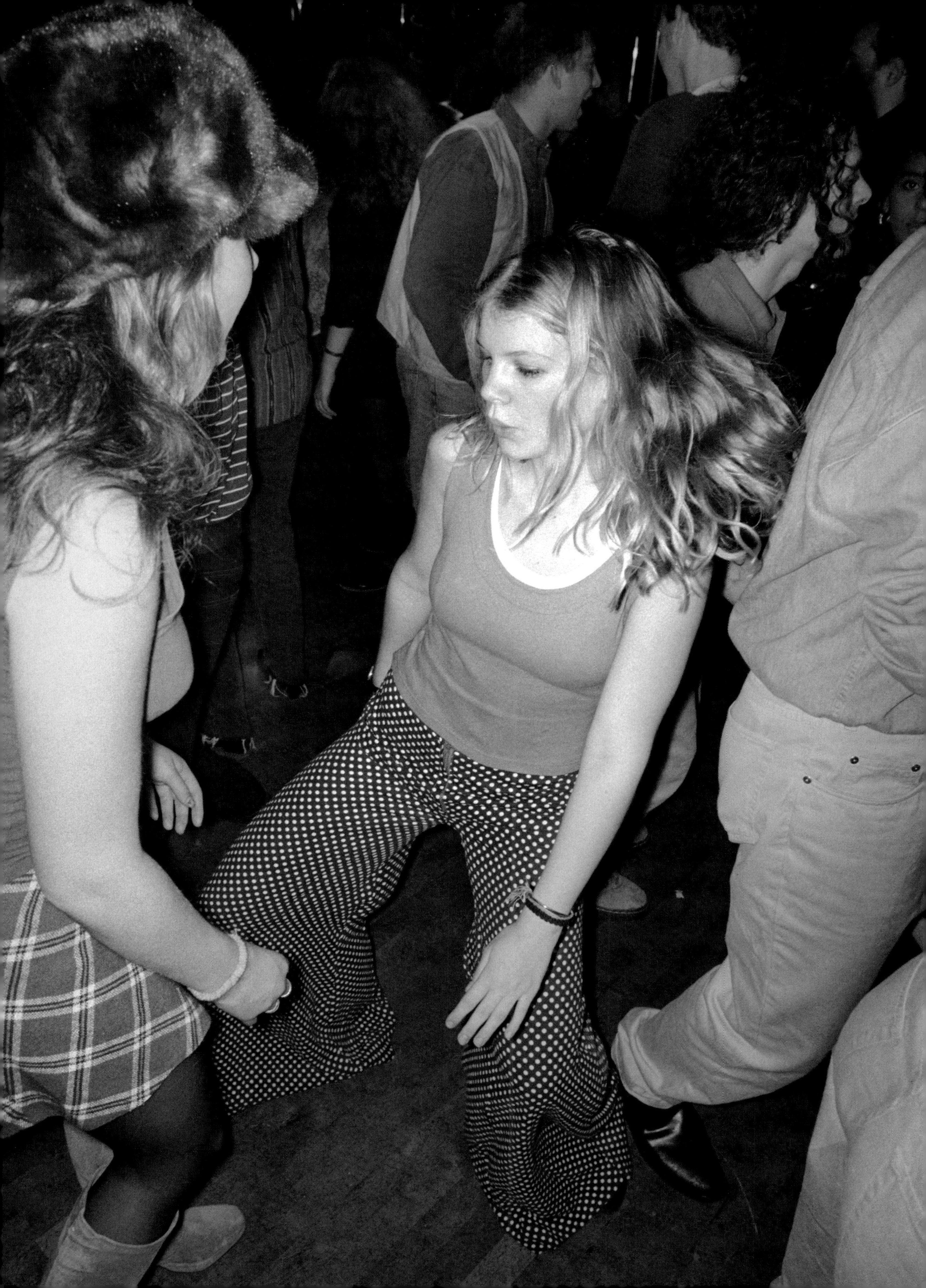

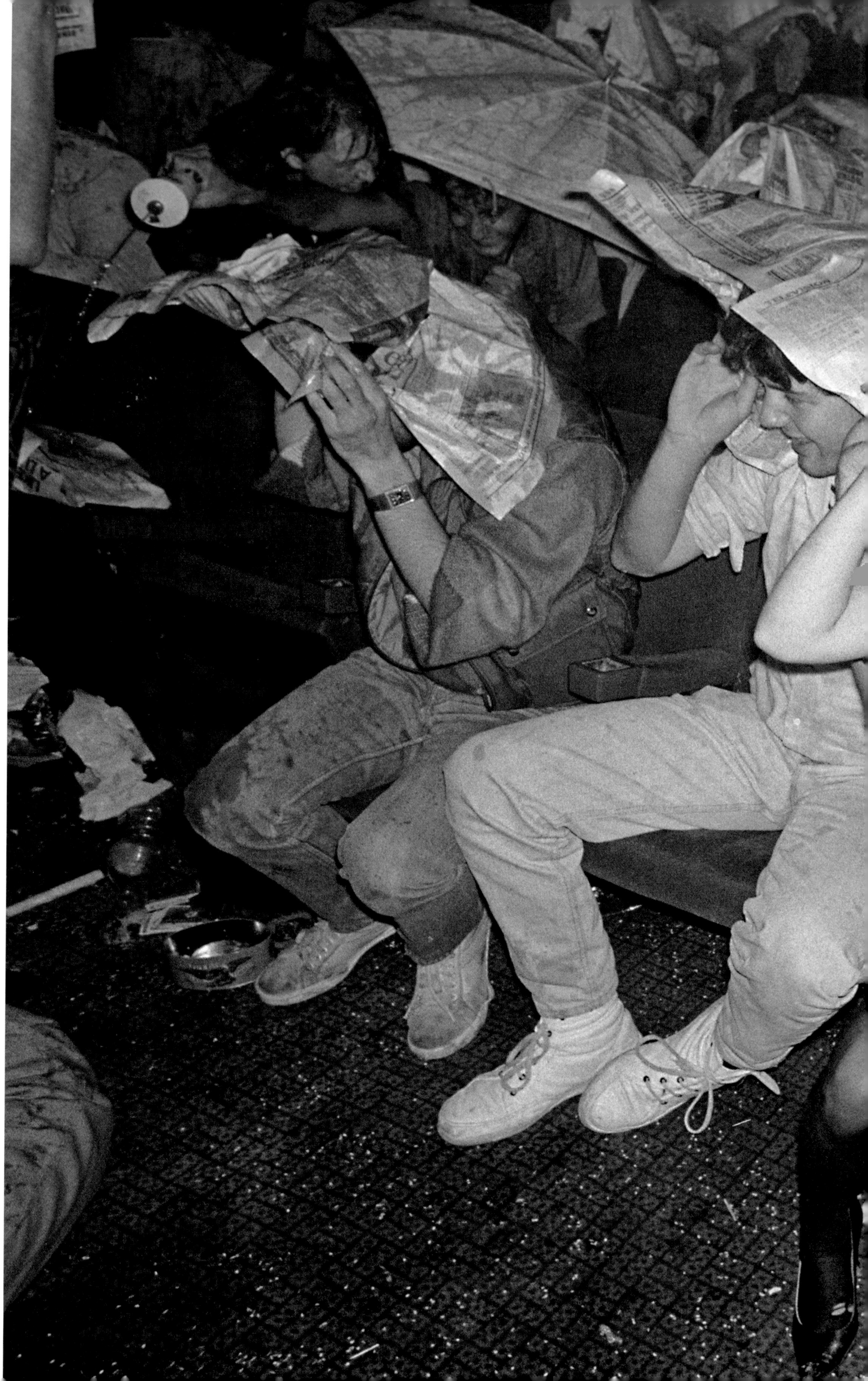

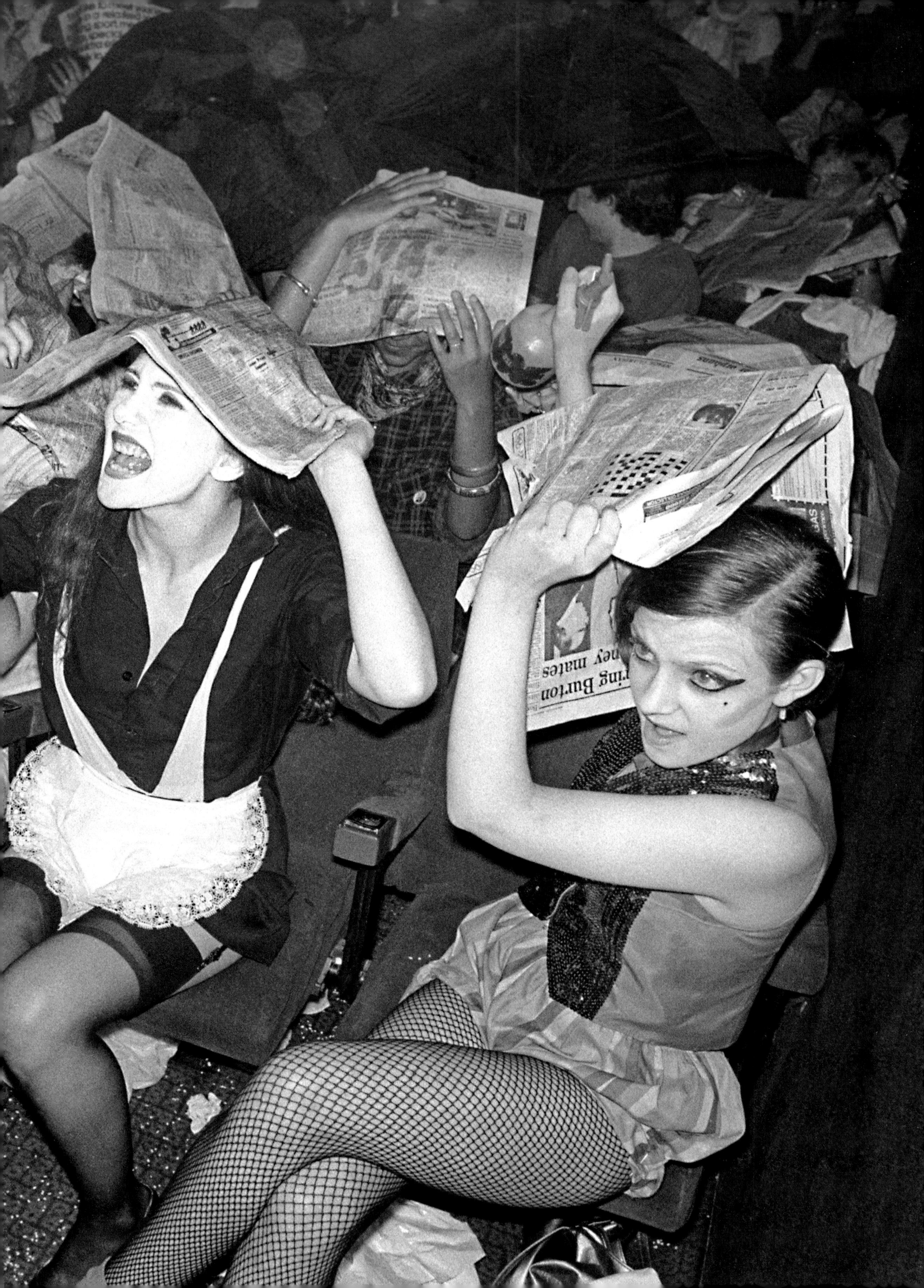

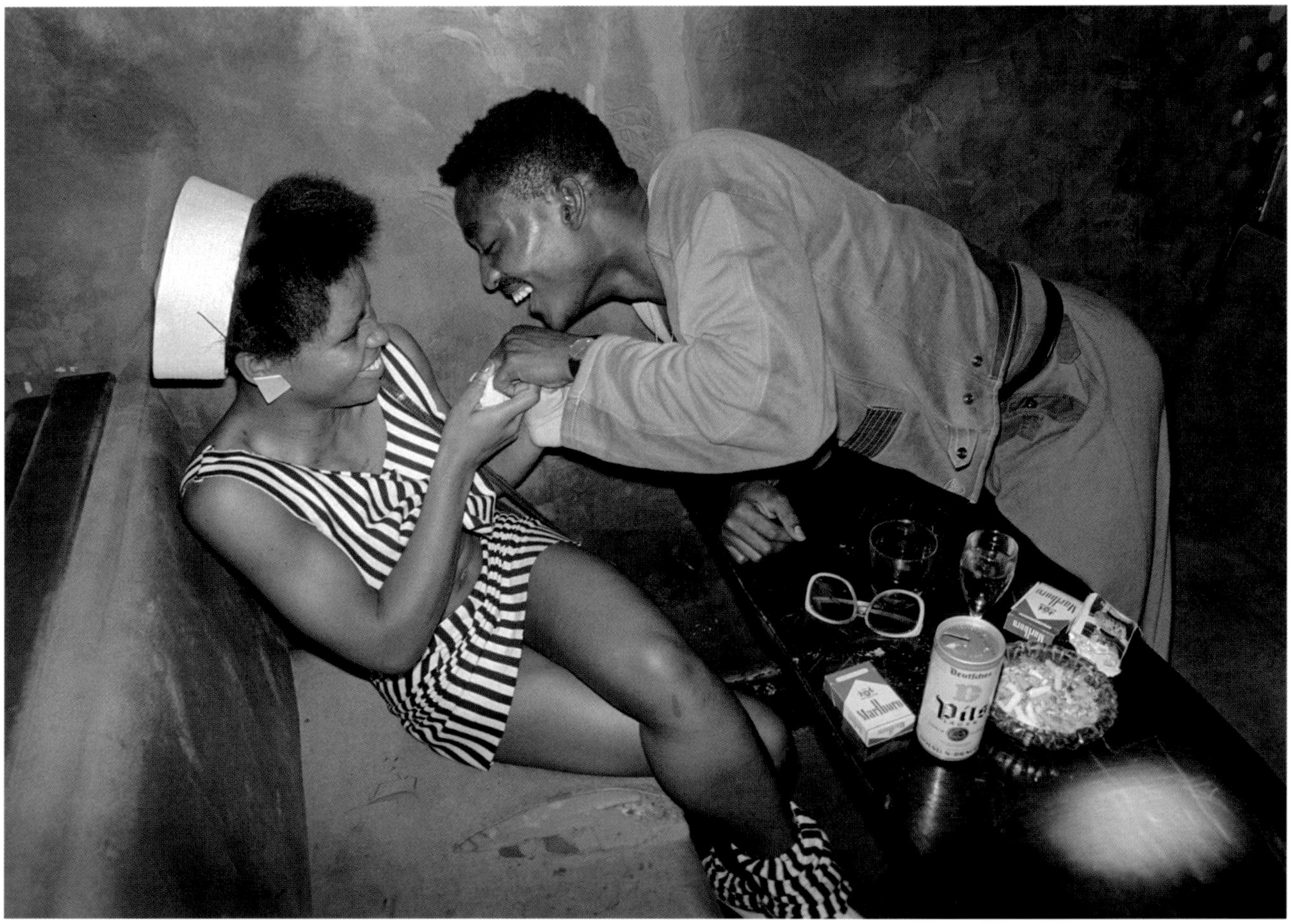
Marlboro
Pils
Marlboro

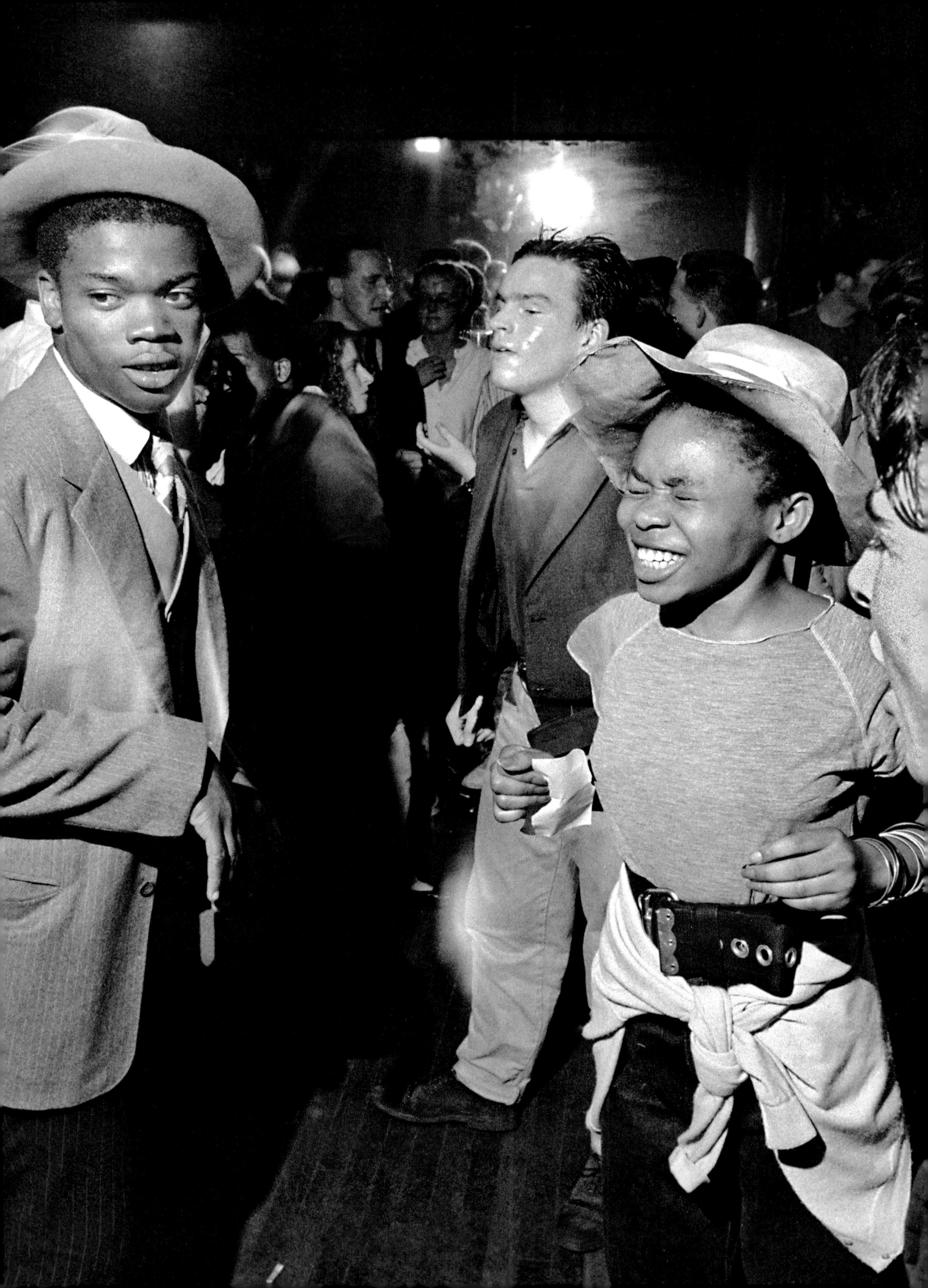

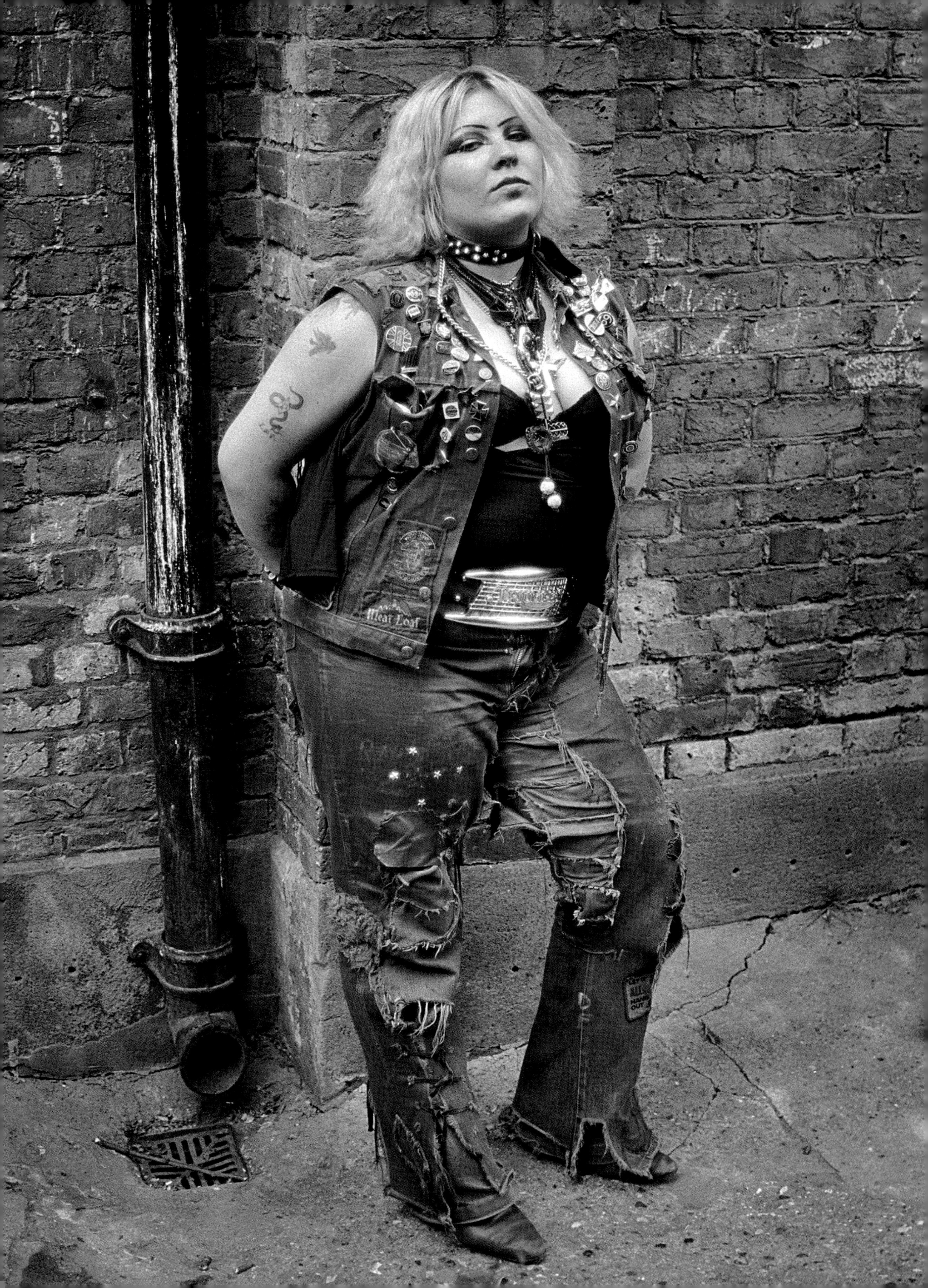
Meat Loaf

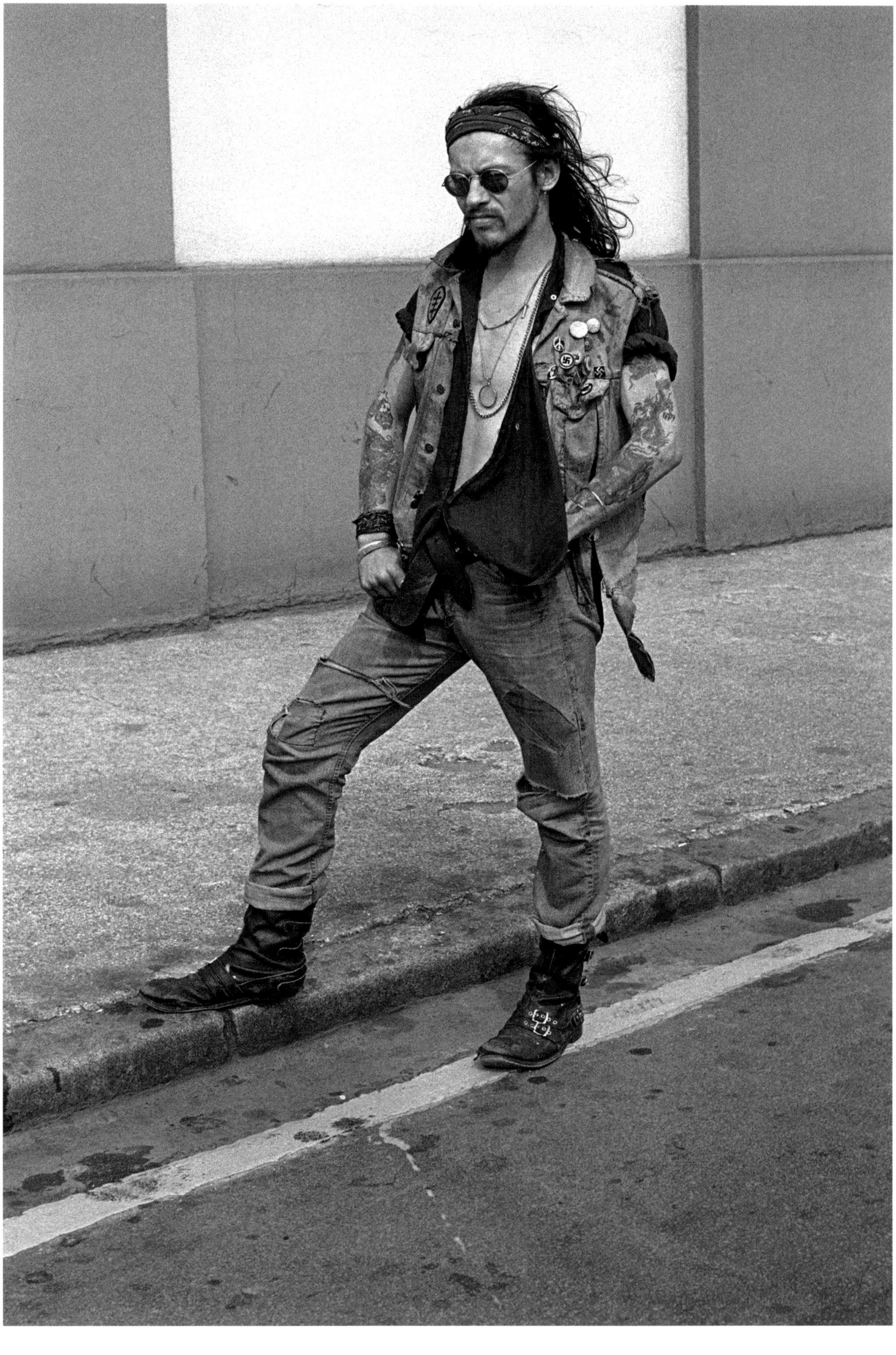

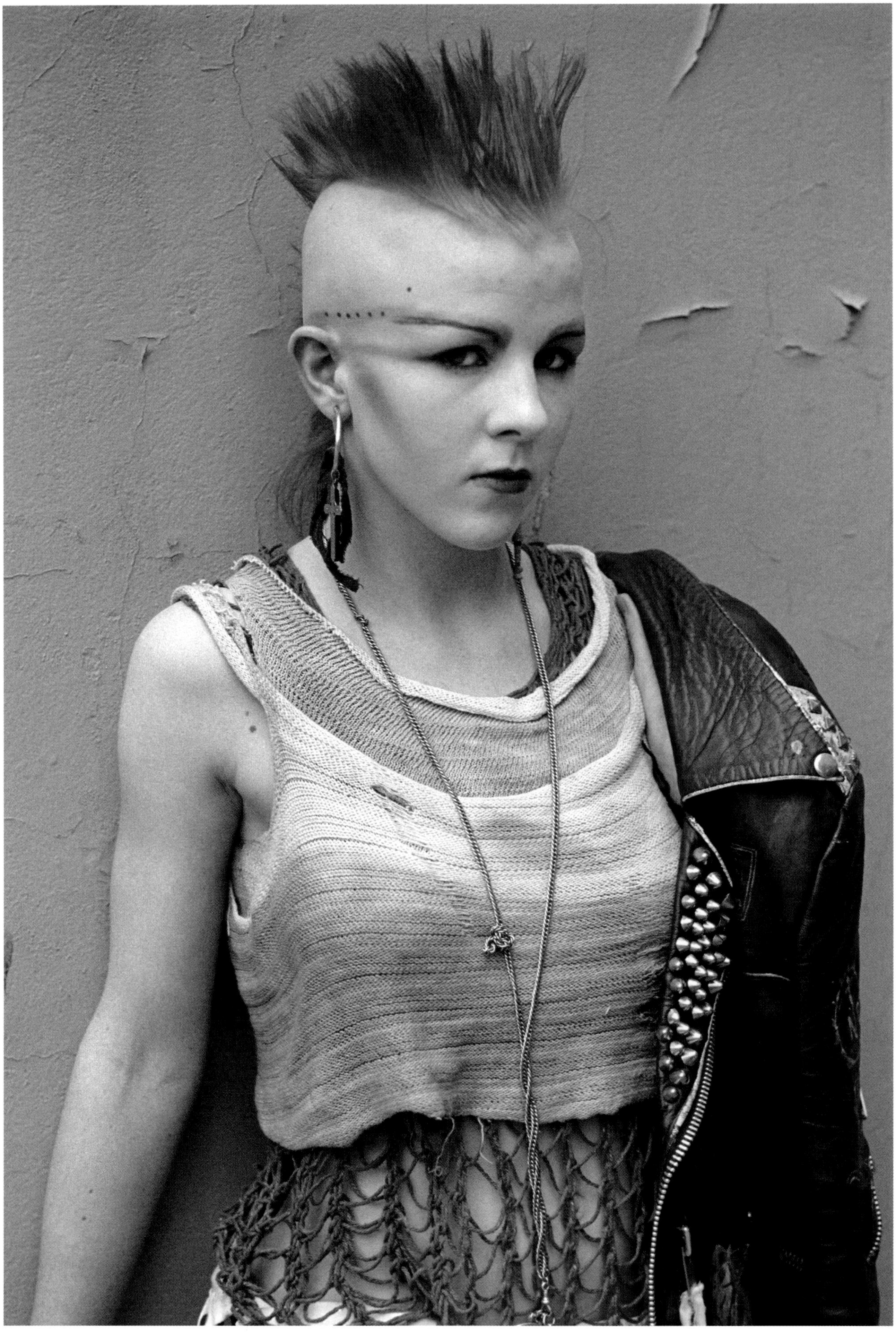

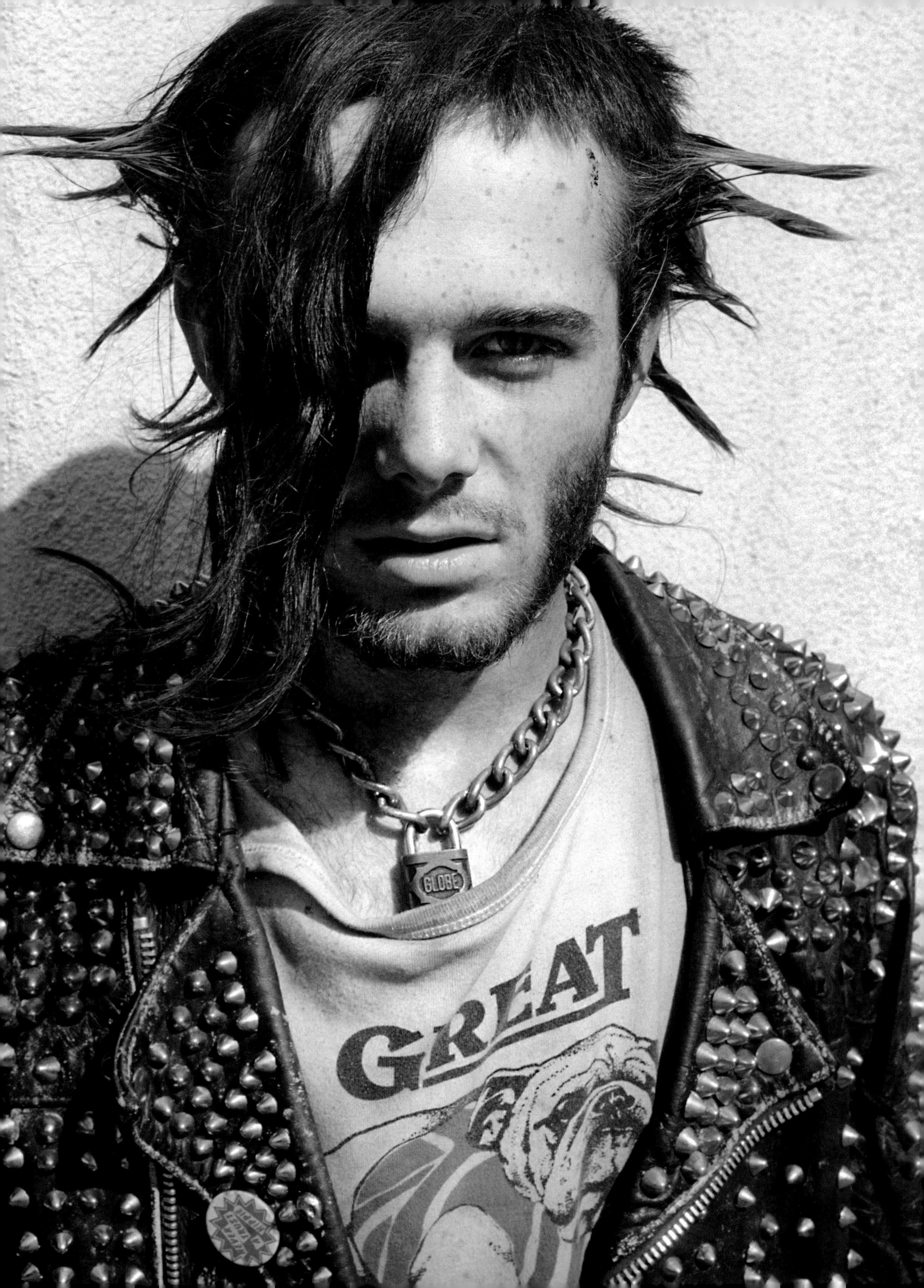
GLOBE
GREAT

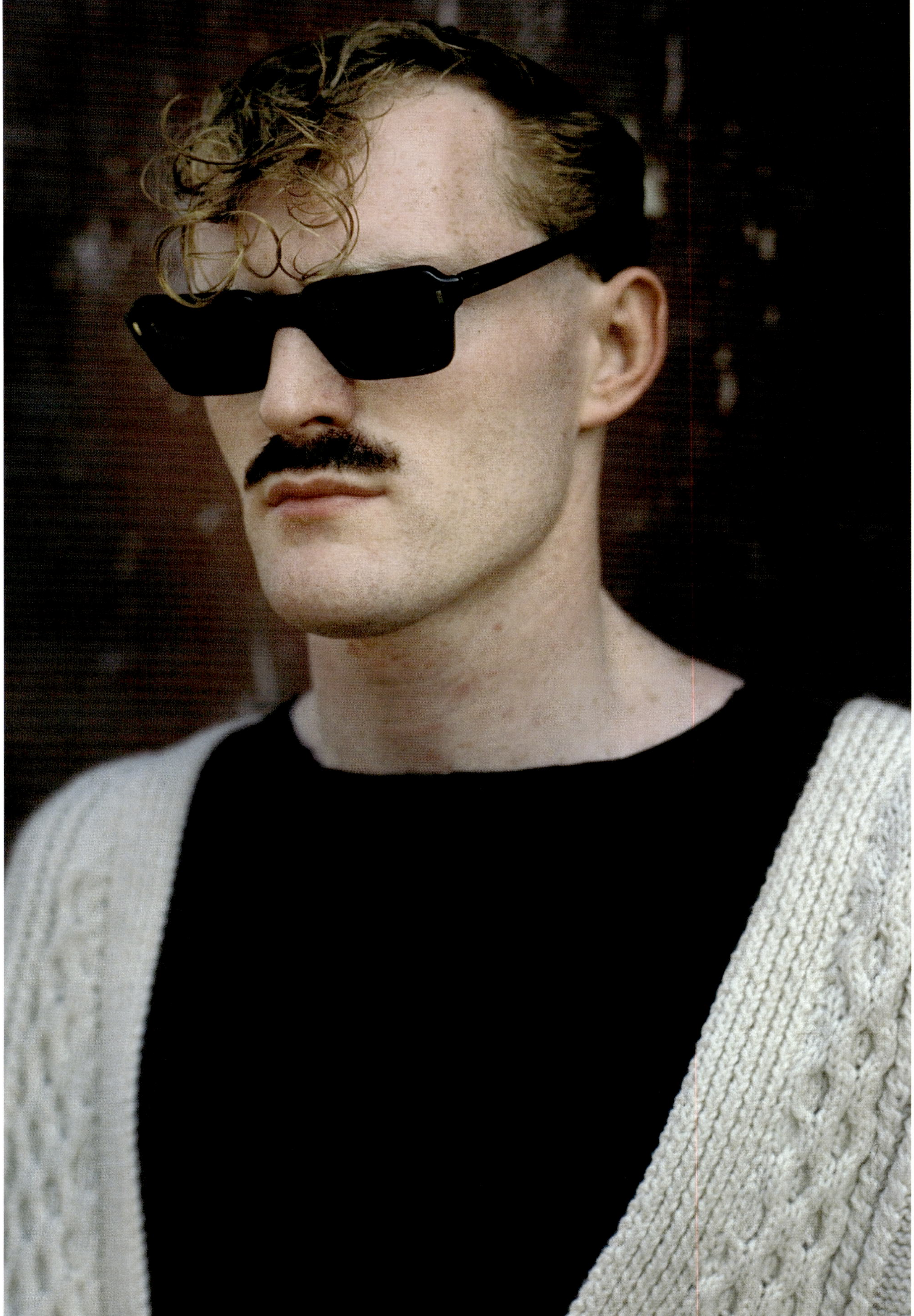

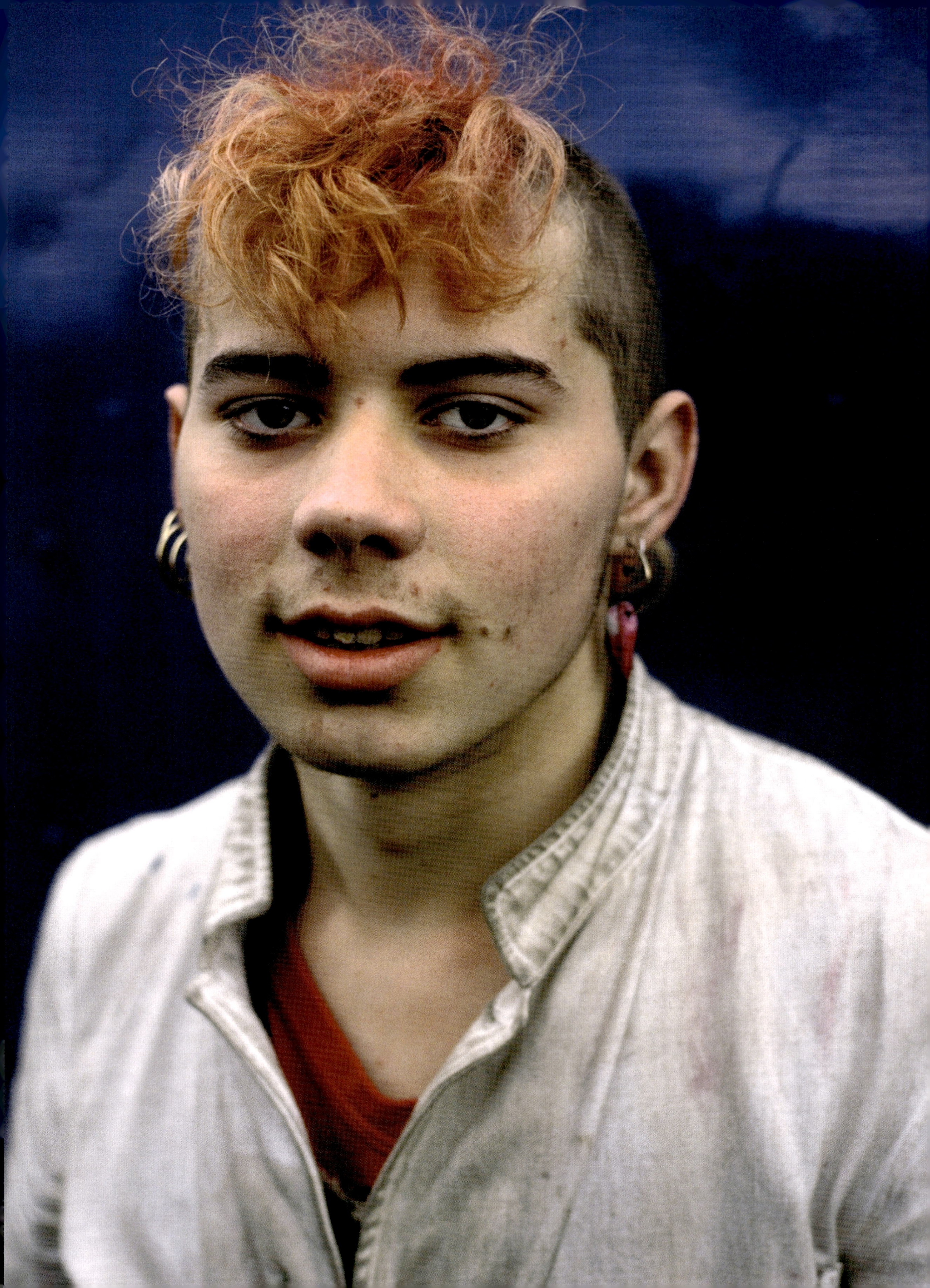

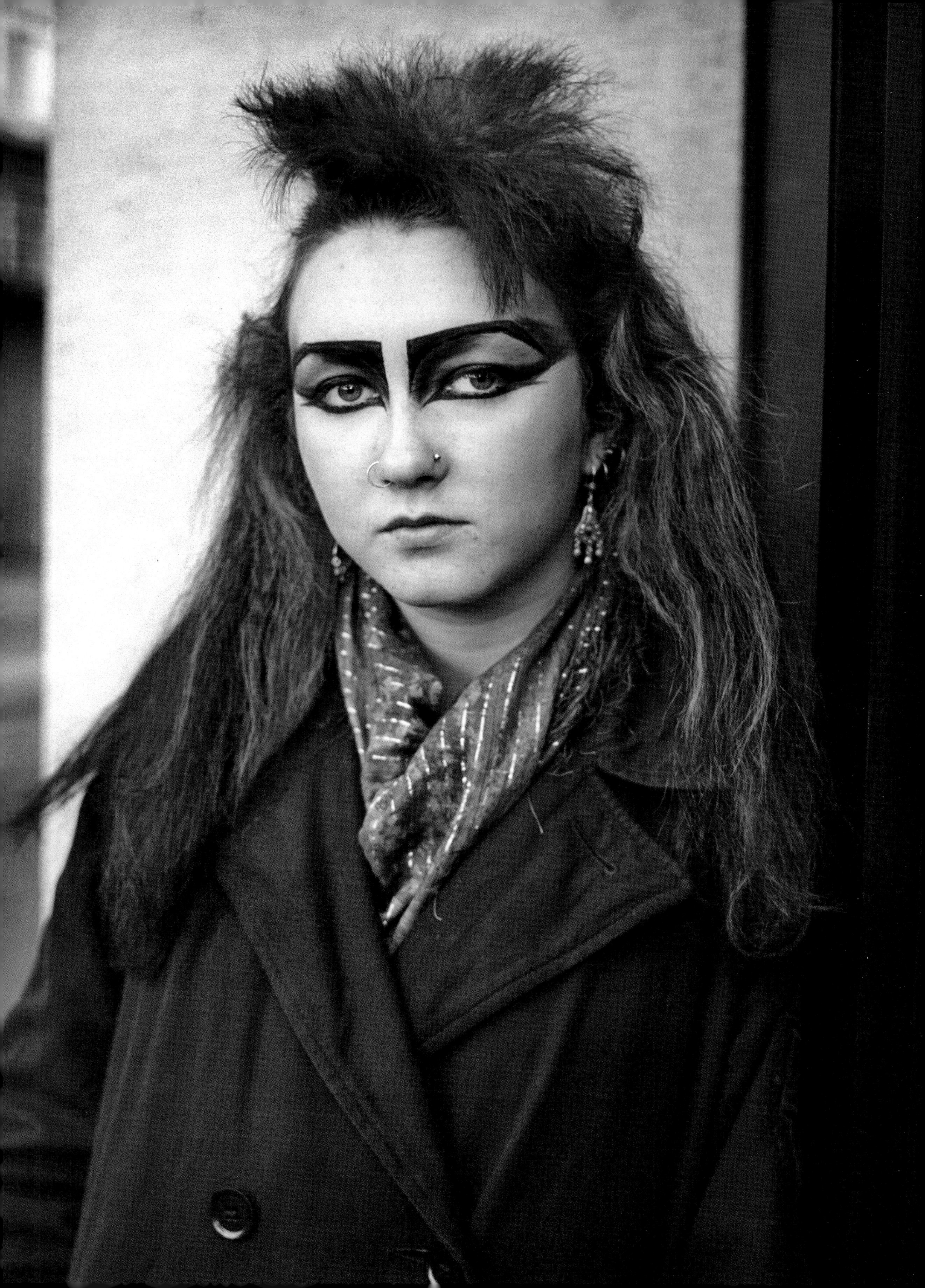

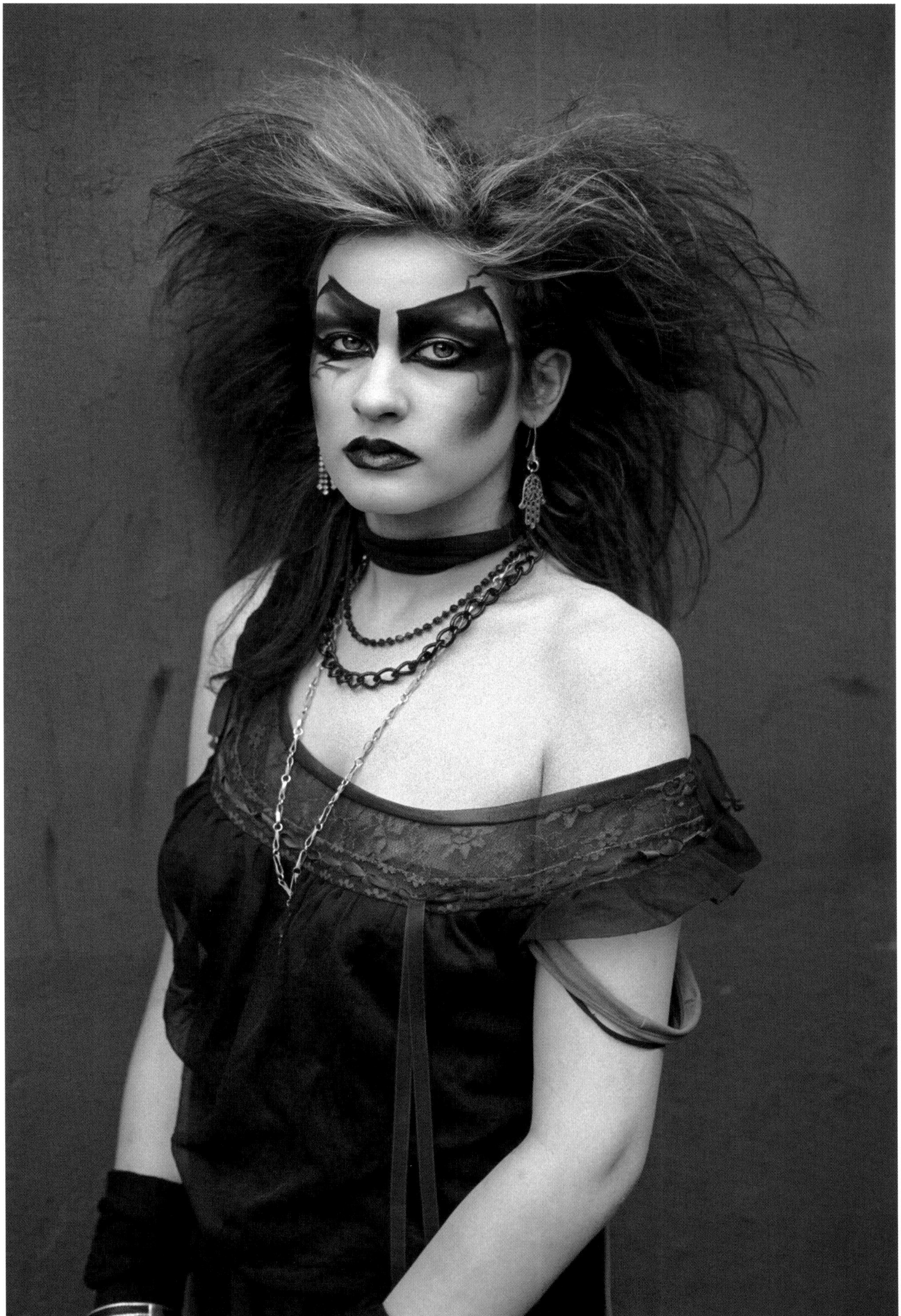

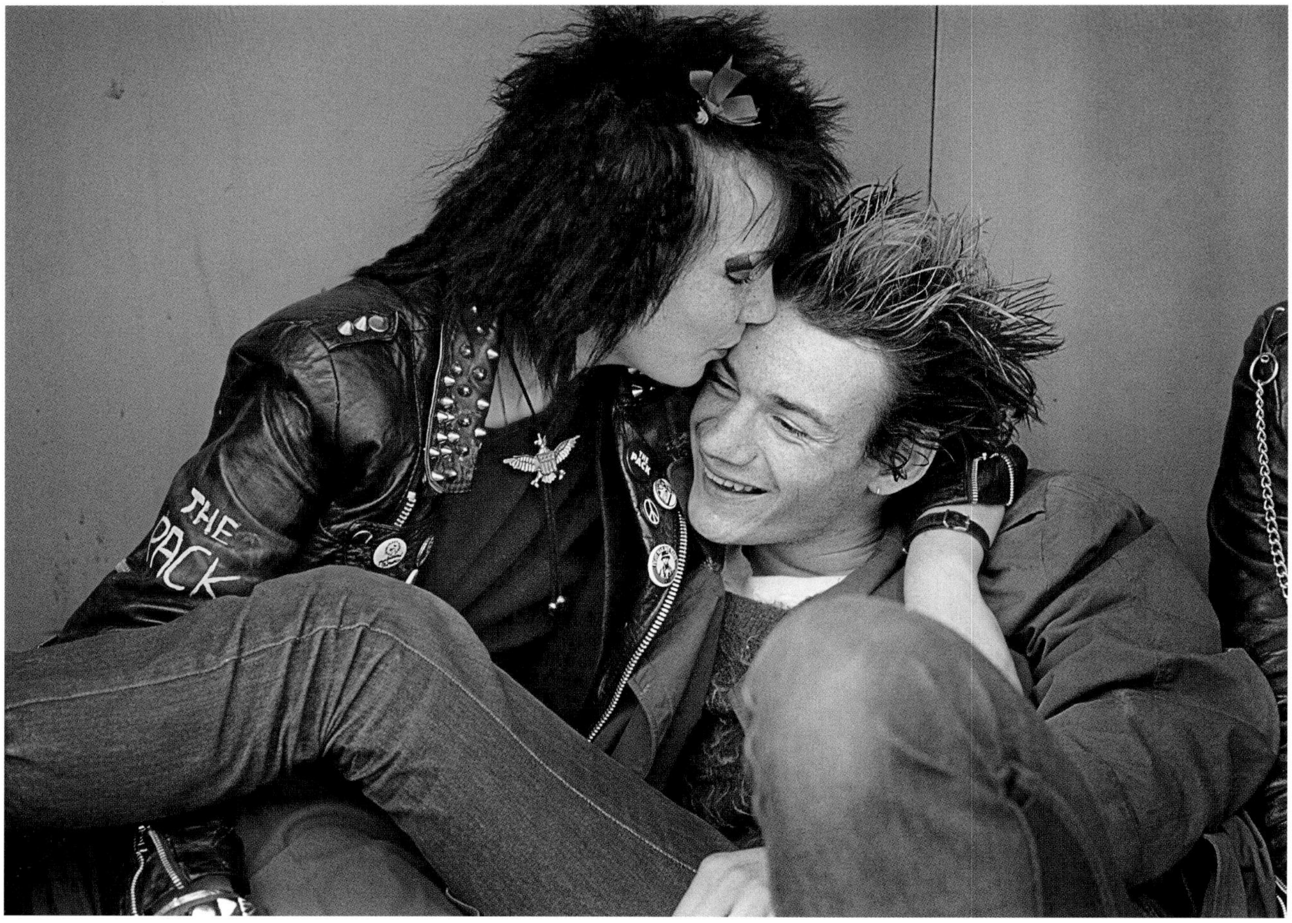
THE
PACK

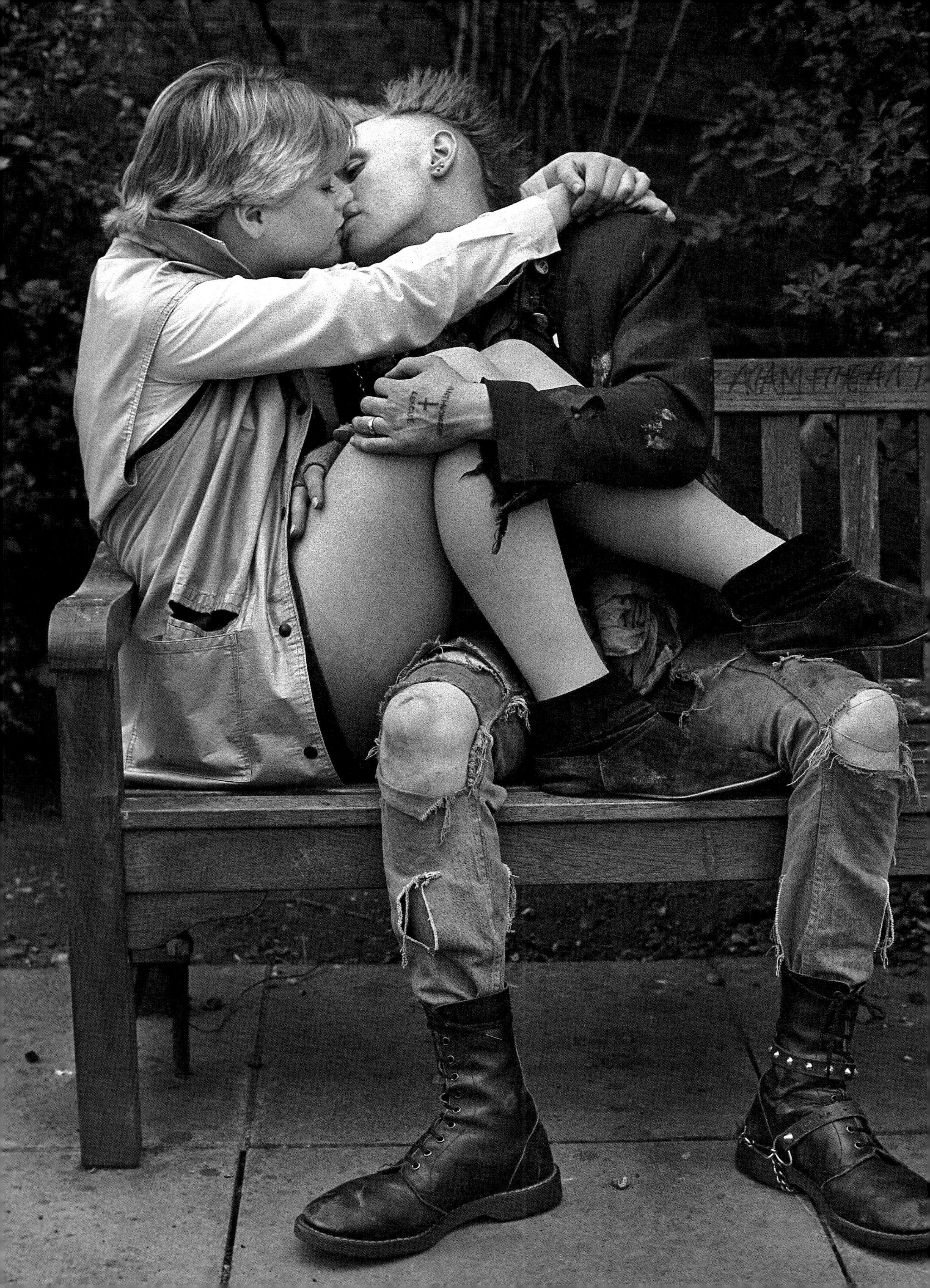

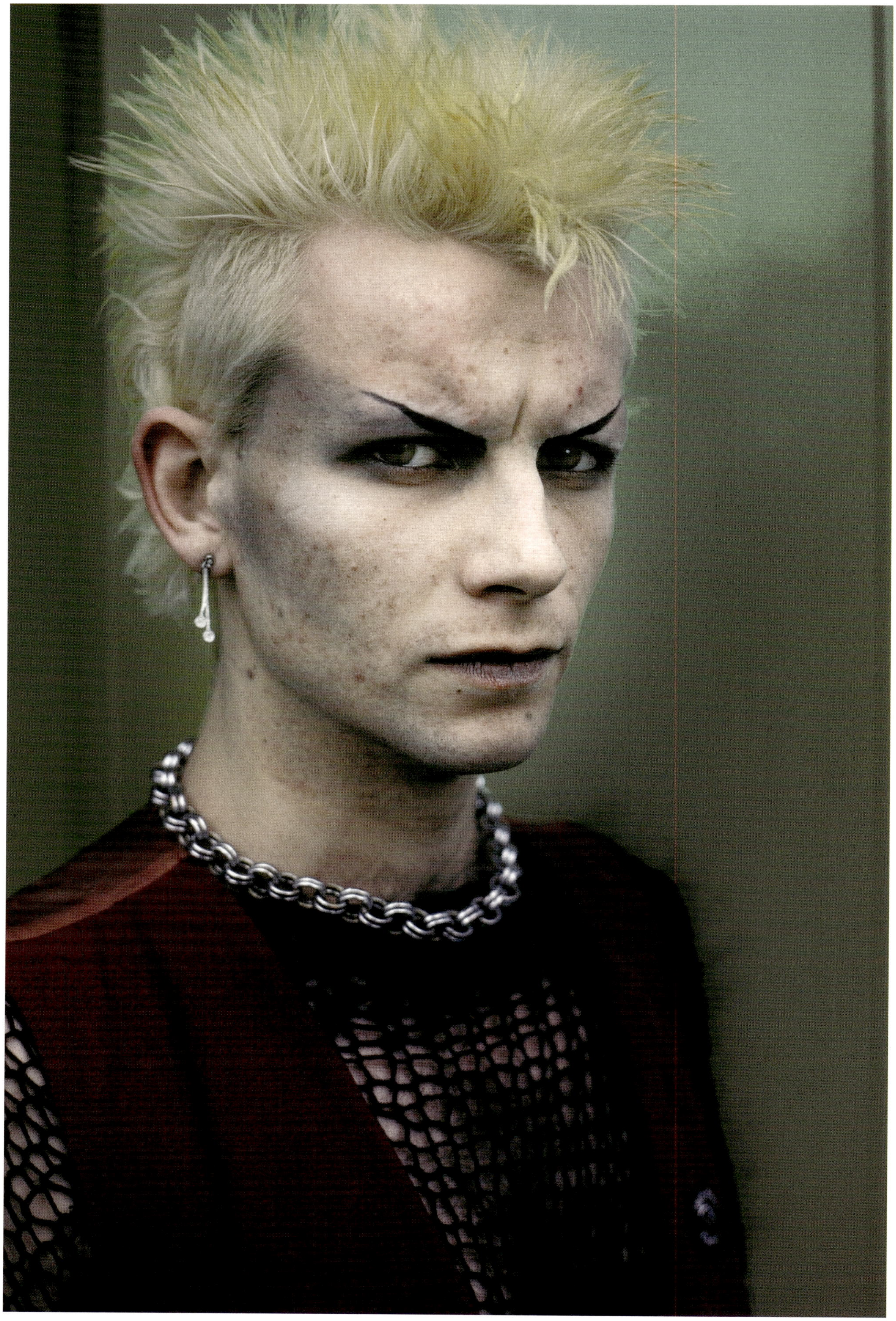

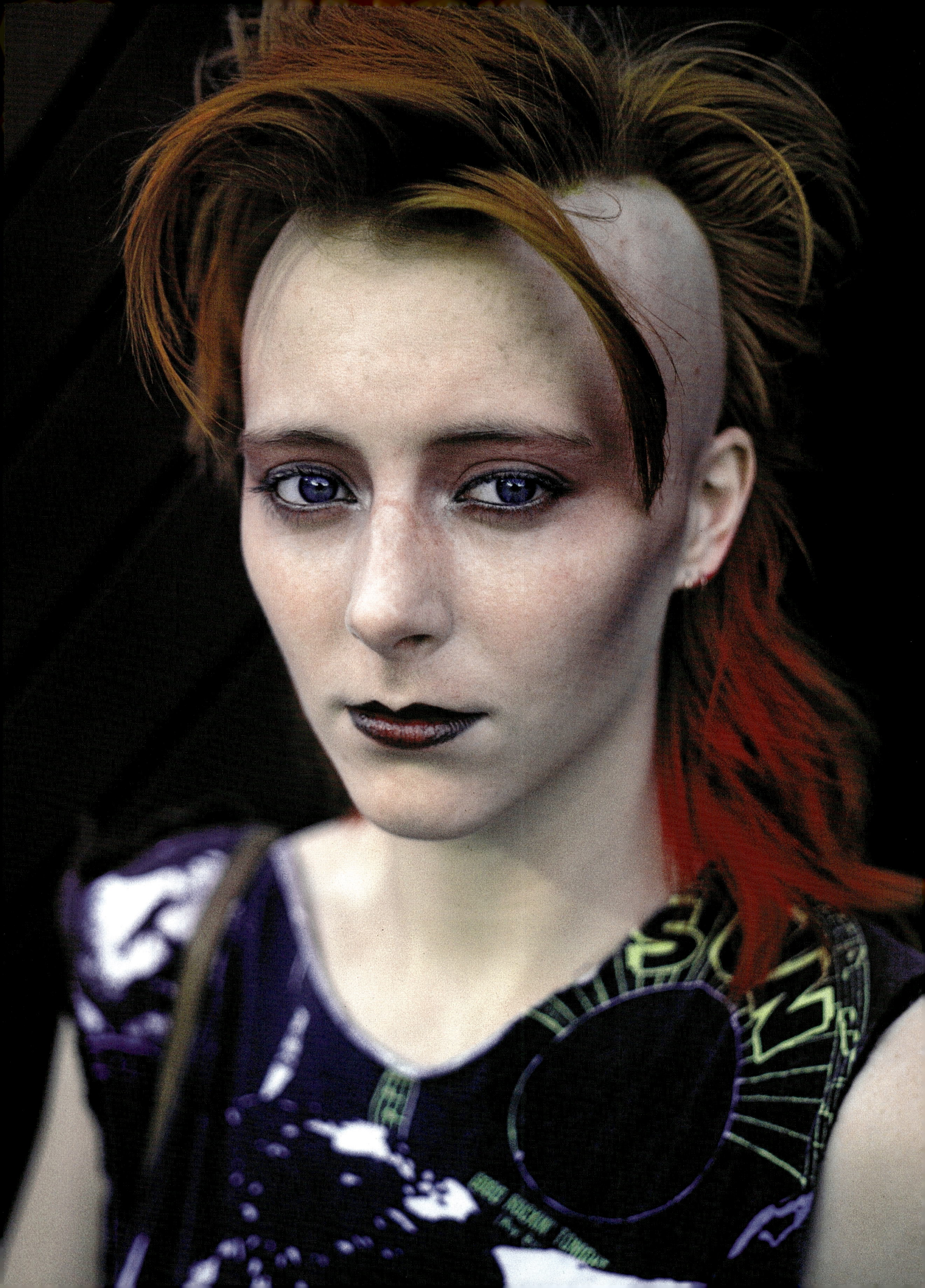

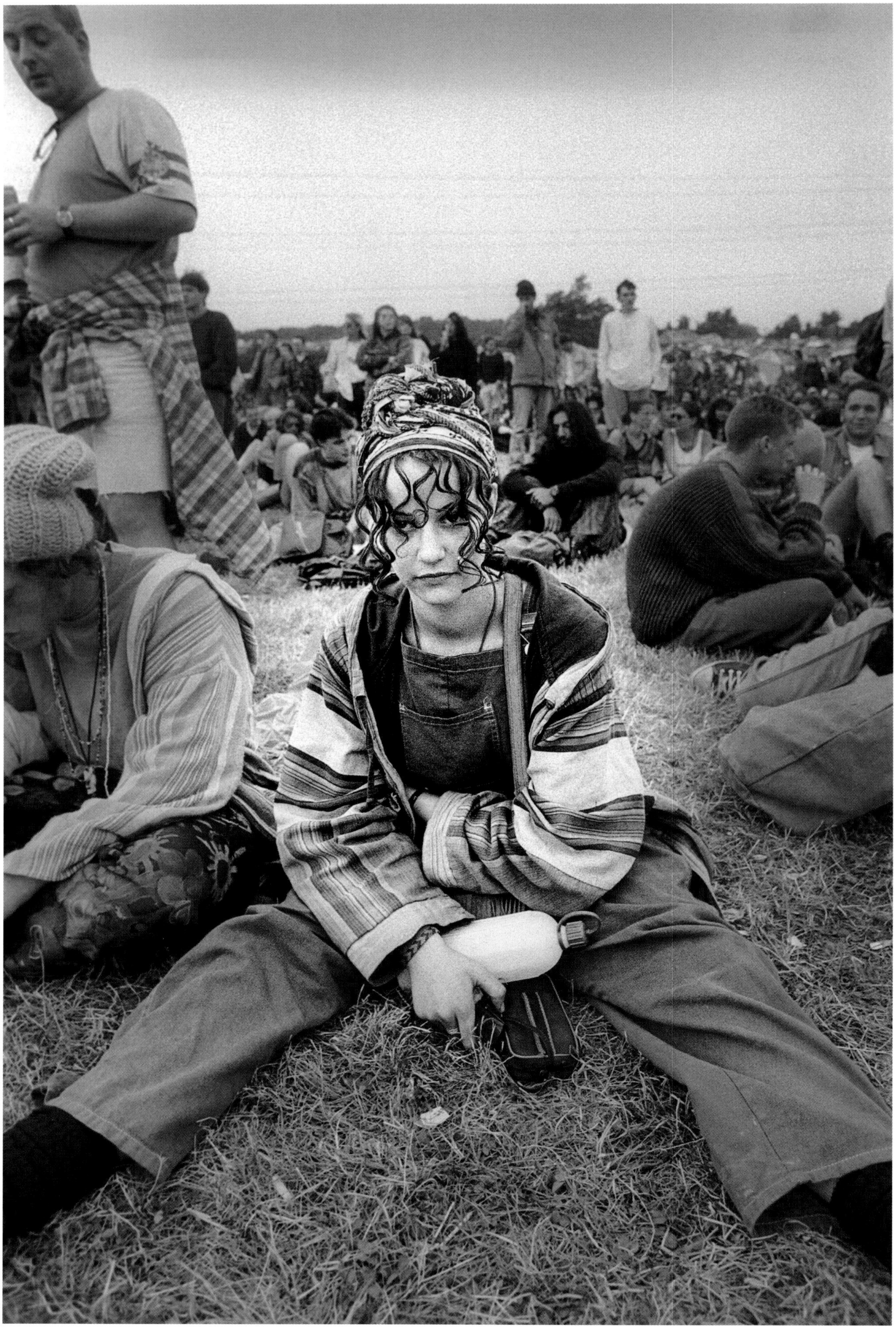

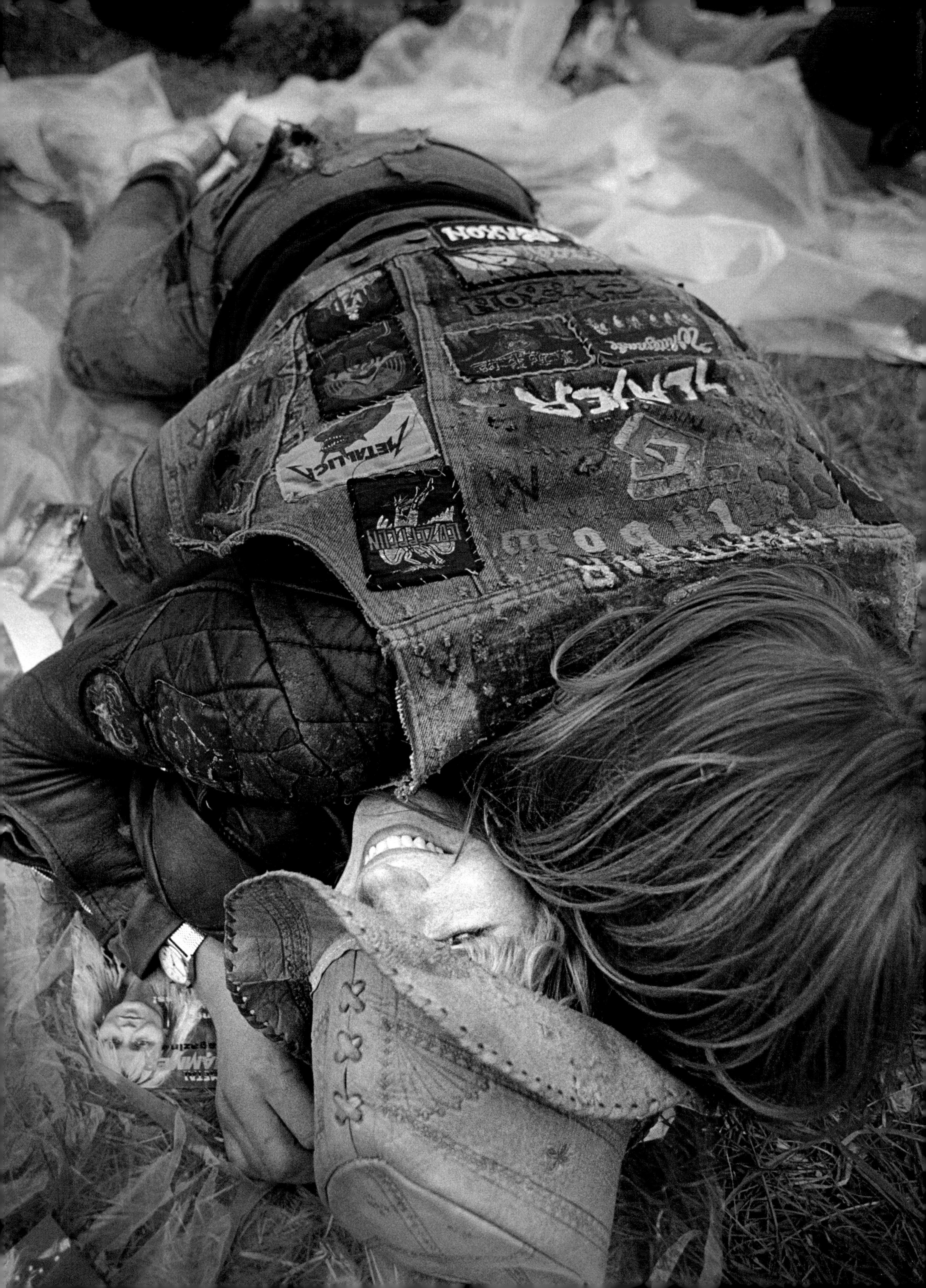
SAXON
METALLICA
SLAYER

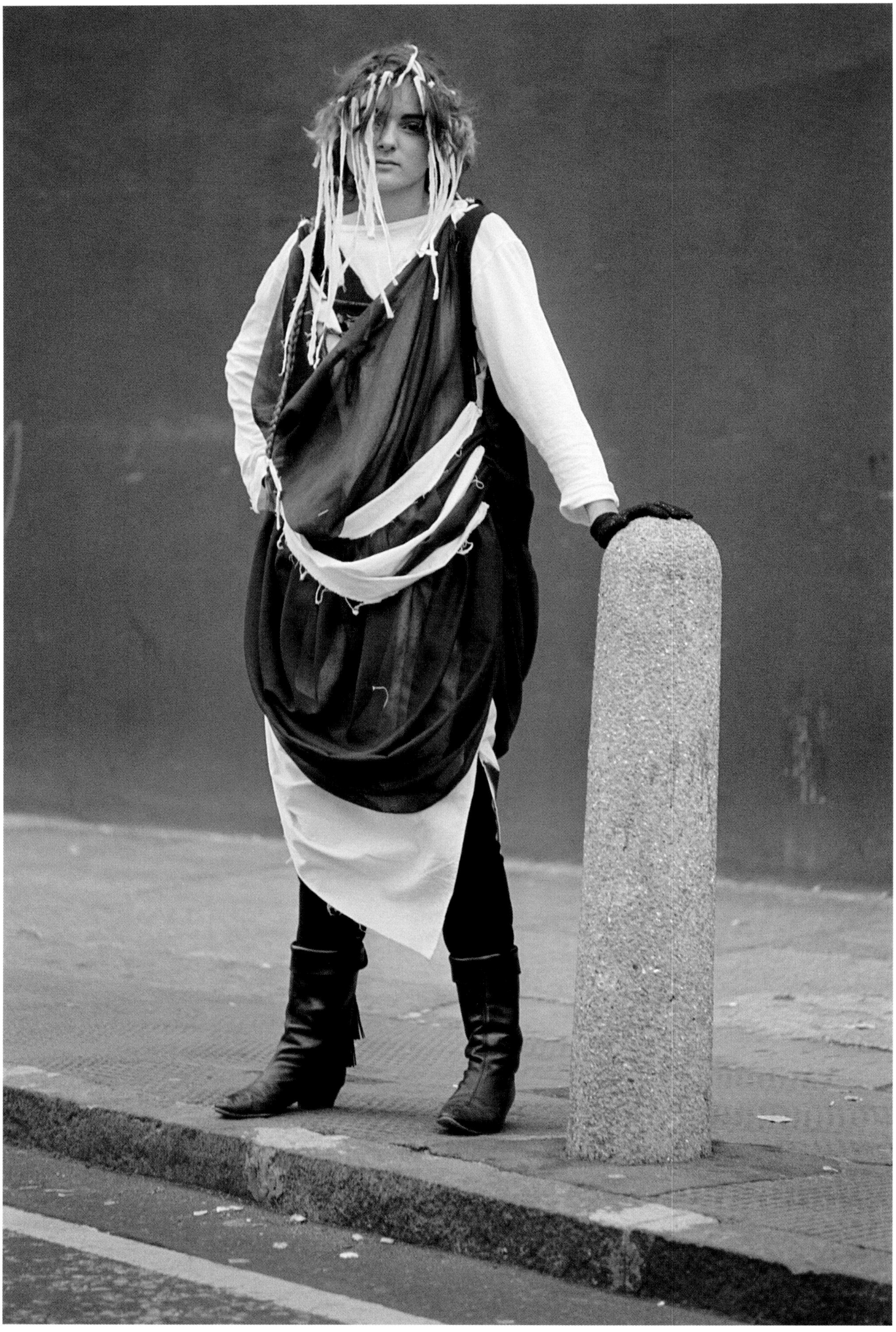

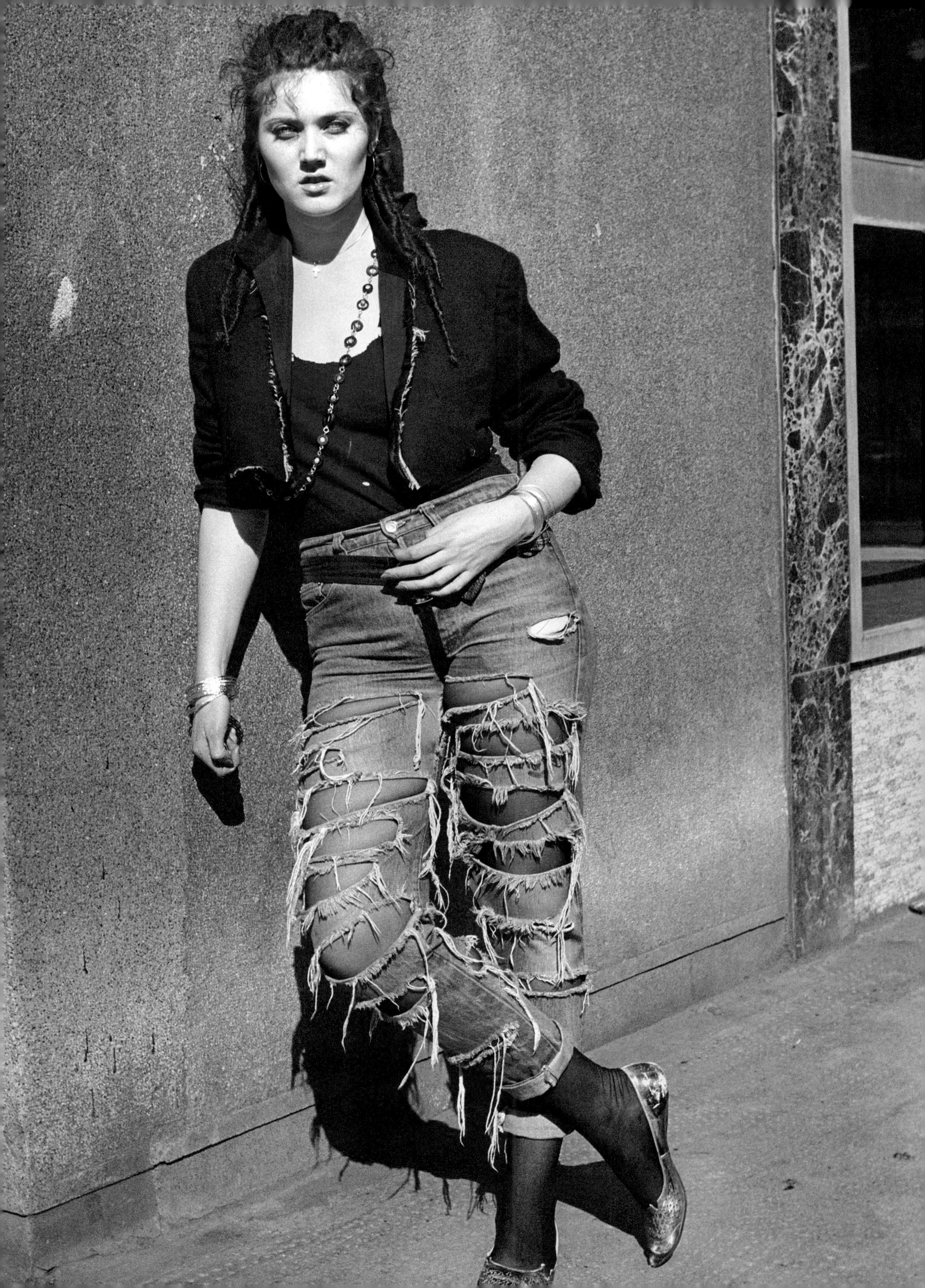

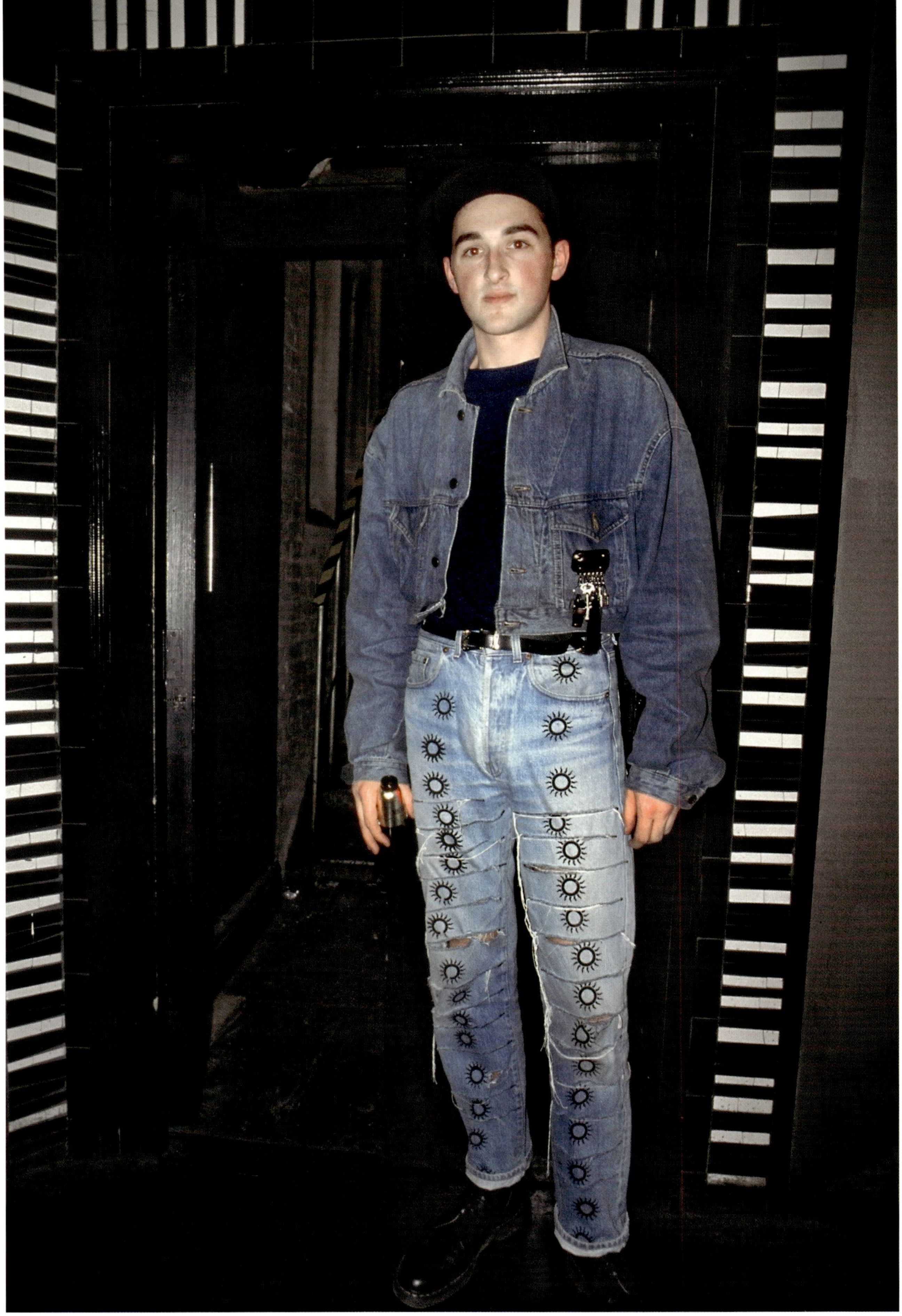

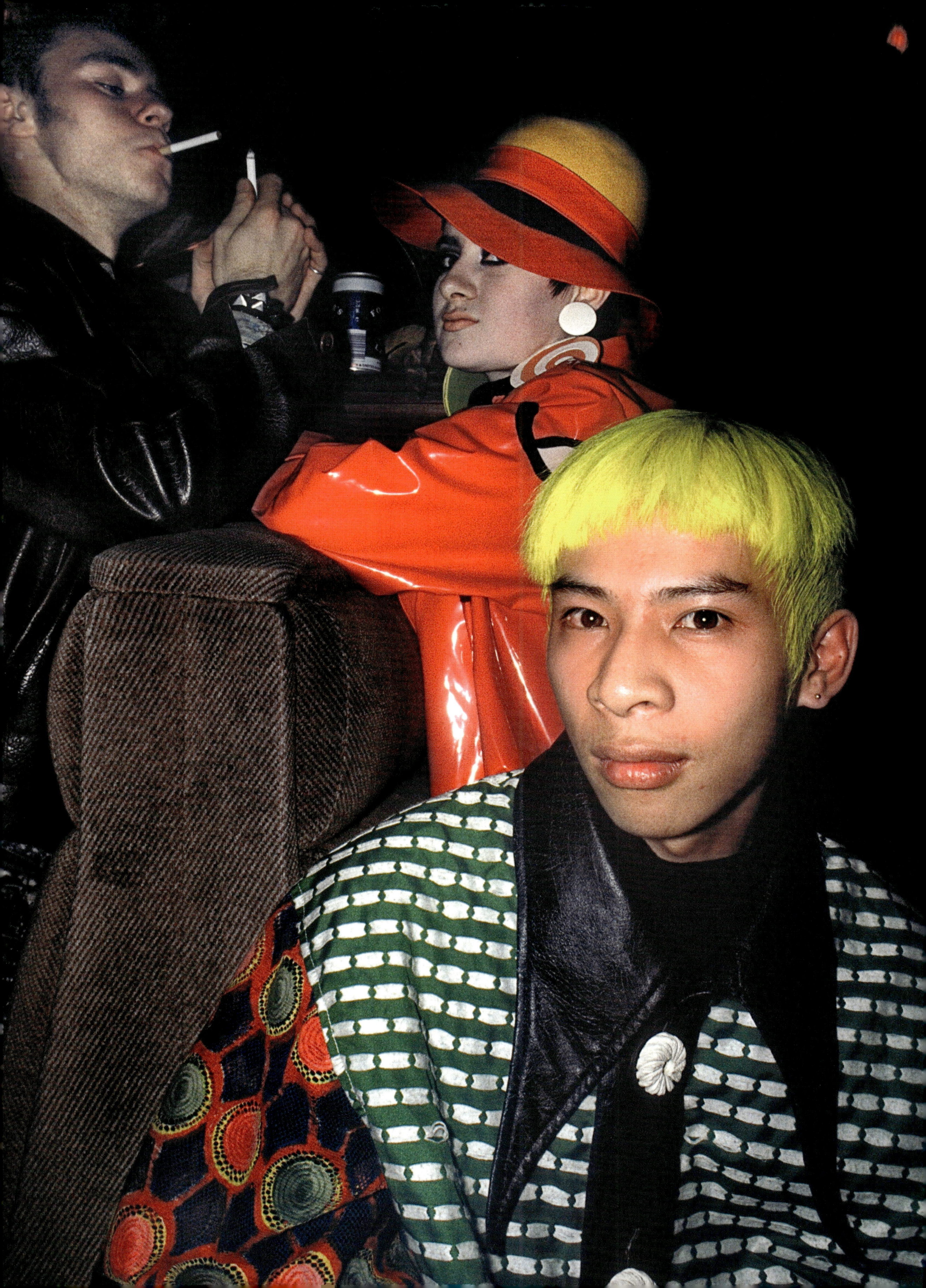

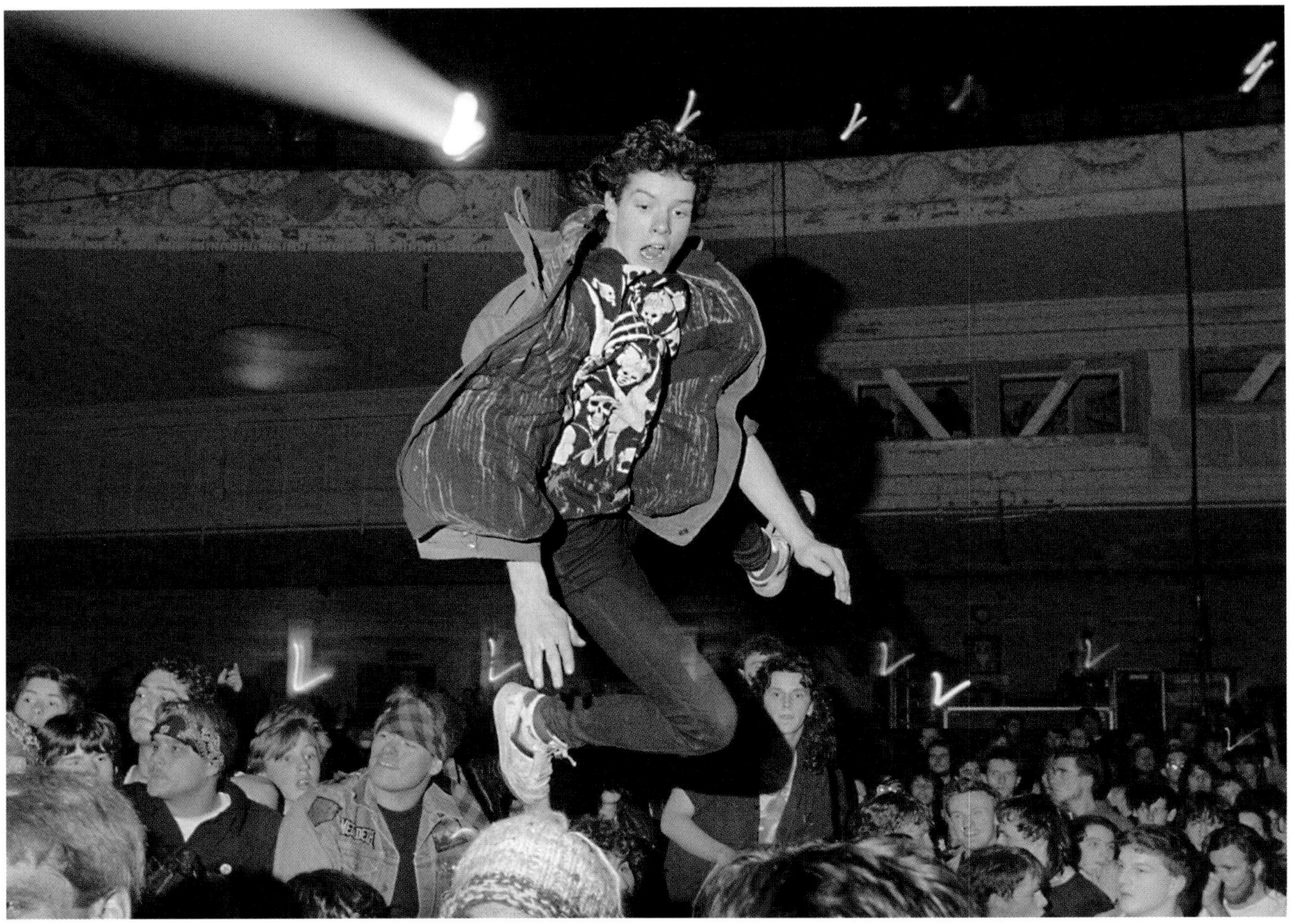

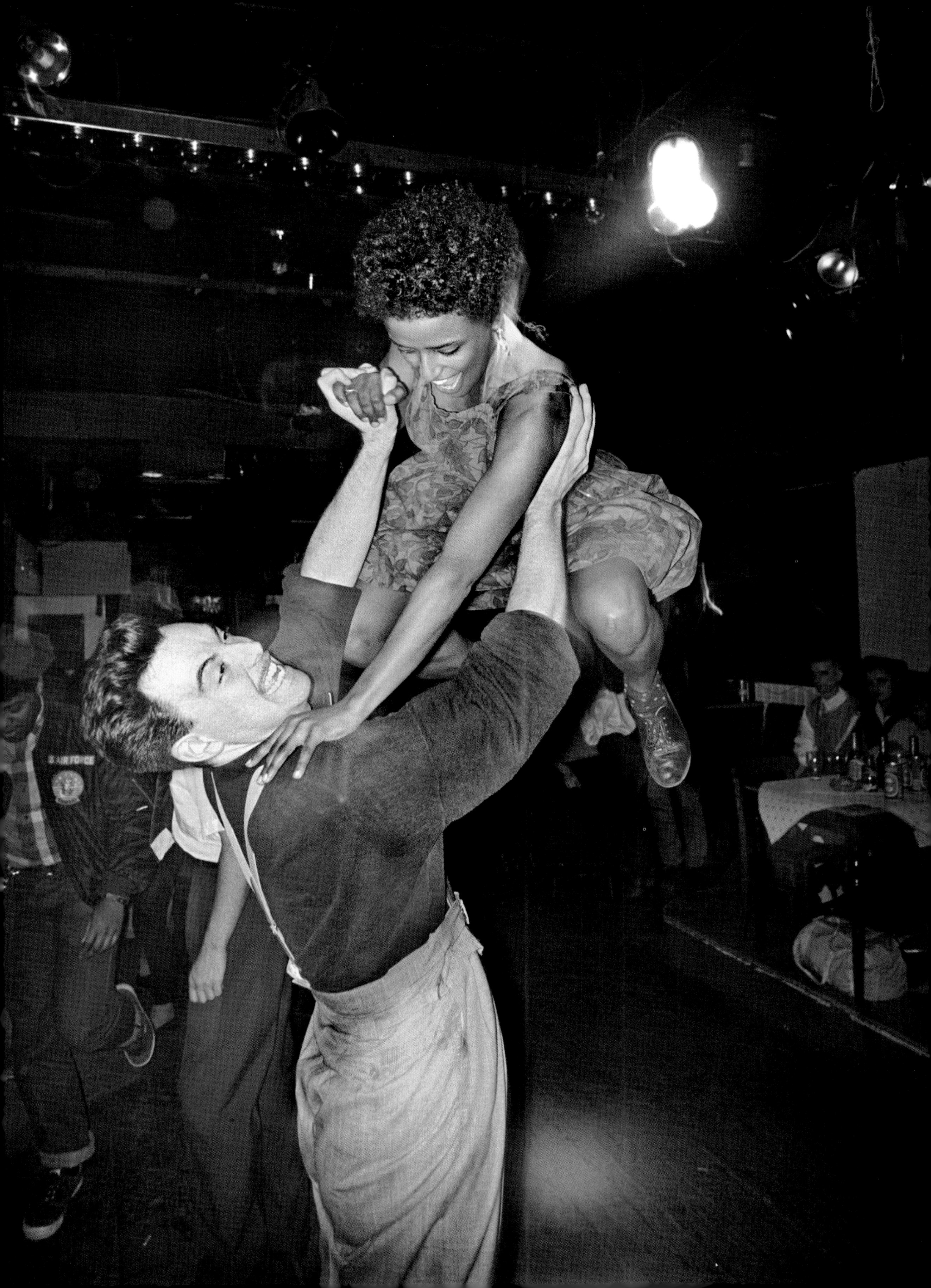
S AIR FORCE

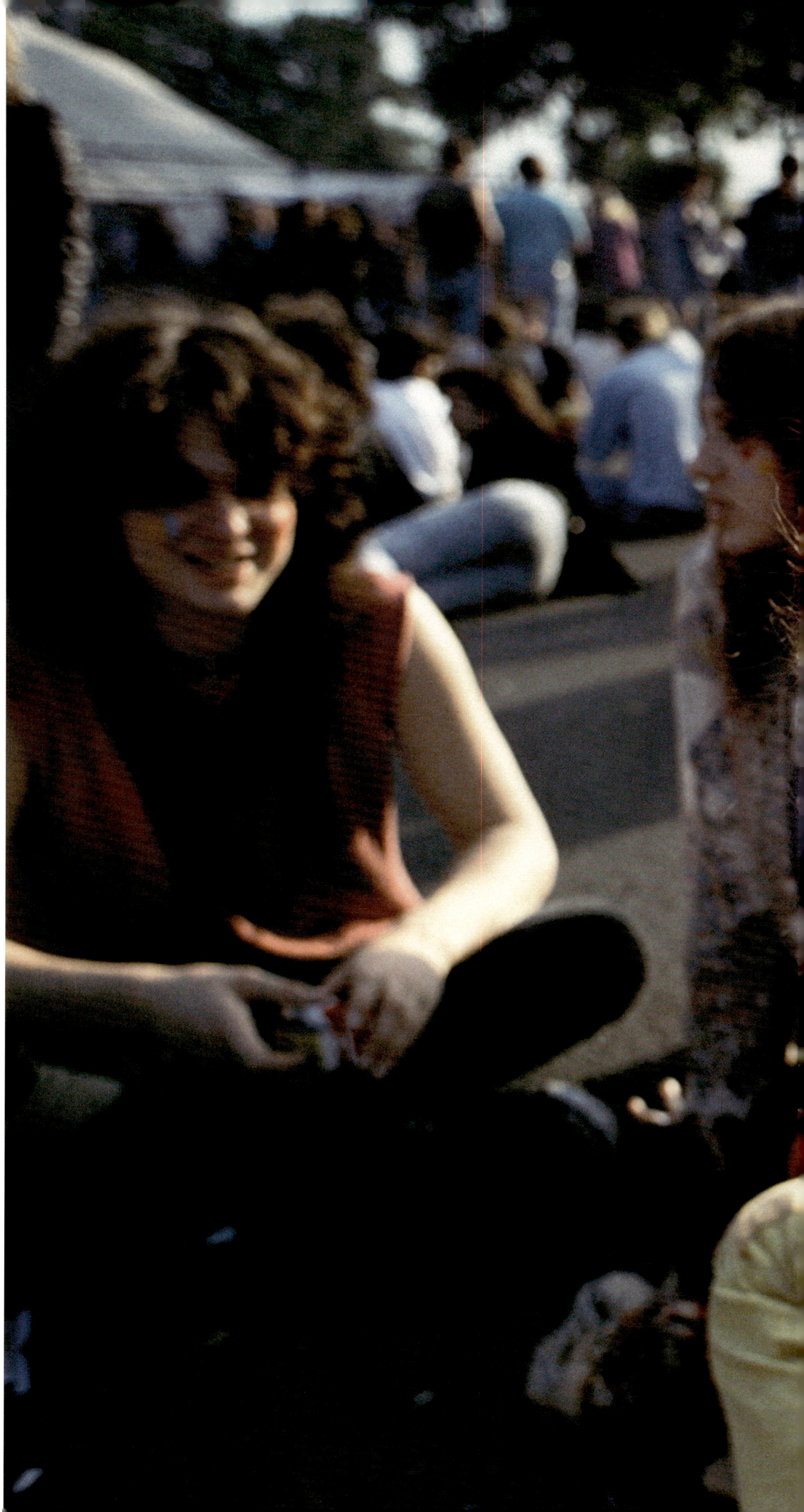

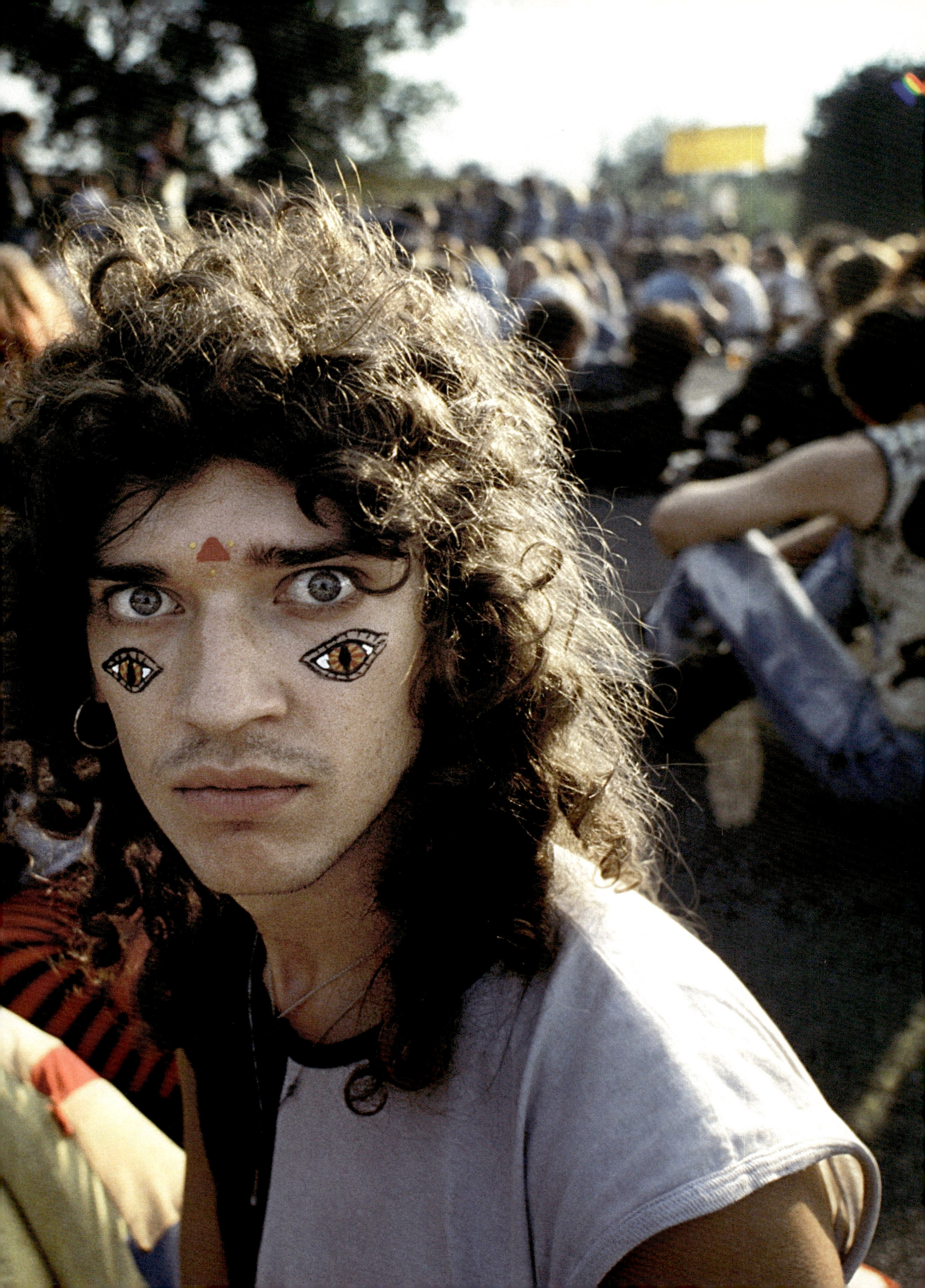

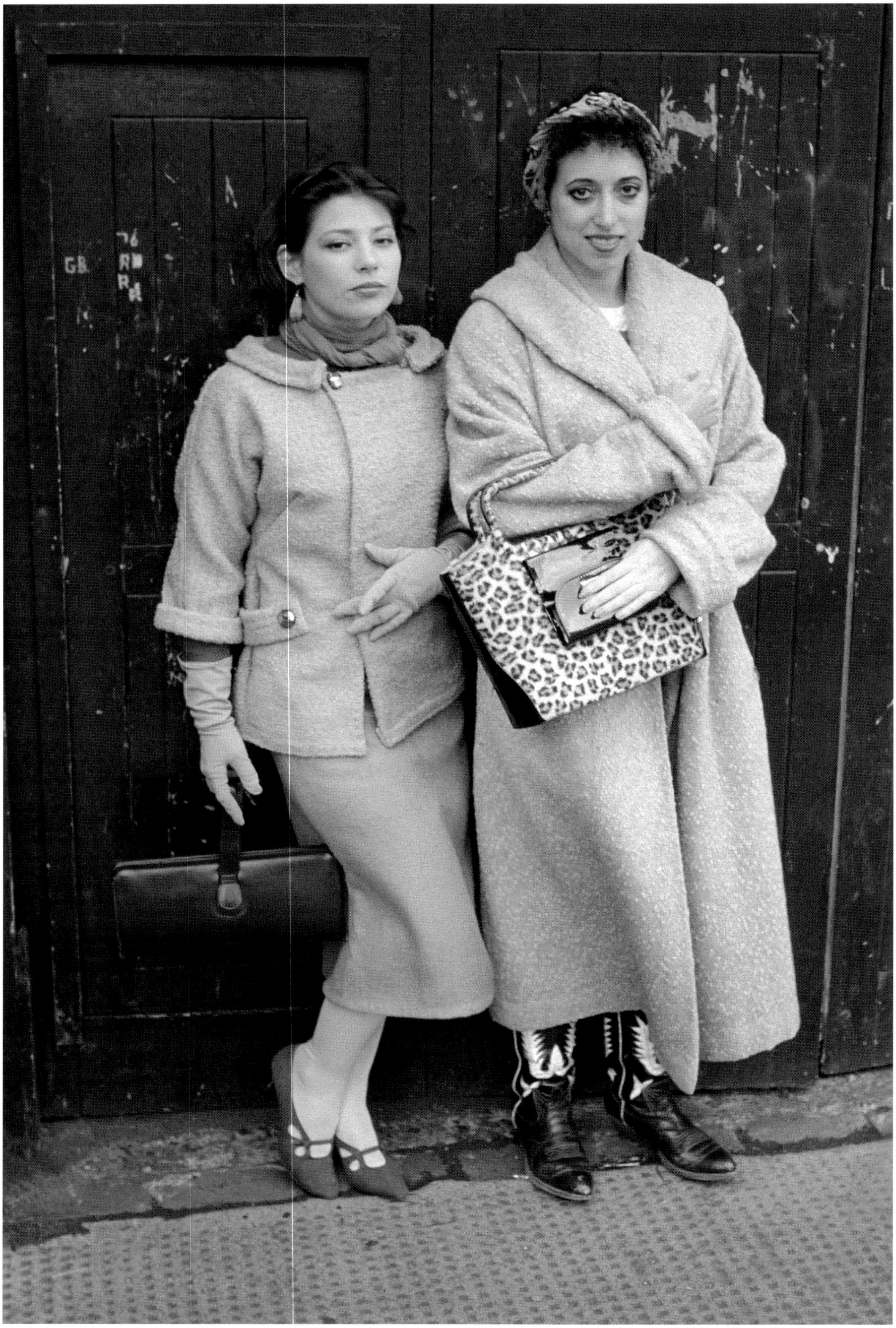

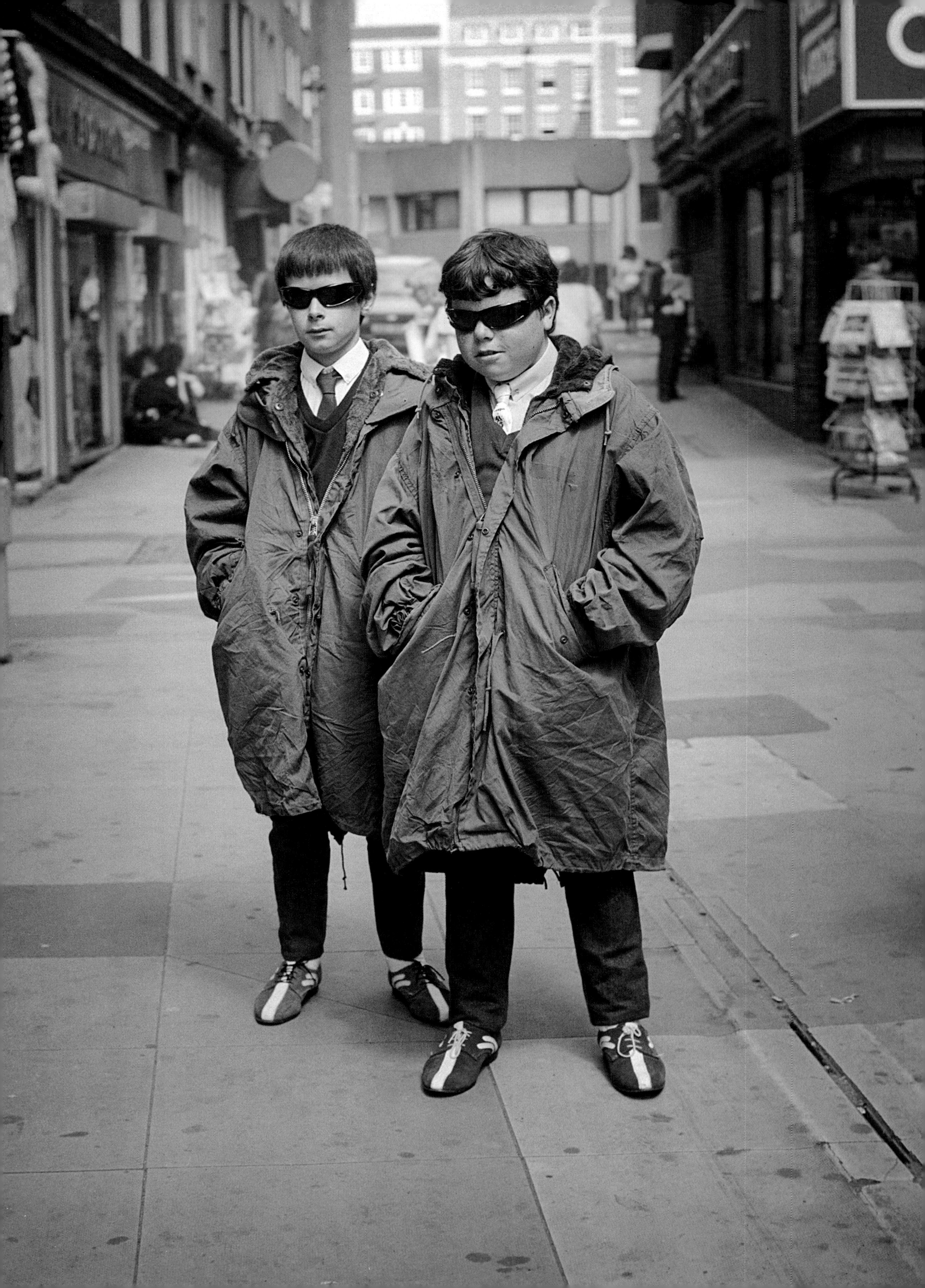

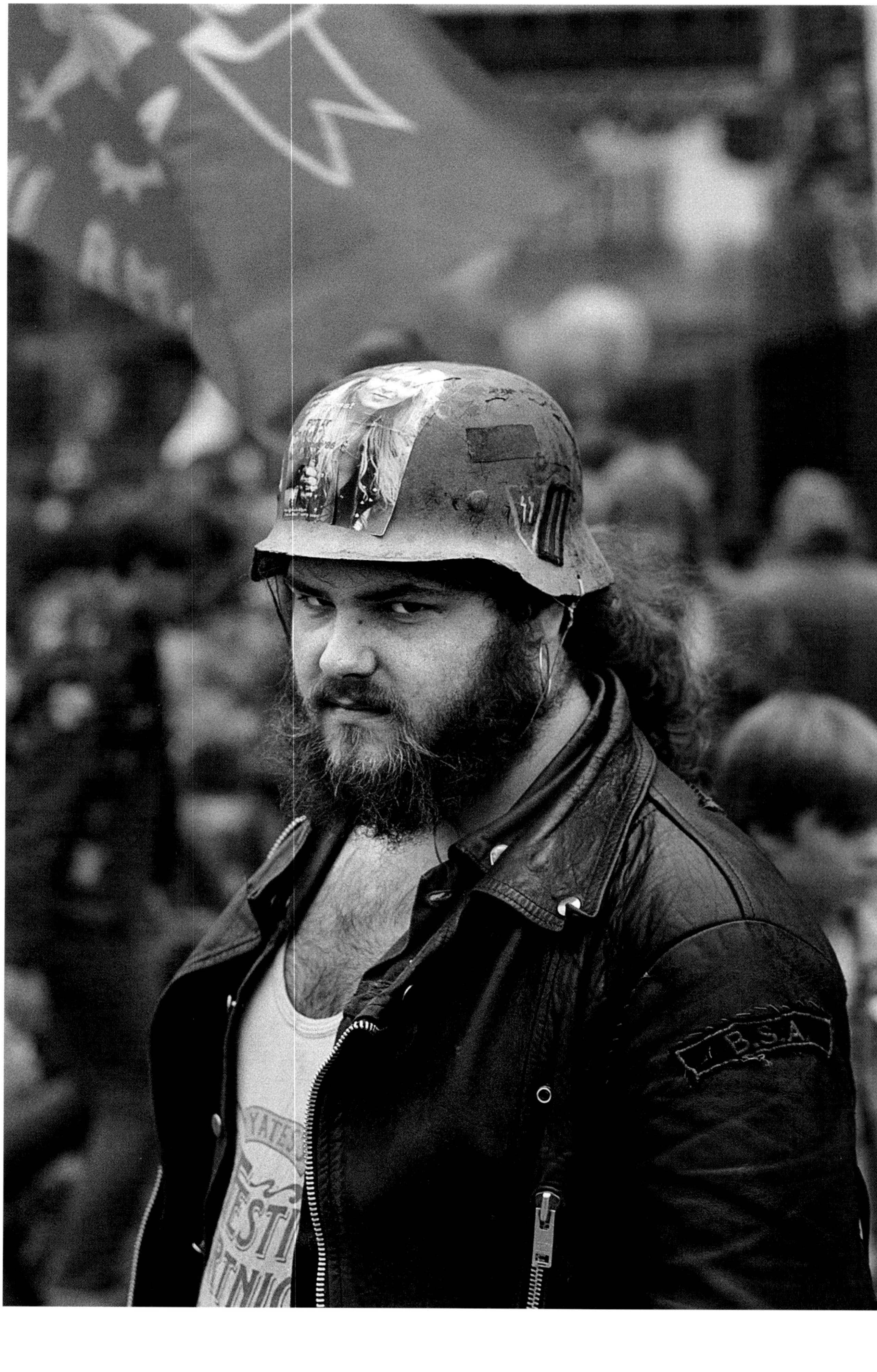
B.S.A

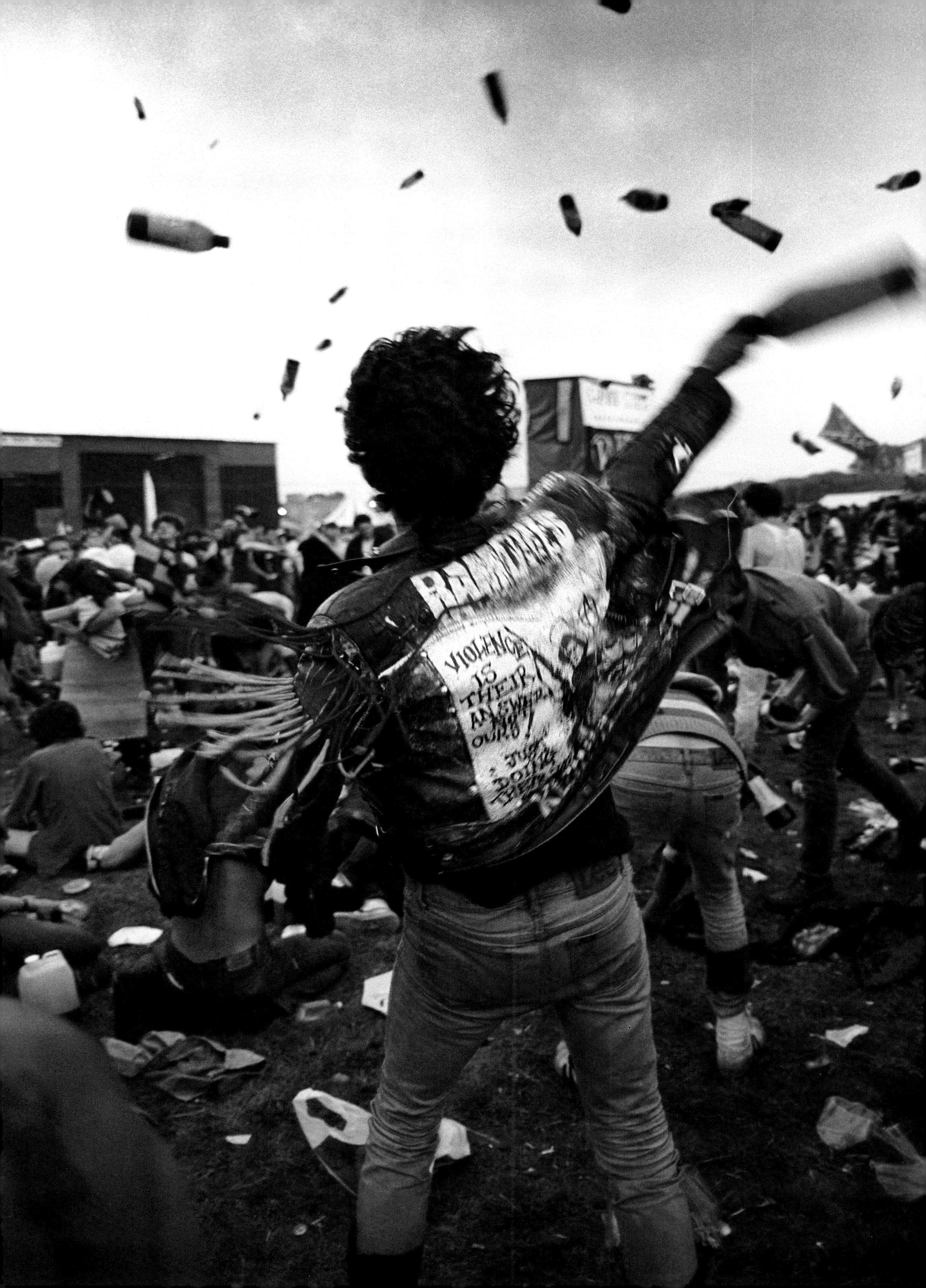
VIOLENCE
IS
THEIR

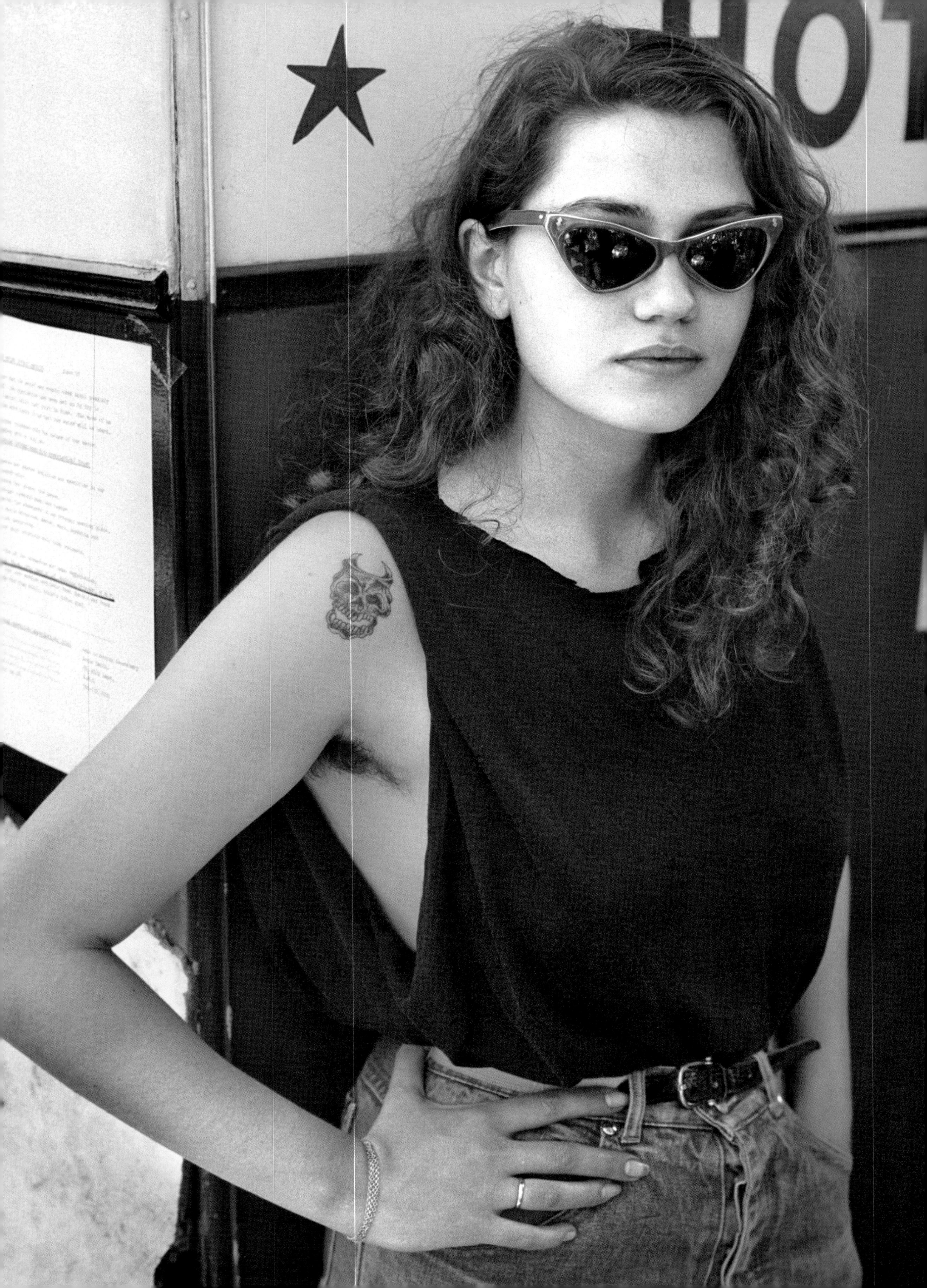

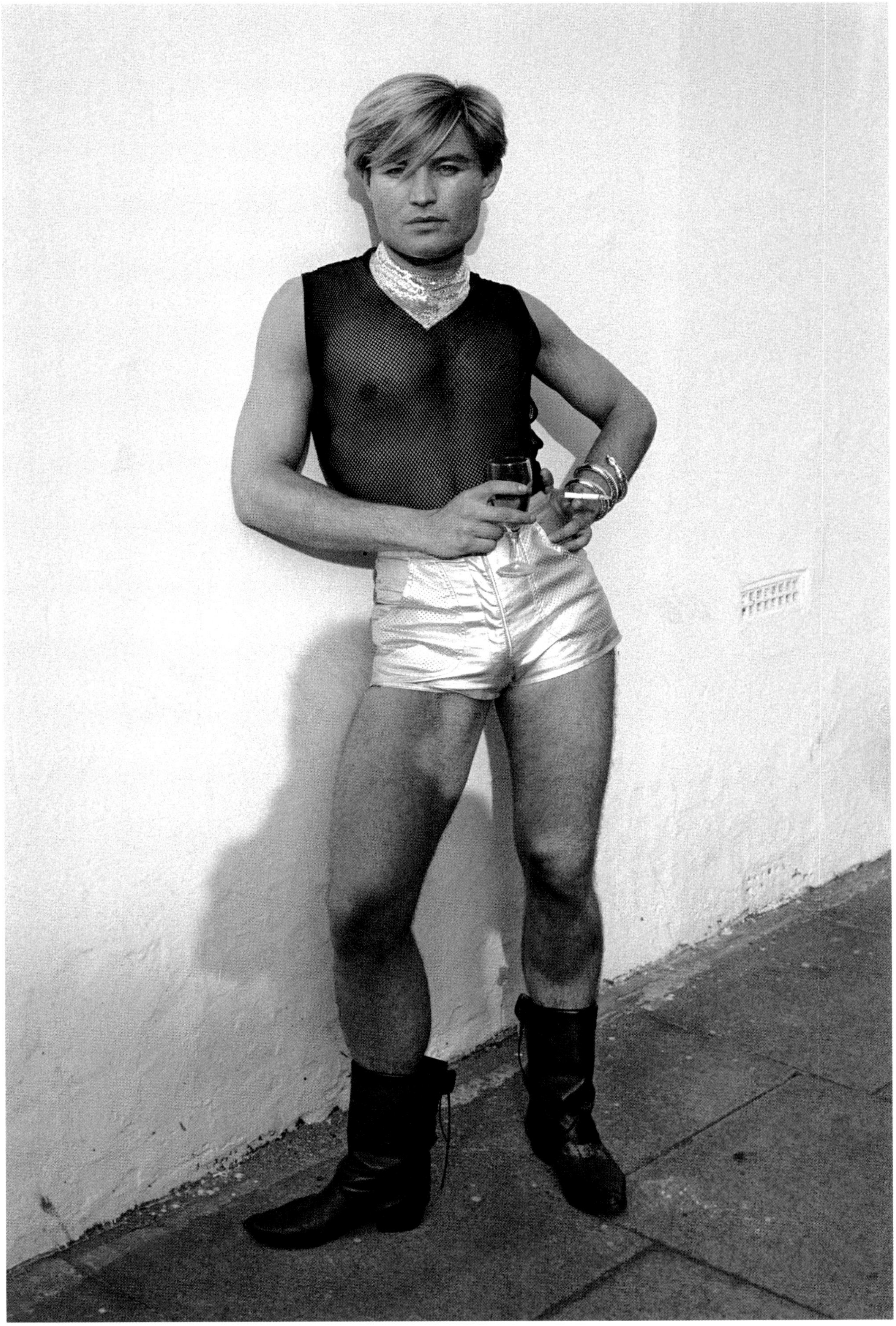

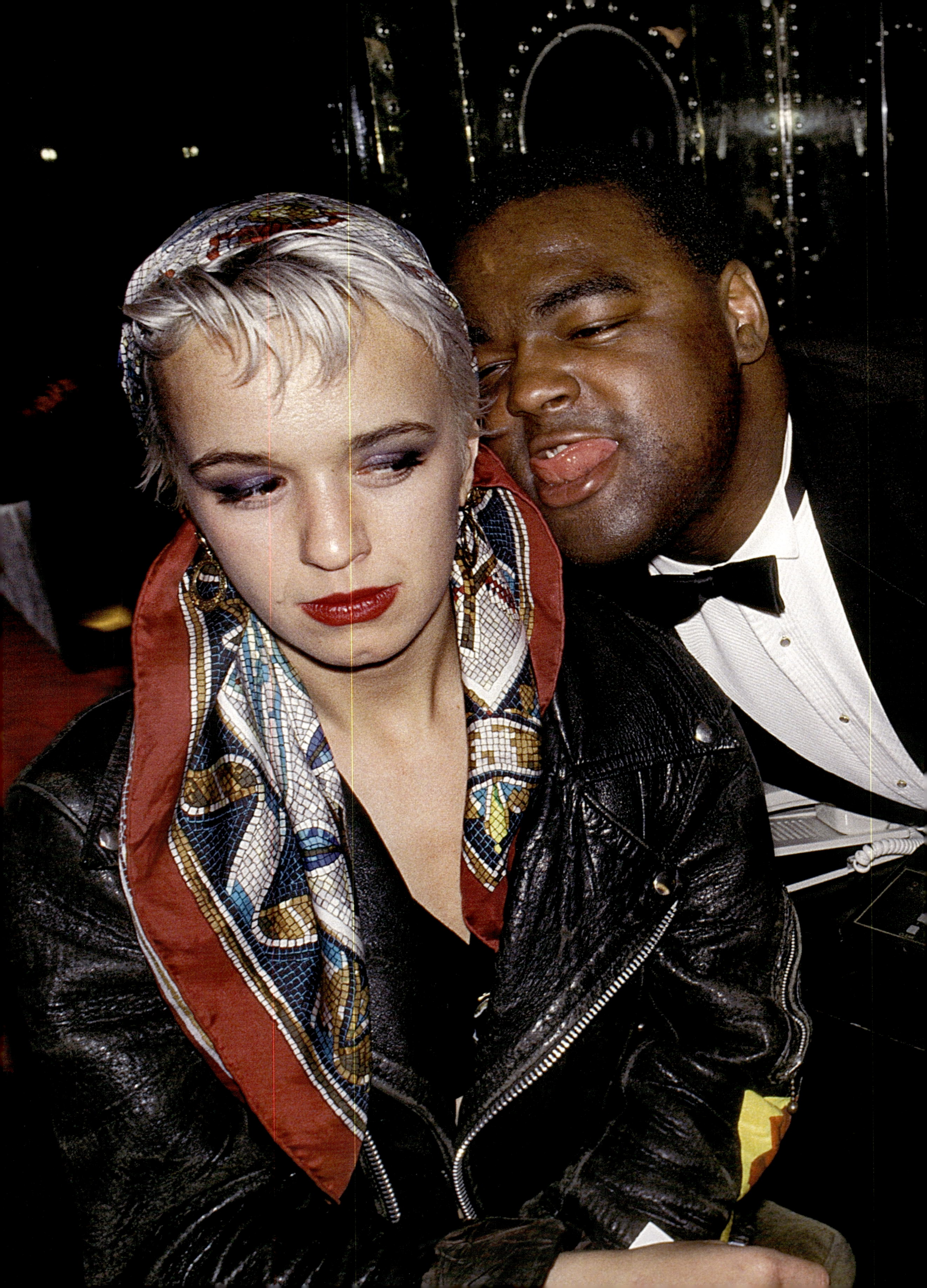

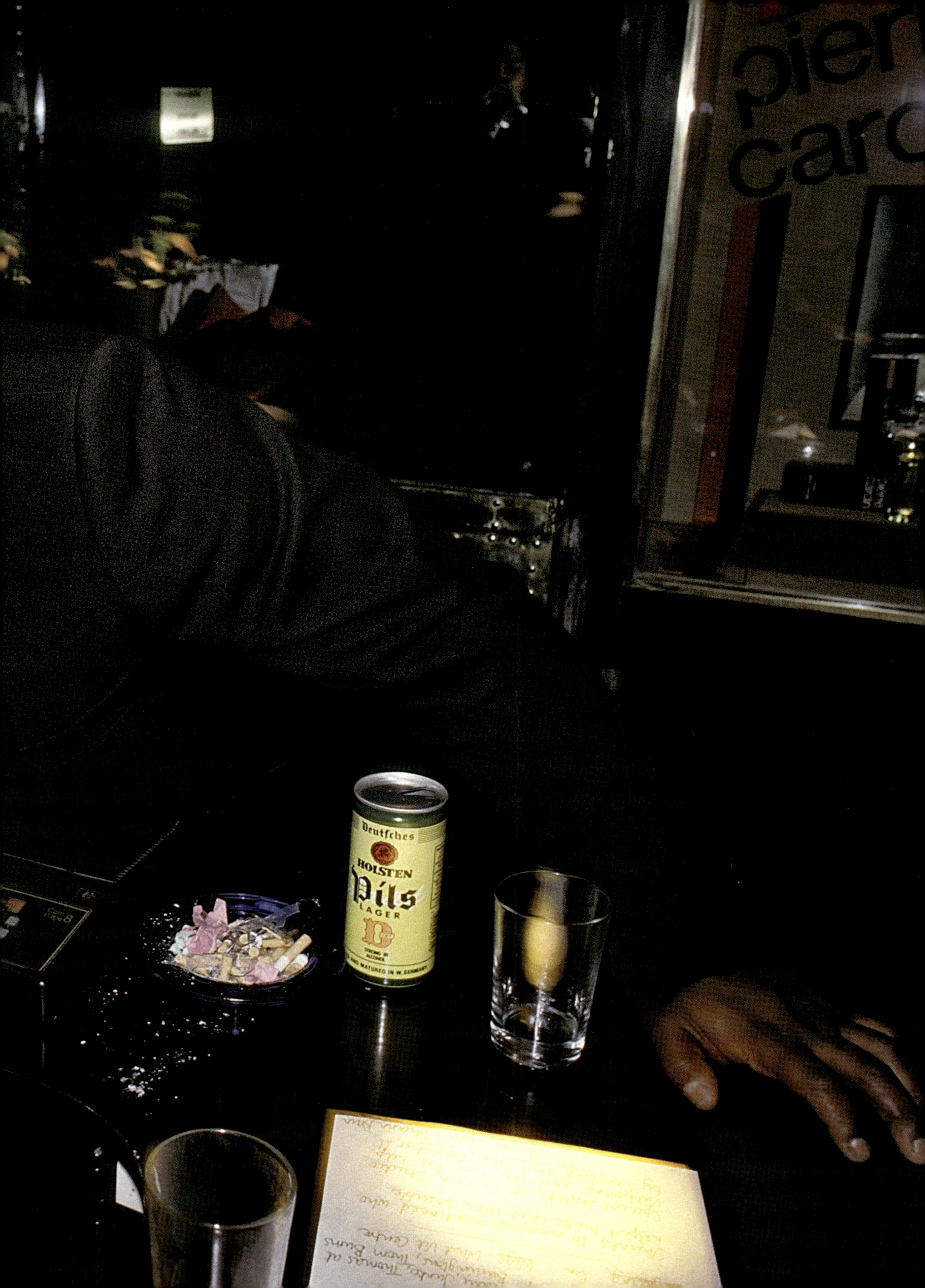
Deutsches
HOLSTEN
Pils
LAGER

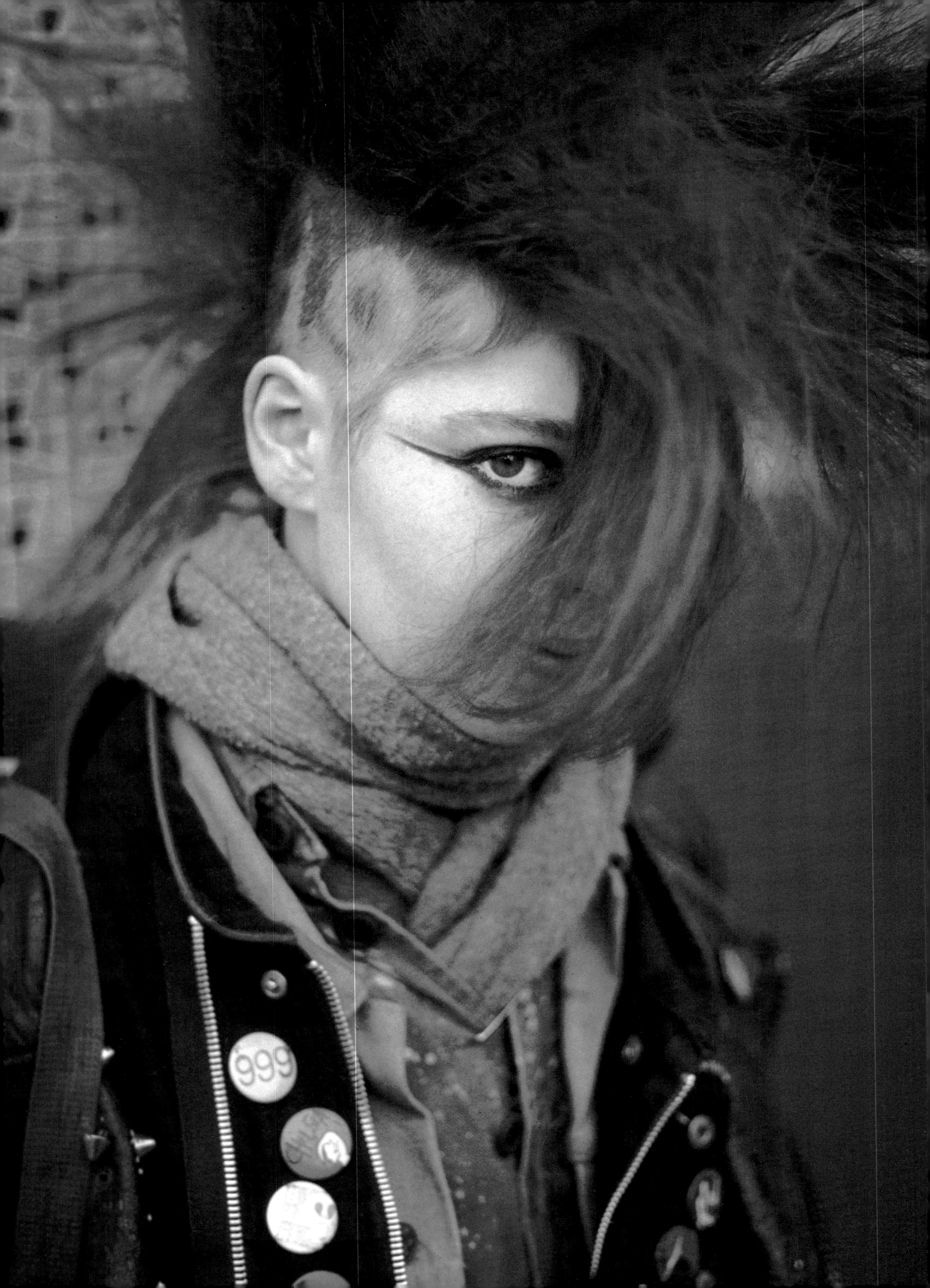
999

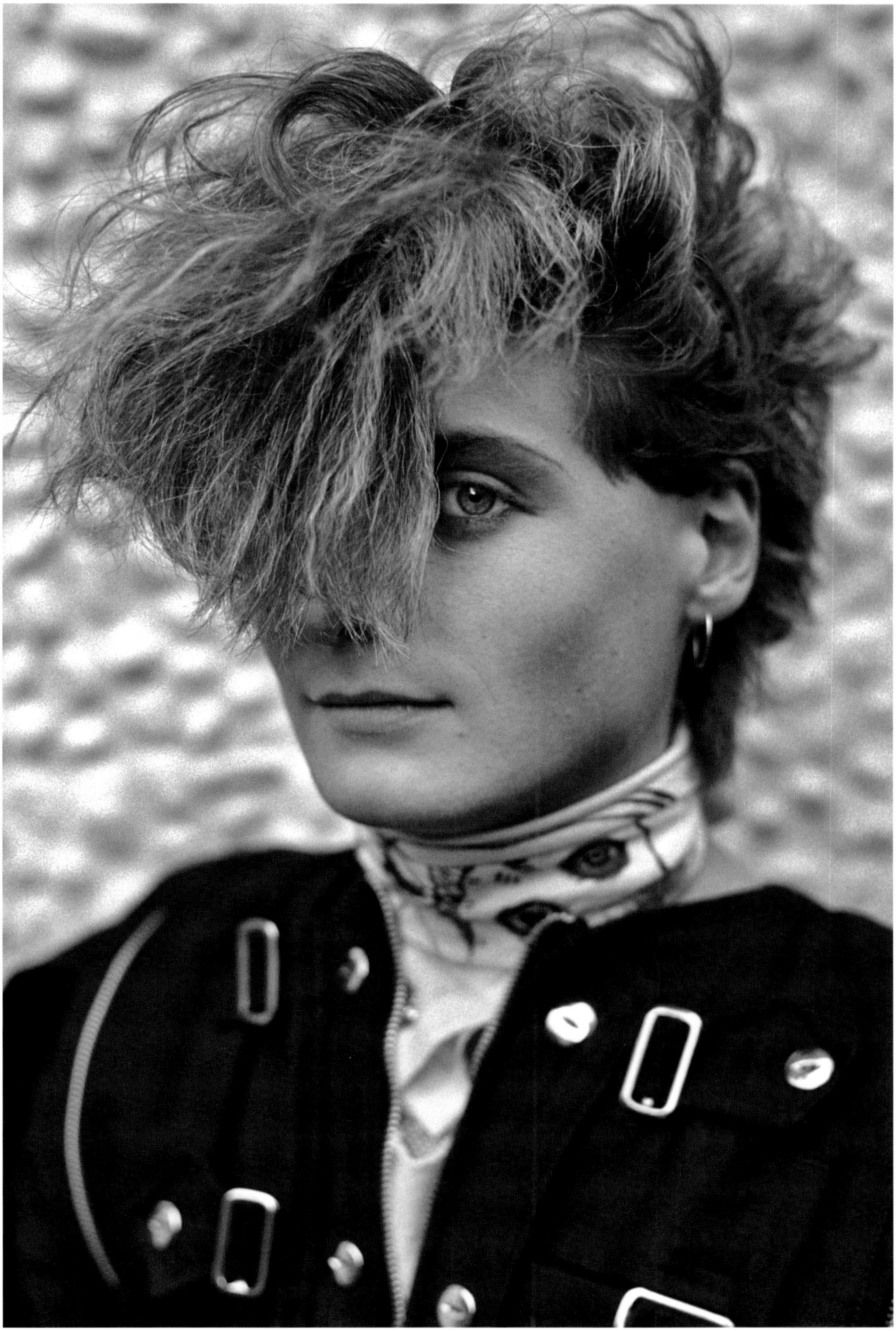

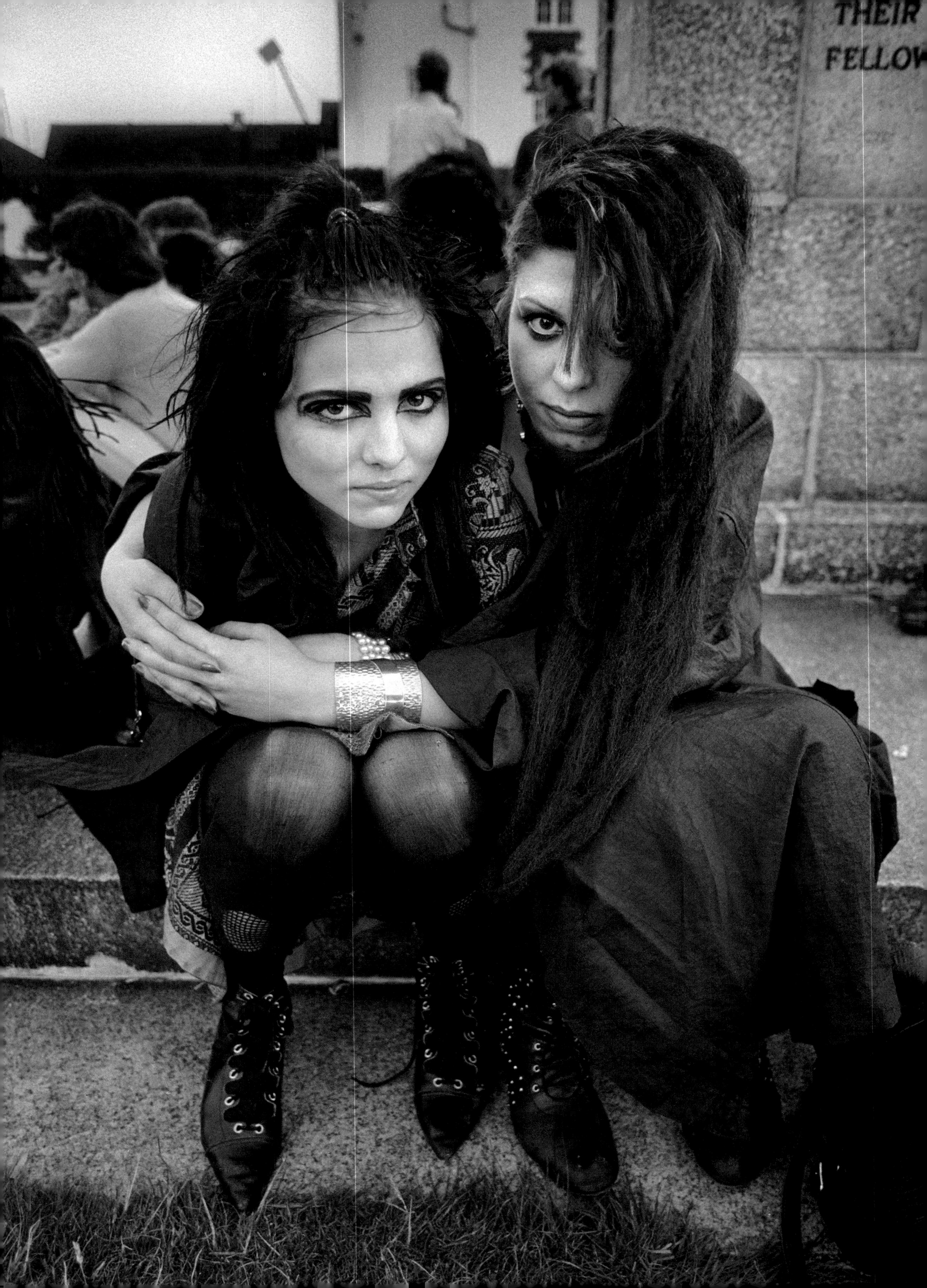
THEIR
FELLOW

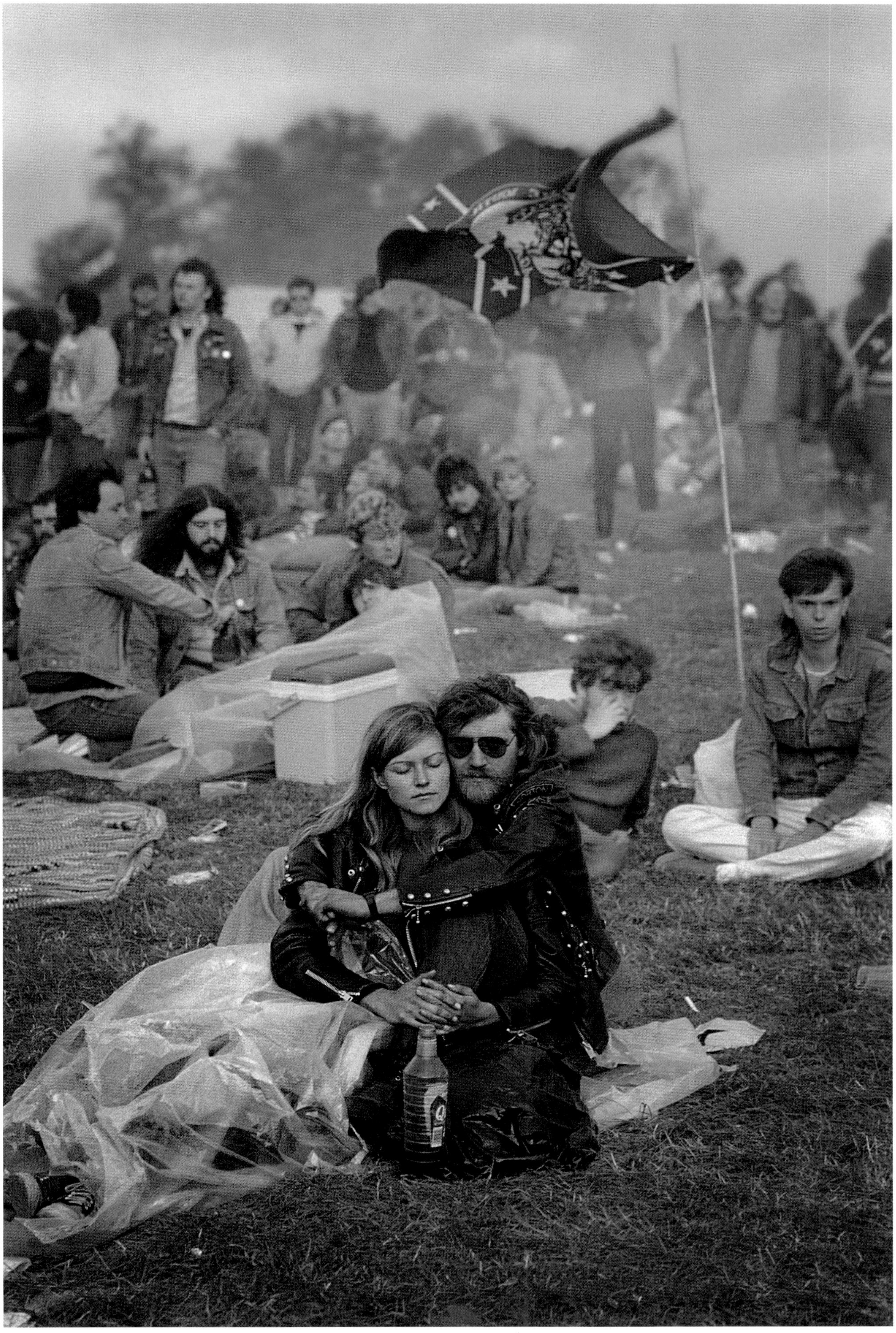

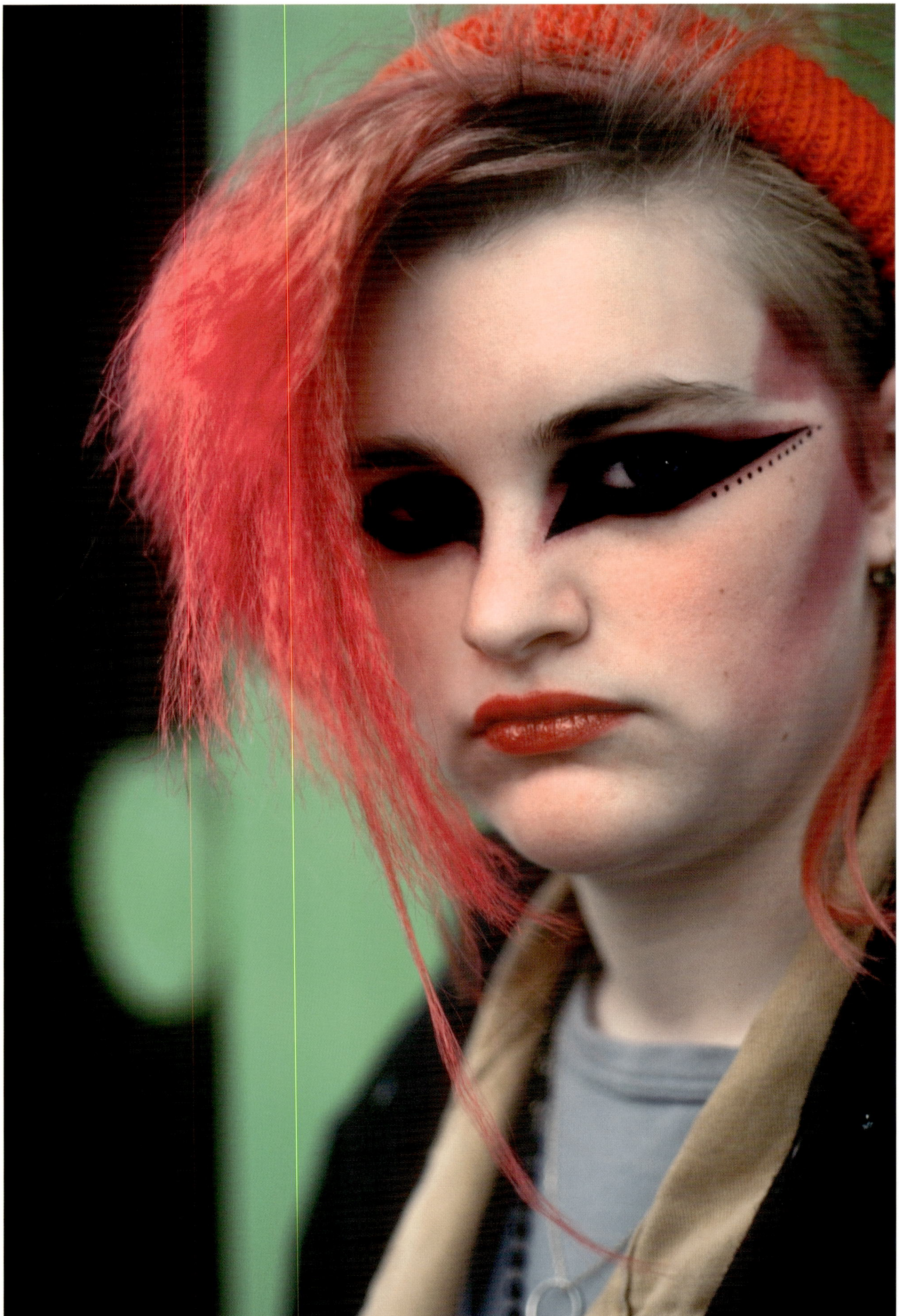

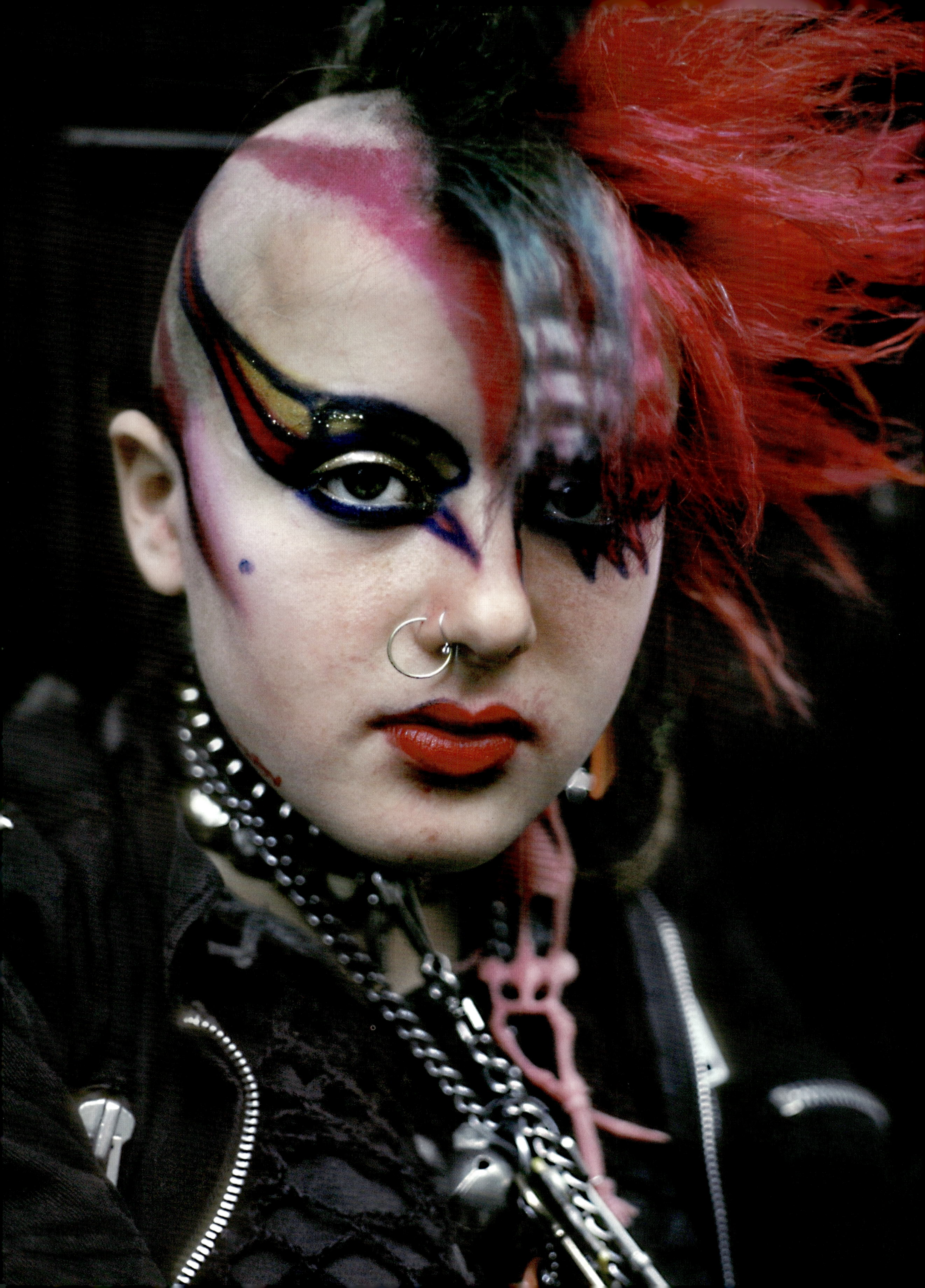

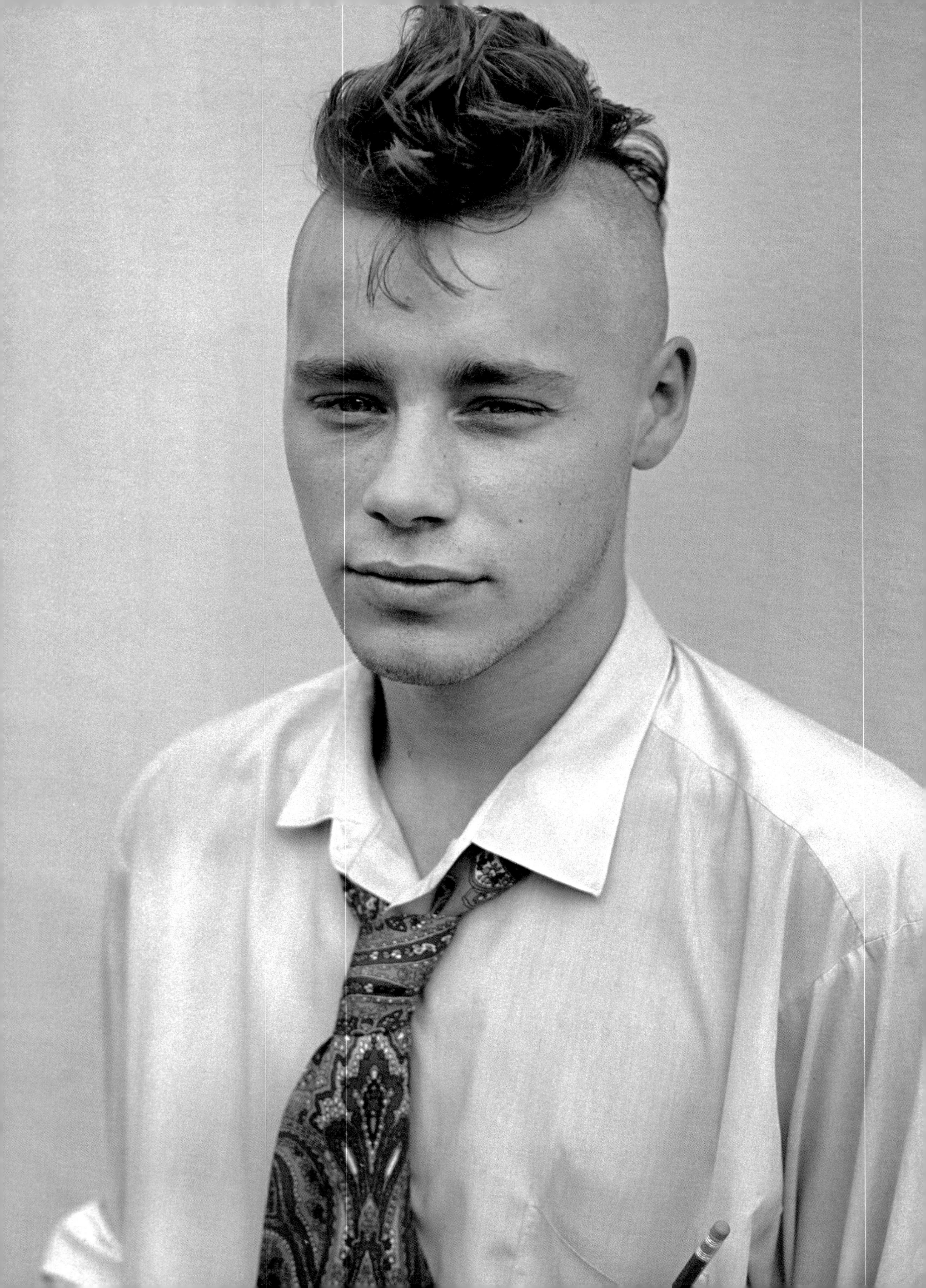

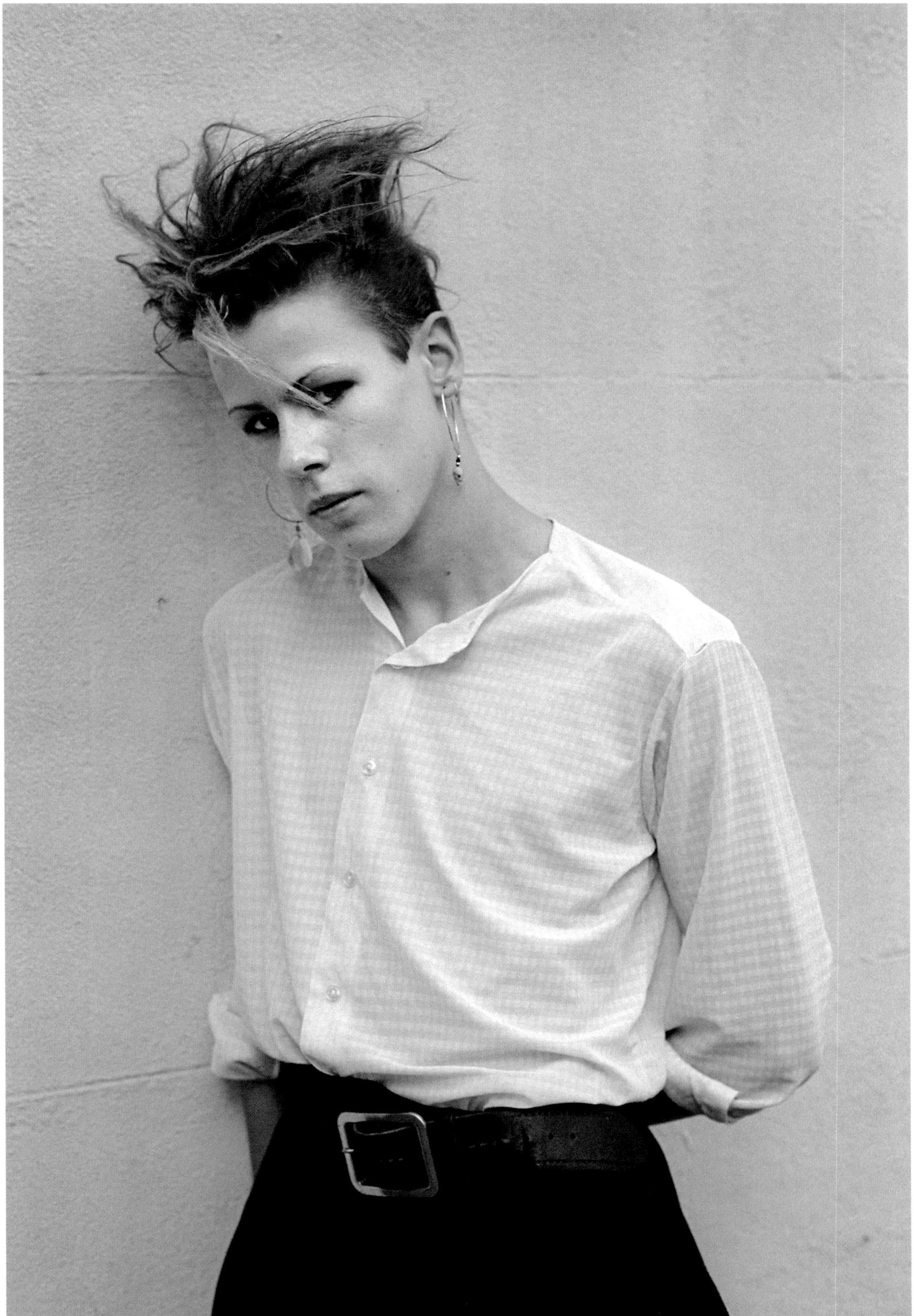

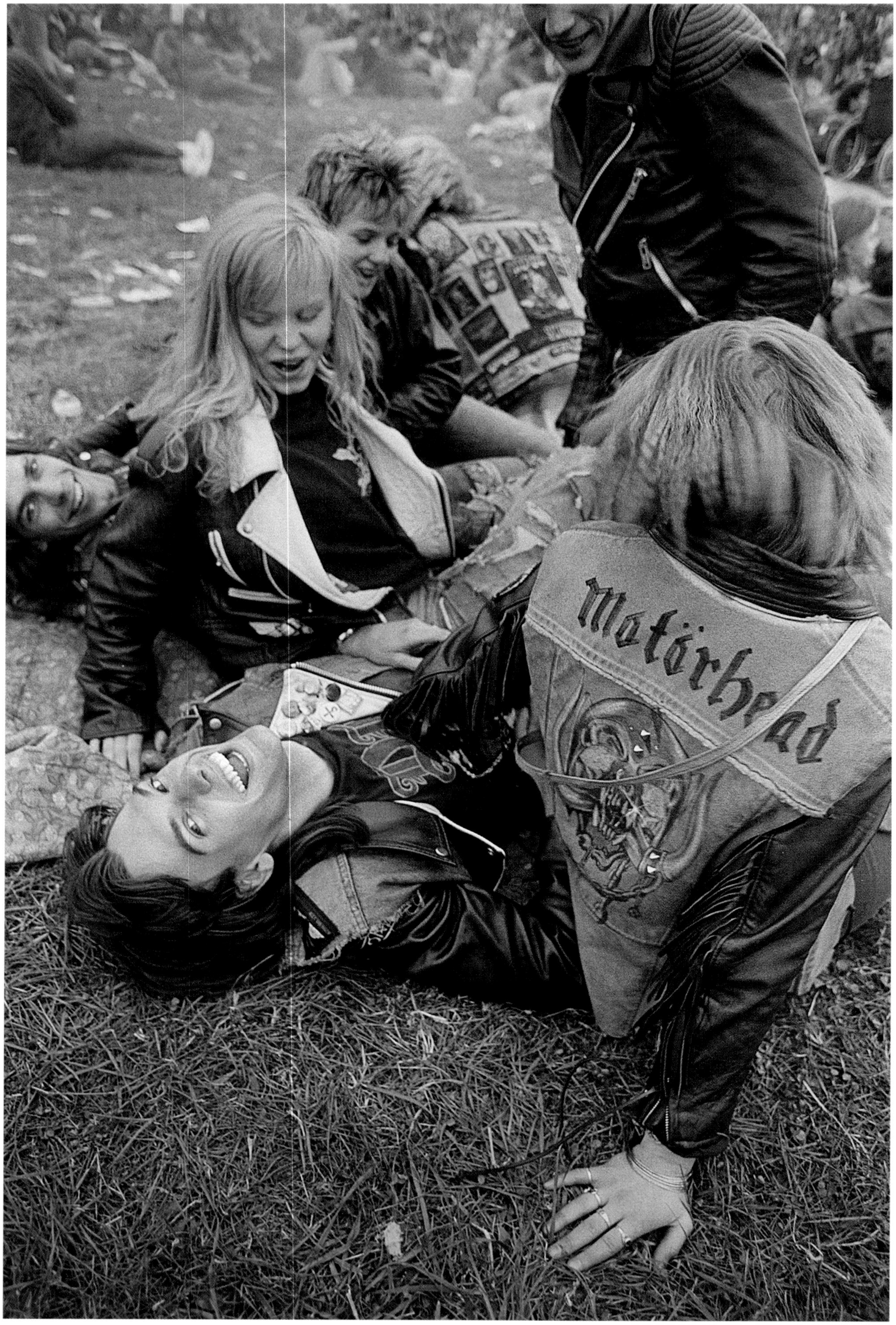
Motörhead

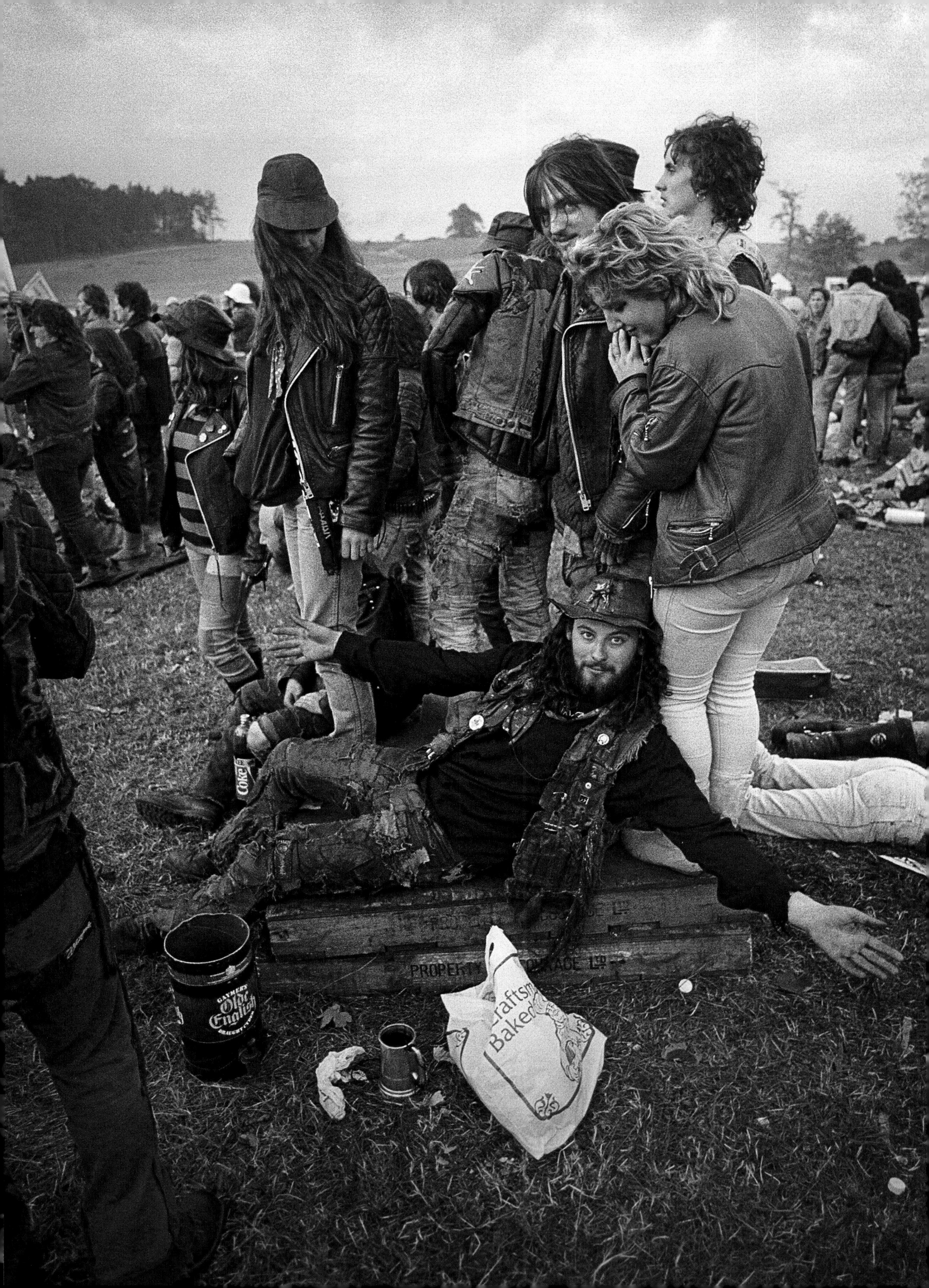
Coke
Olde English
PROPERTY
Baked

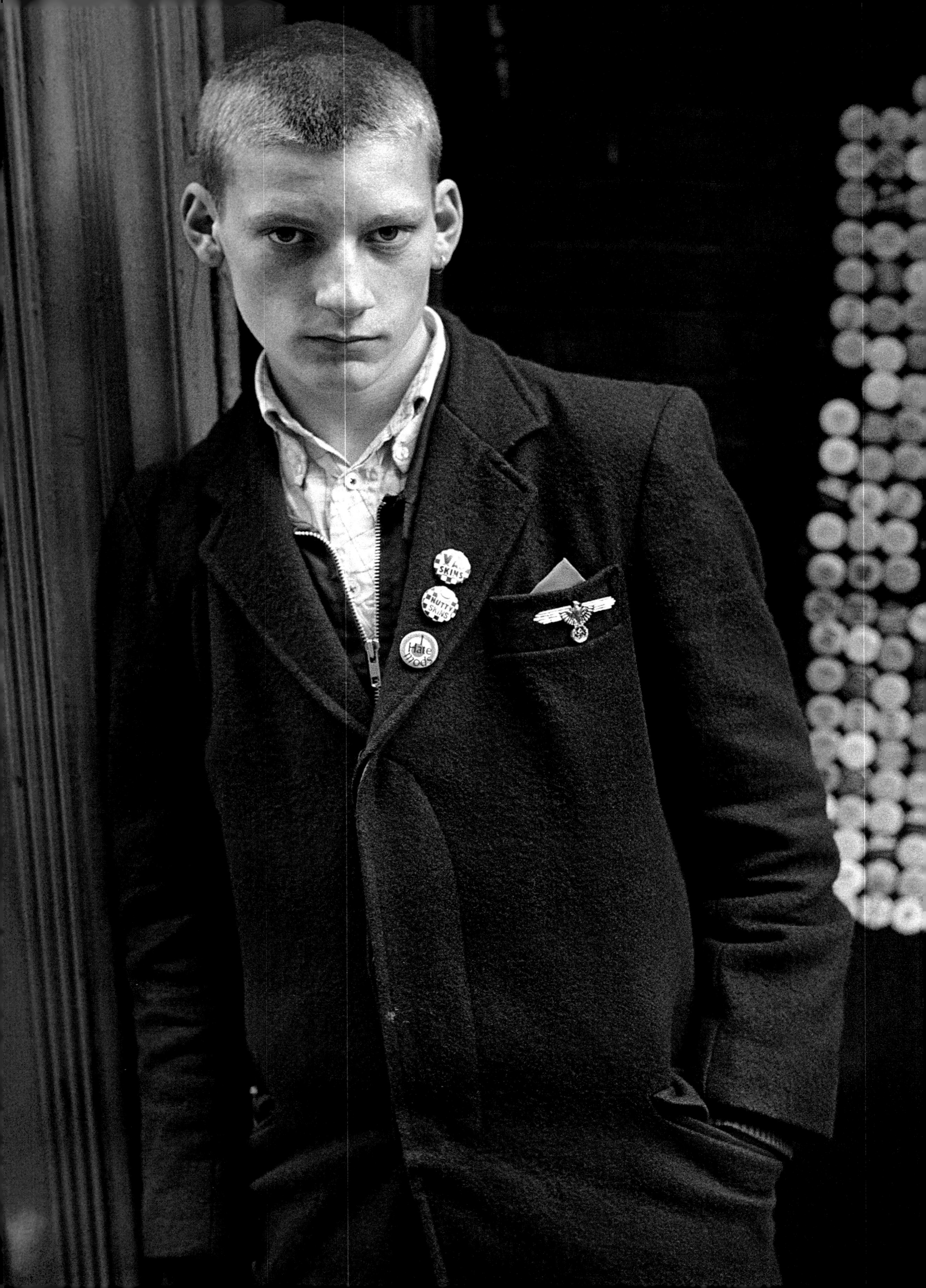
SKINS
NUTTY SKINS
I Hate mods

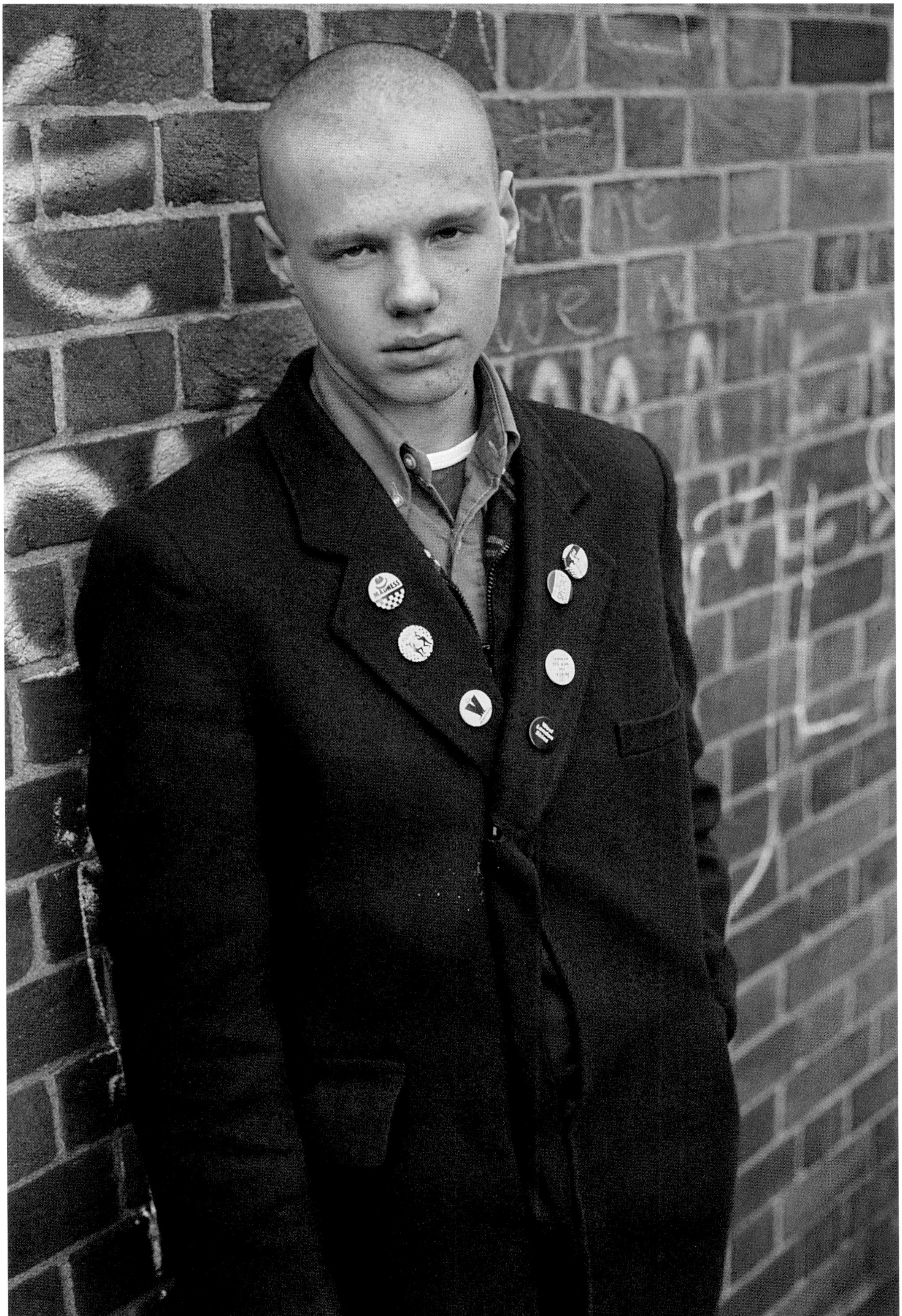

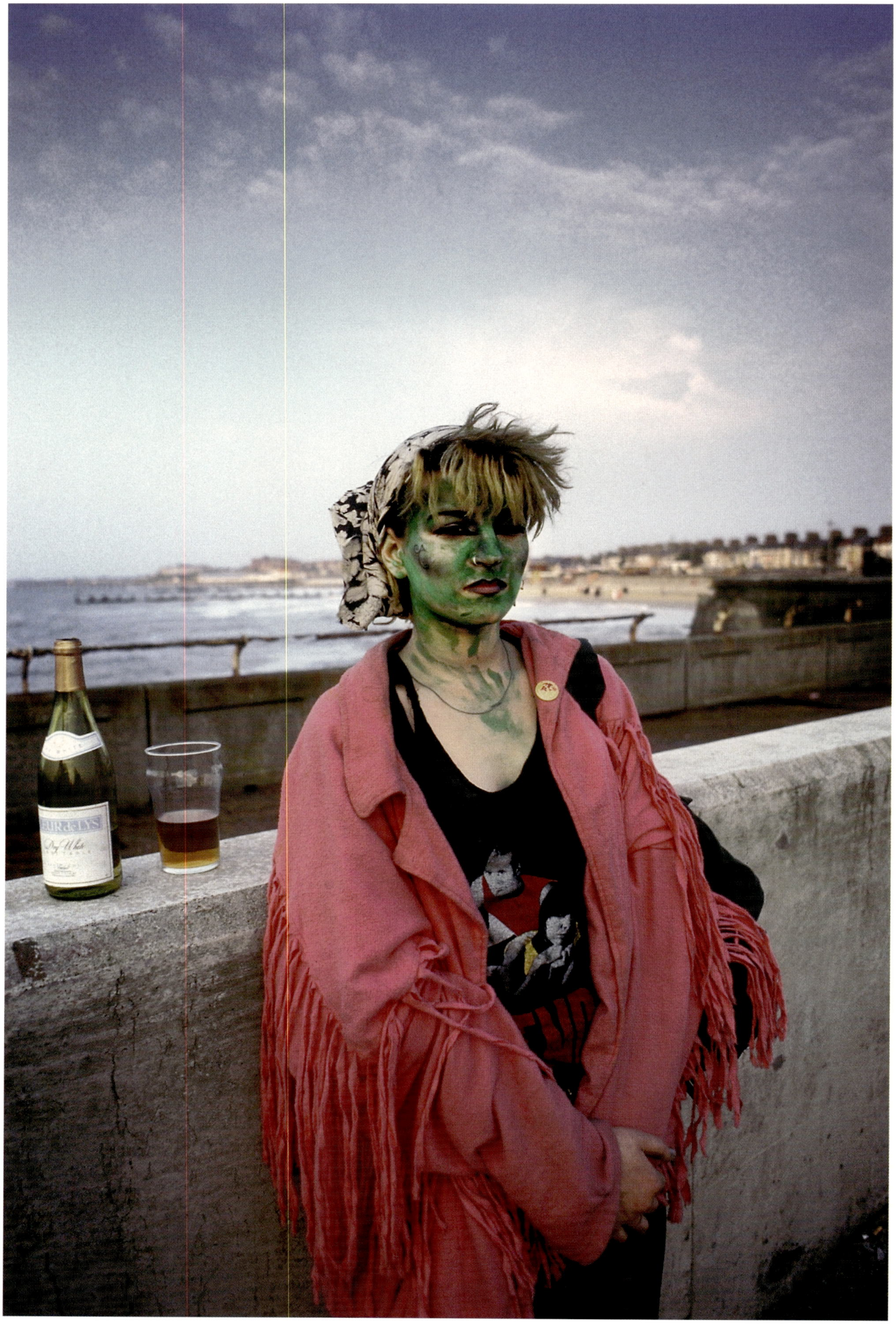

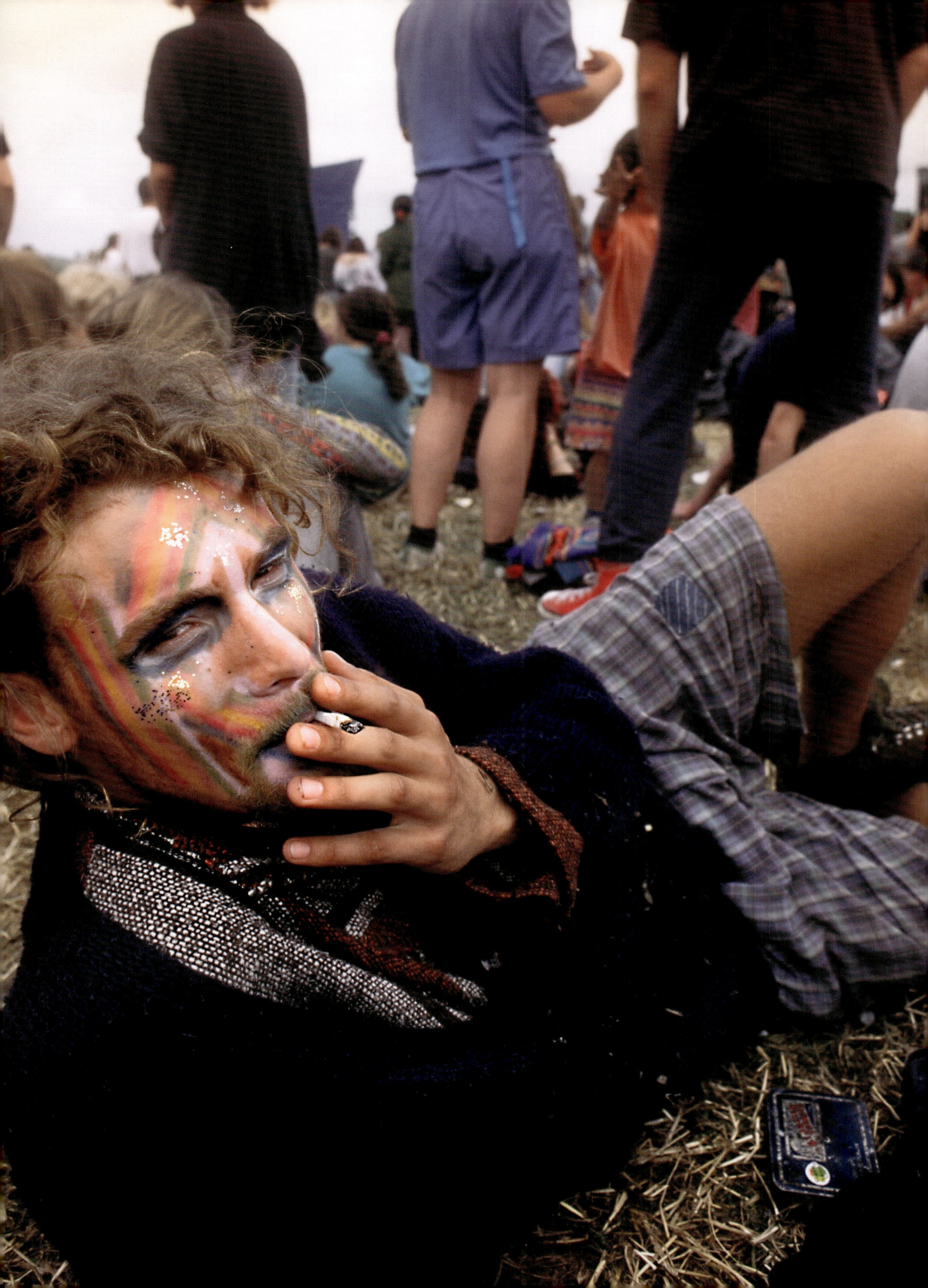

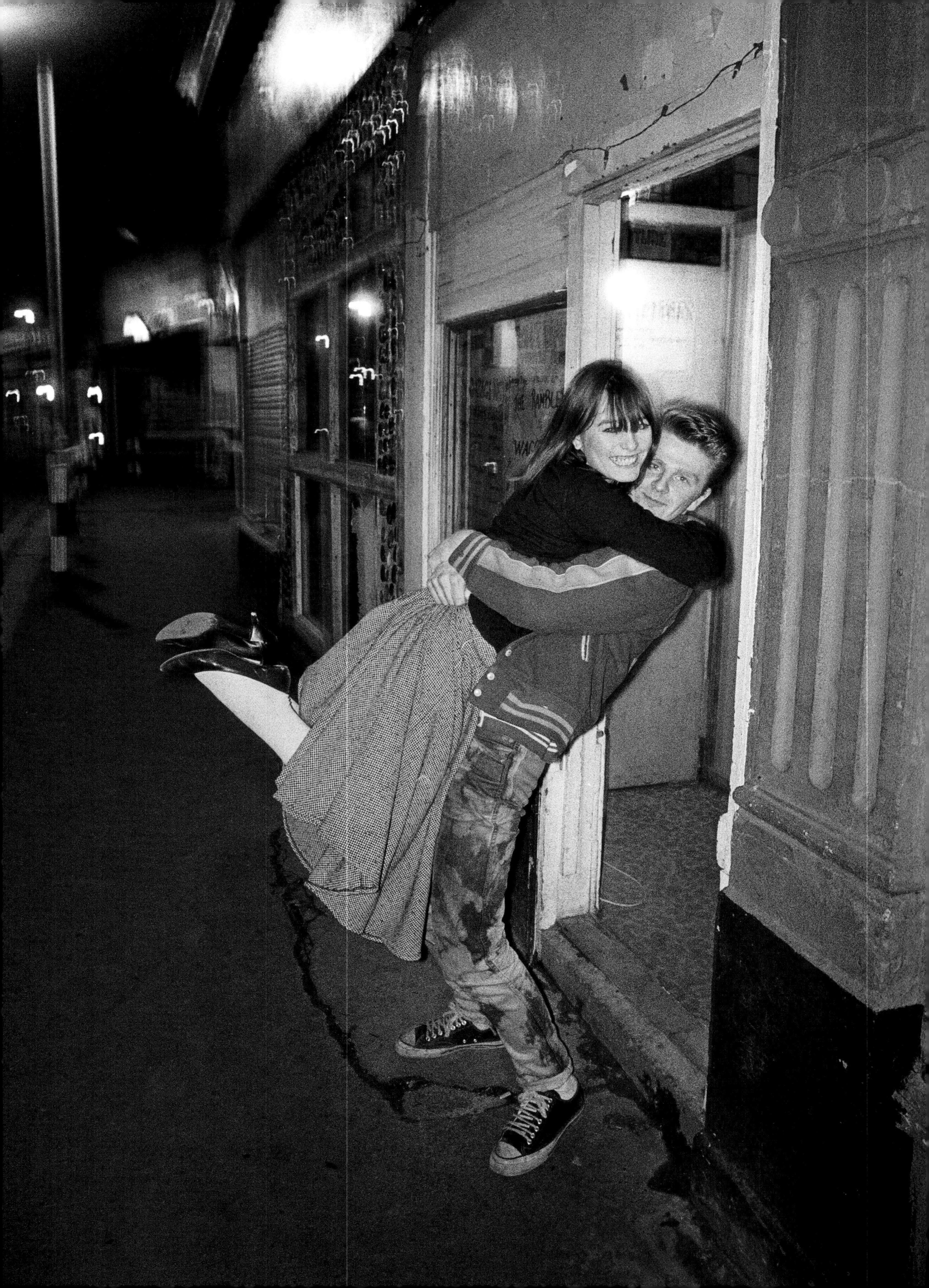

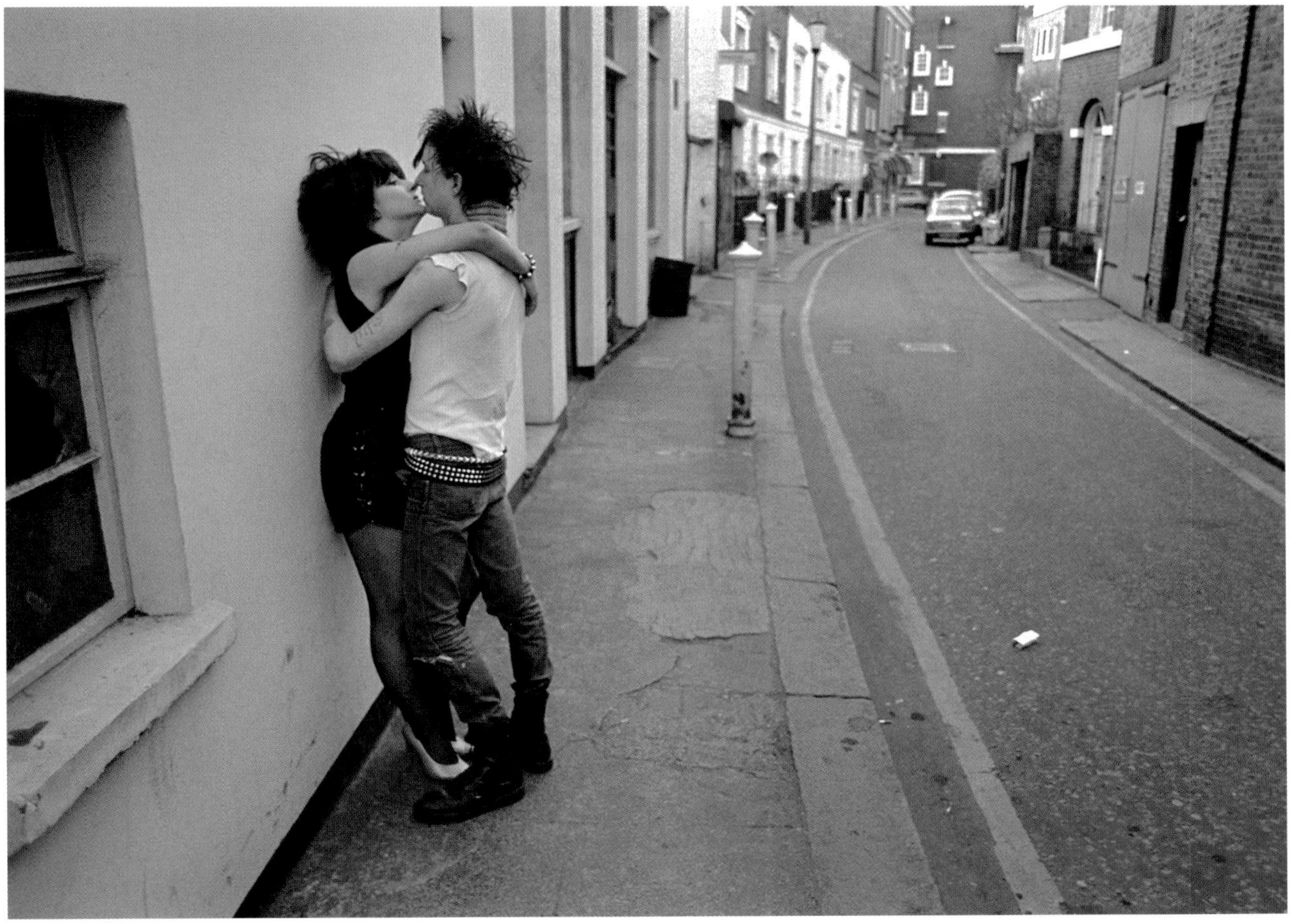

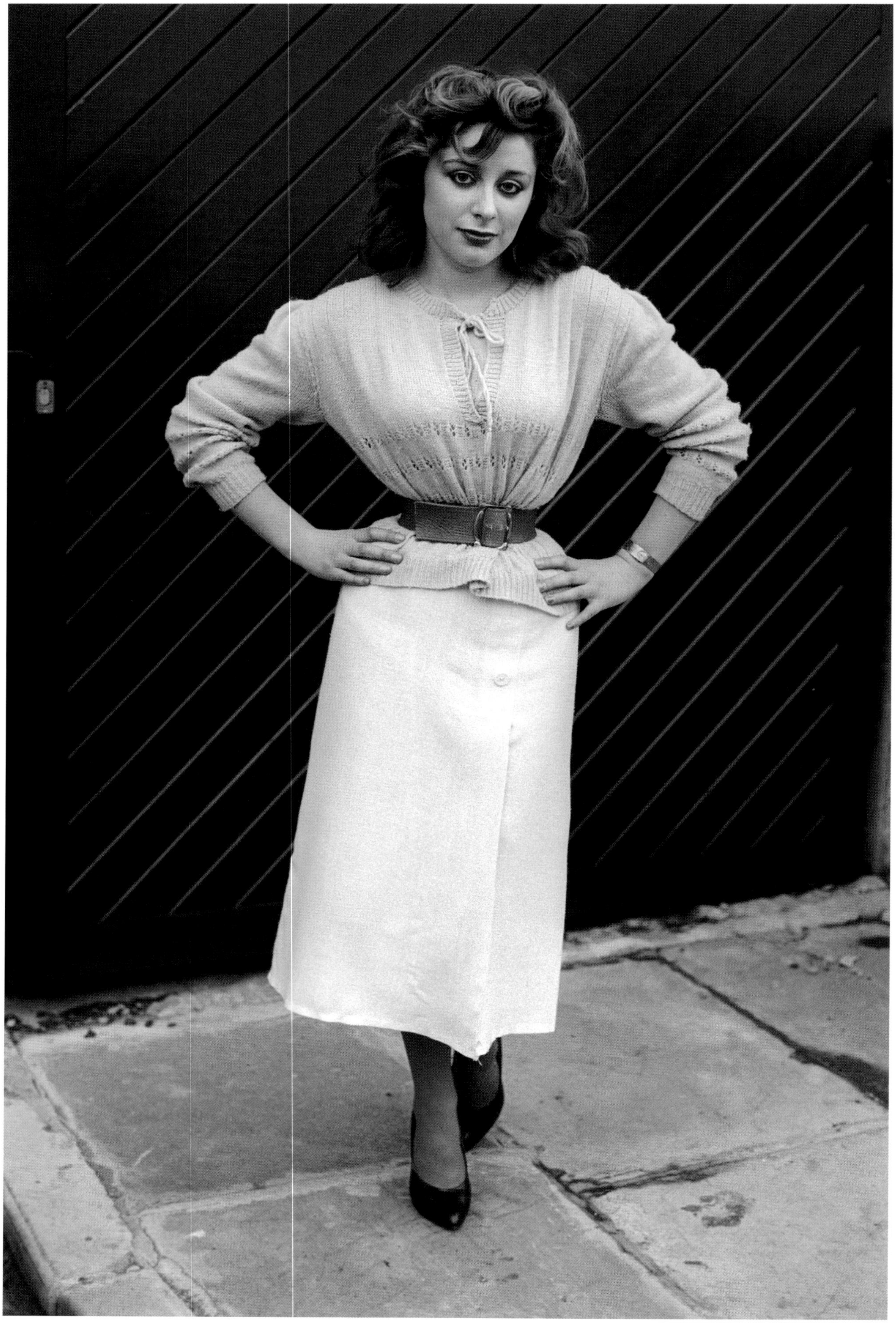

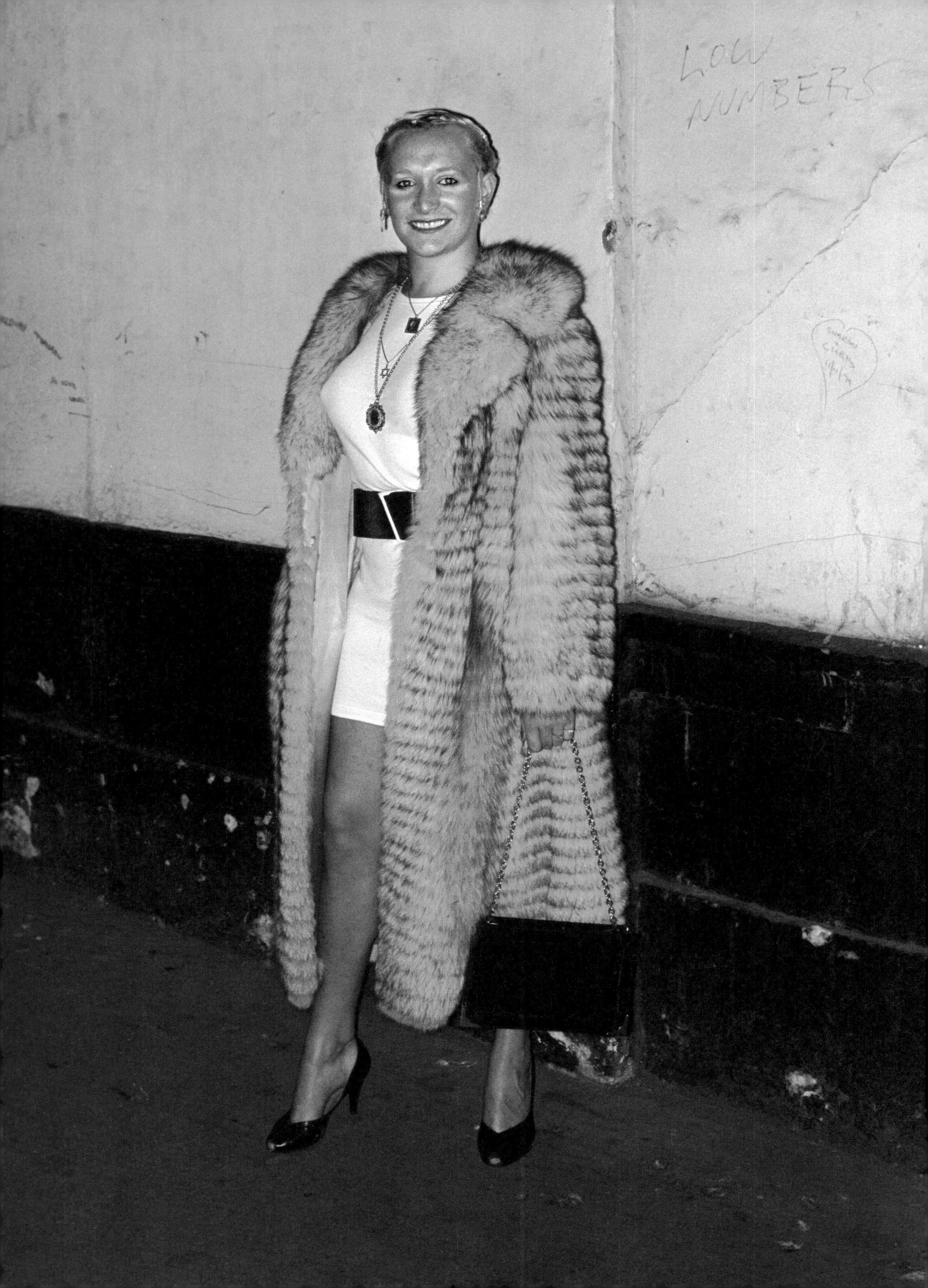
LOW NUMBERS

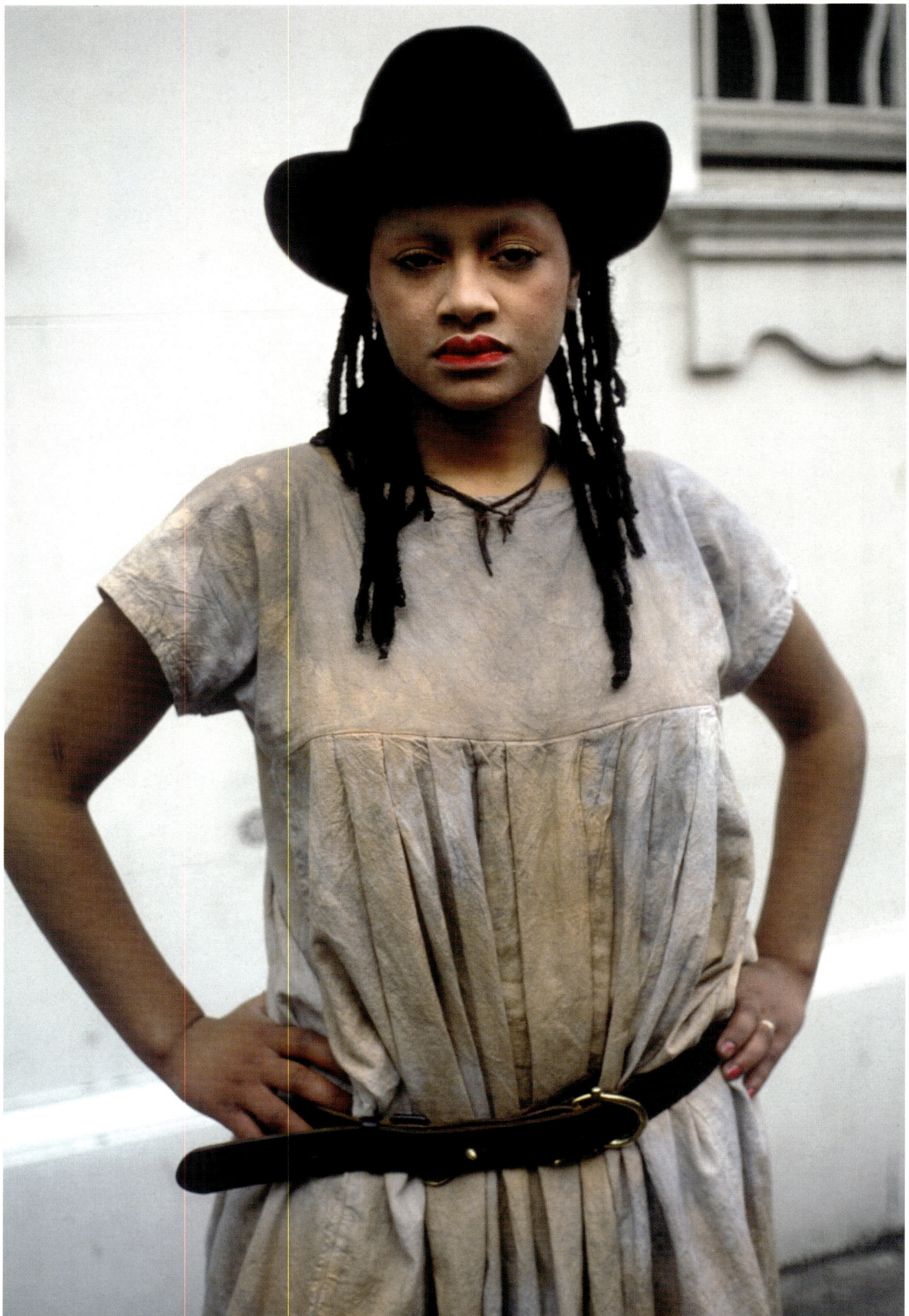

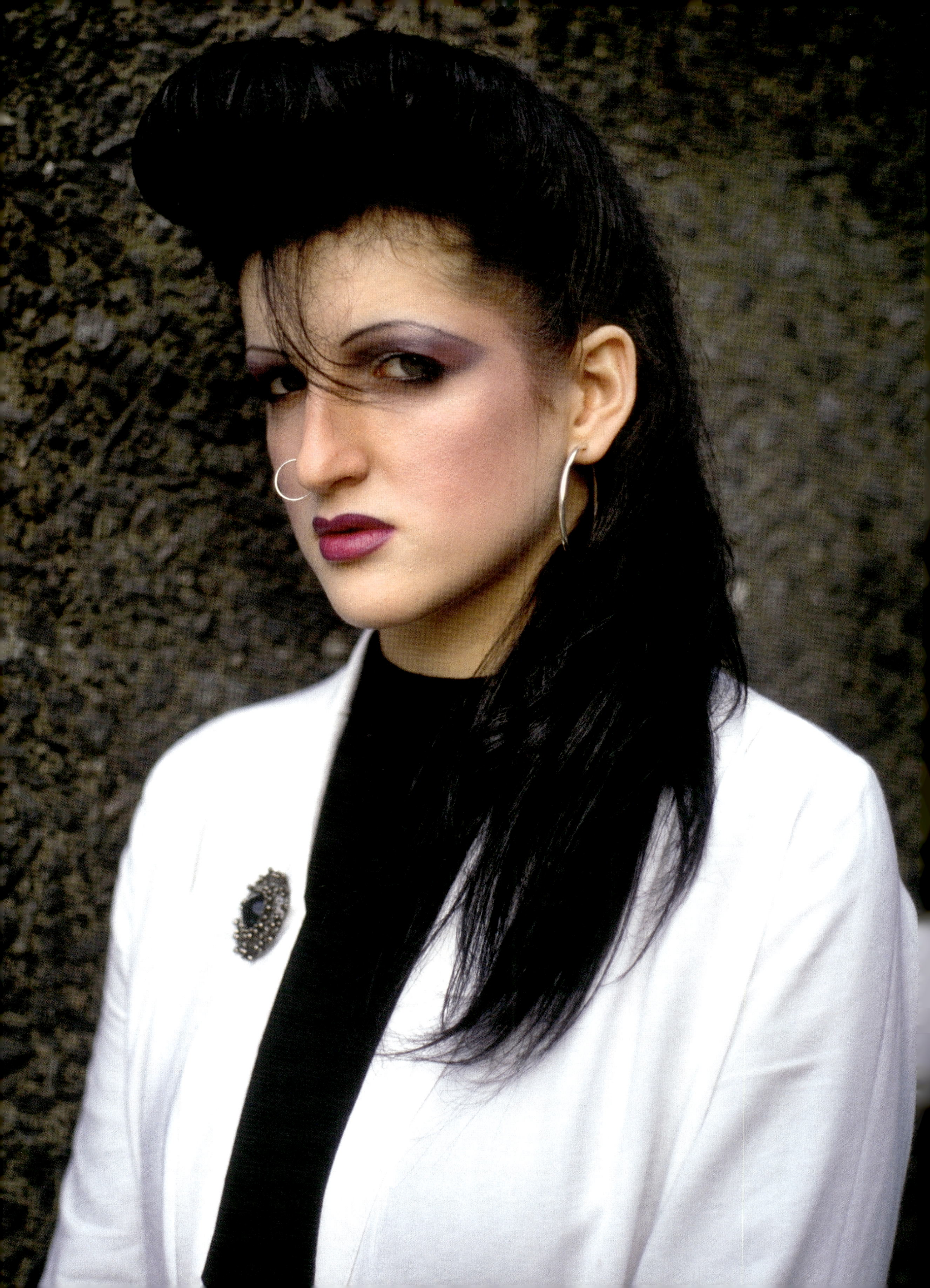

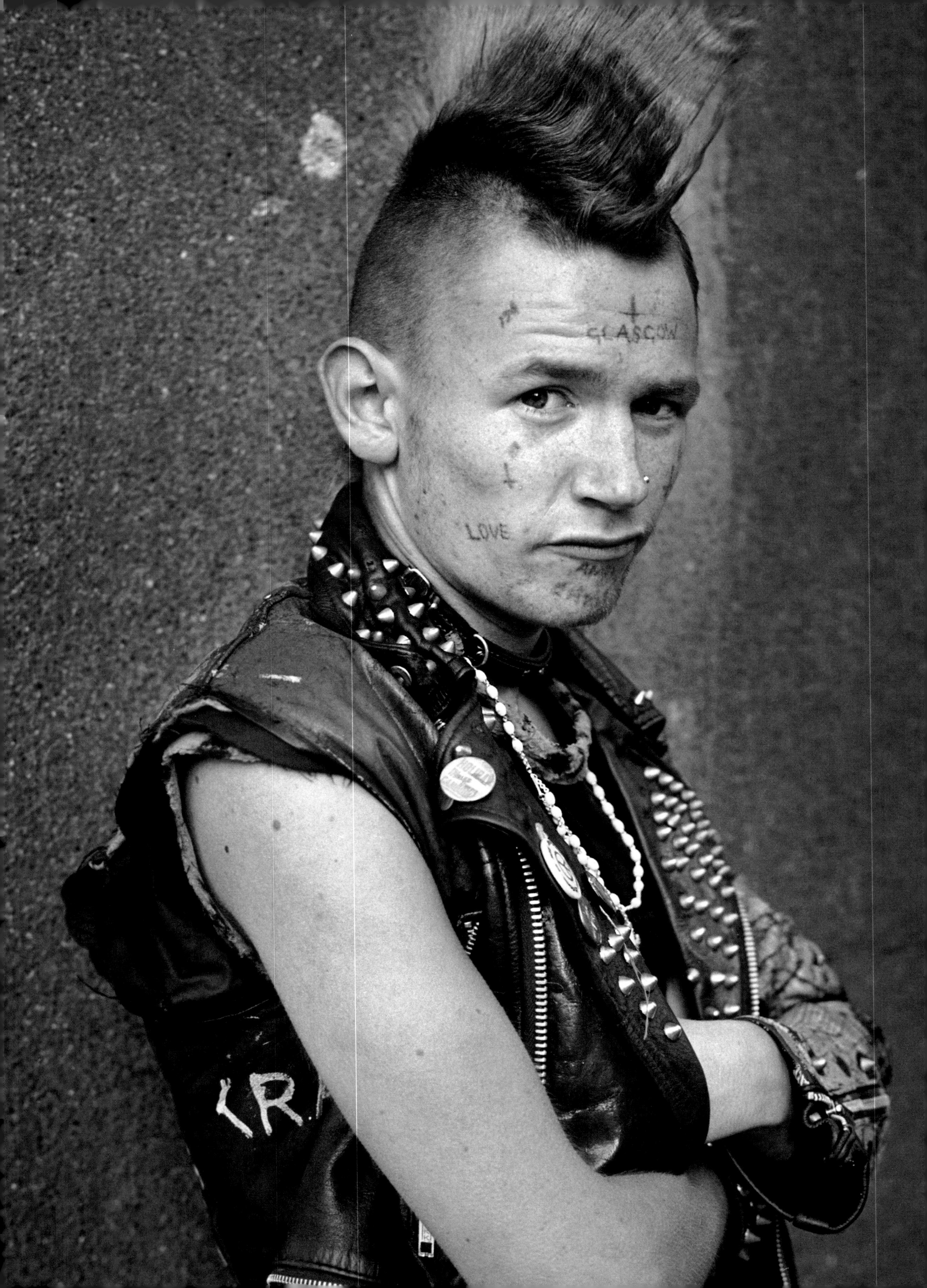
LOVE

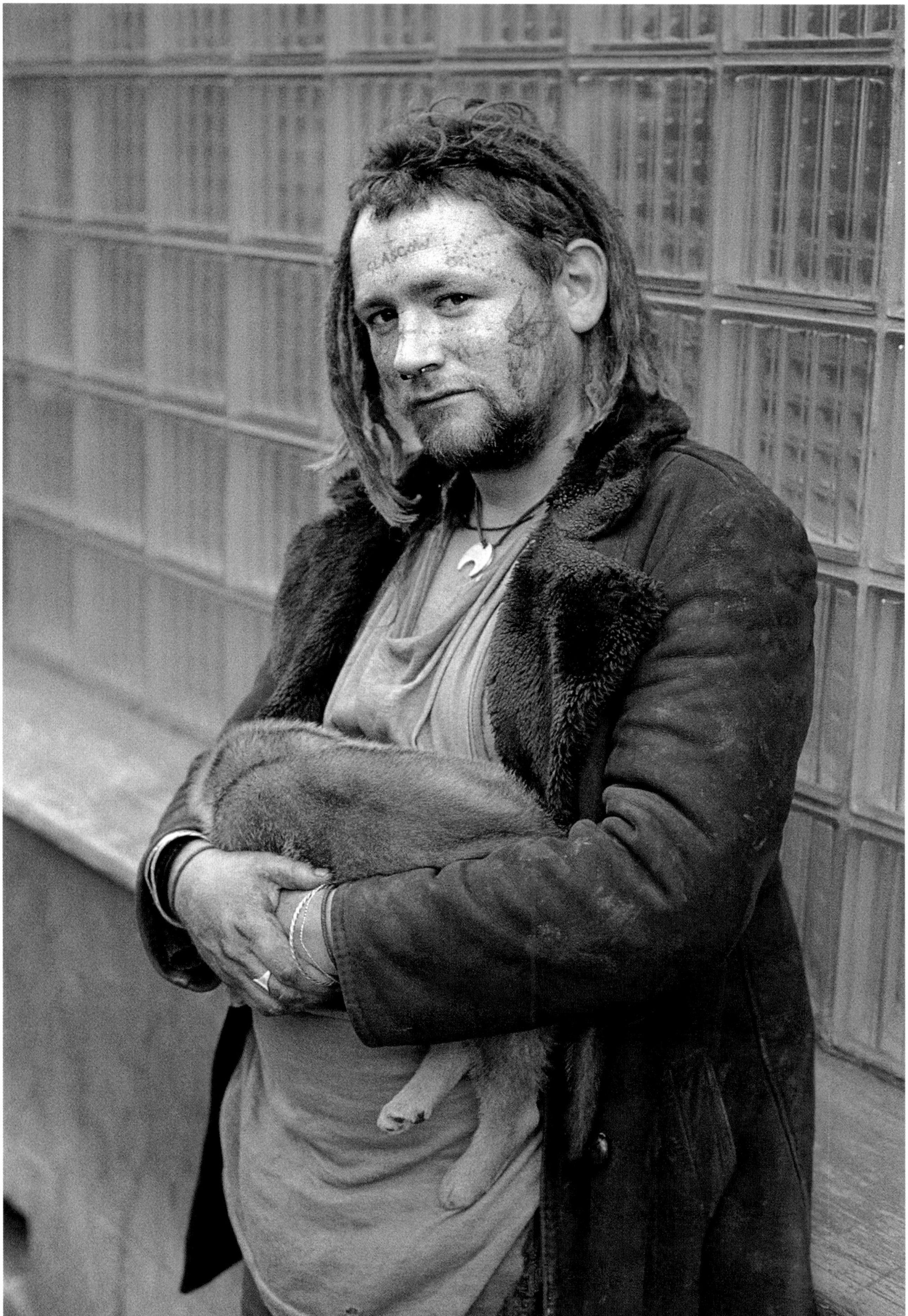

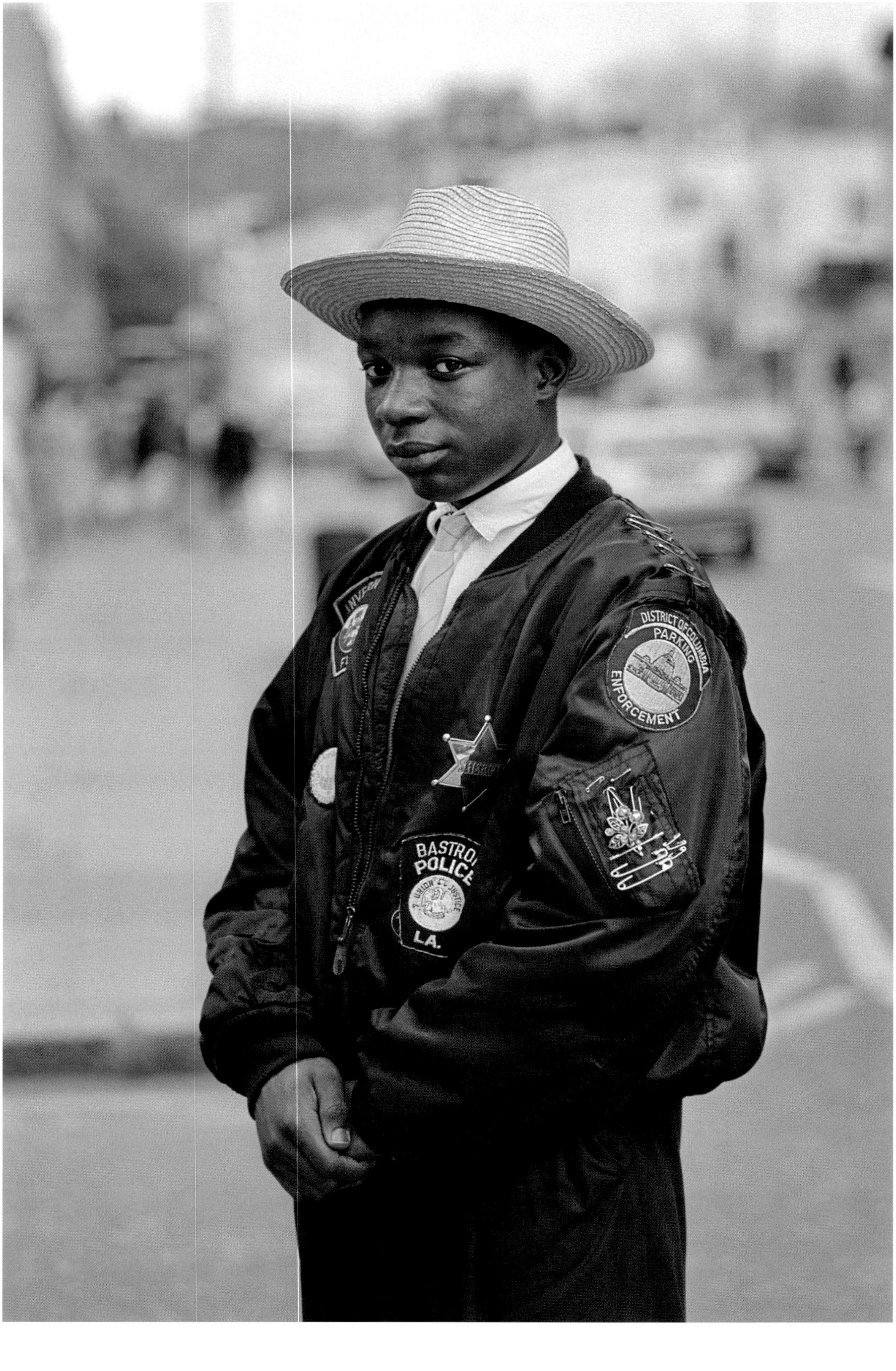
DISTRICT OF COLUMBIA
PARKING
ENFORCEMENT
POLICE
LA.

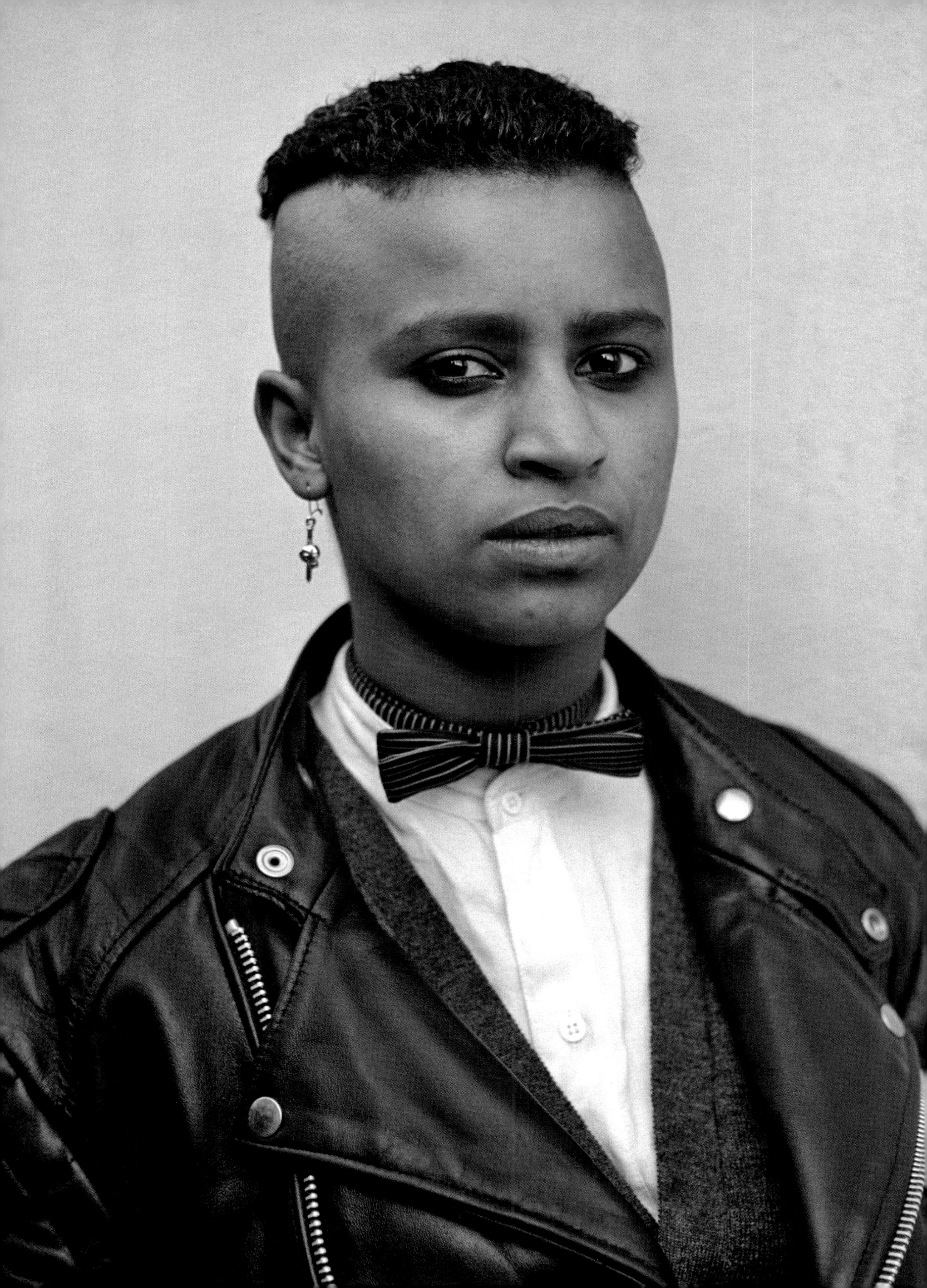

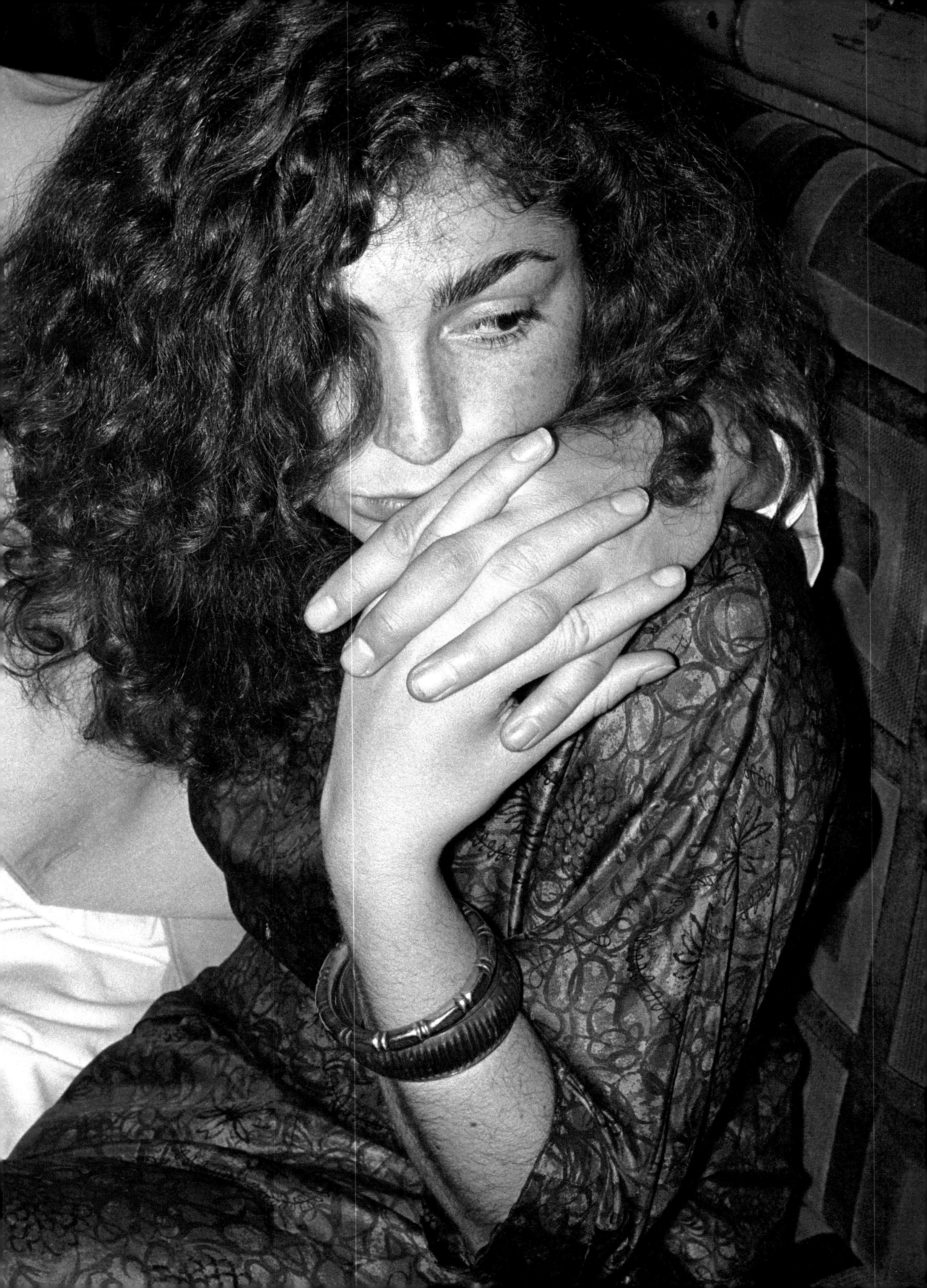

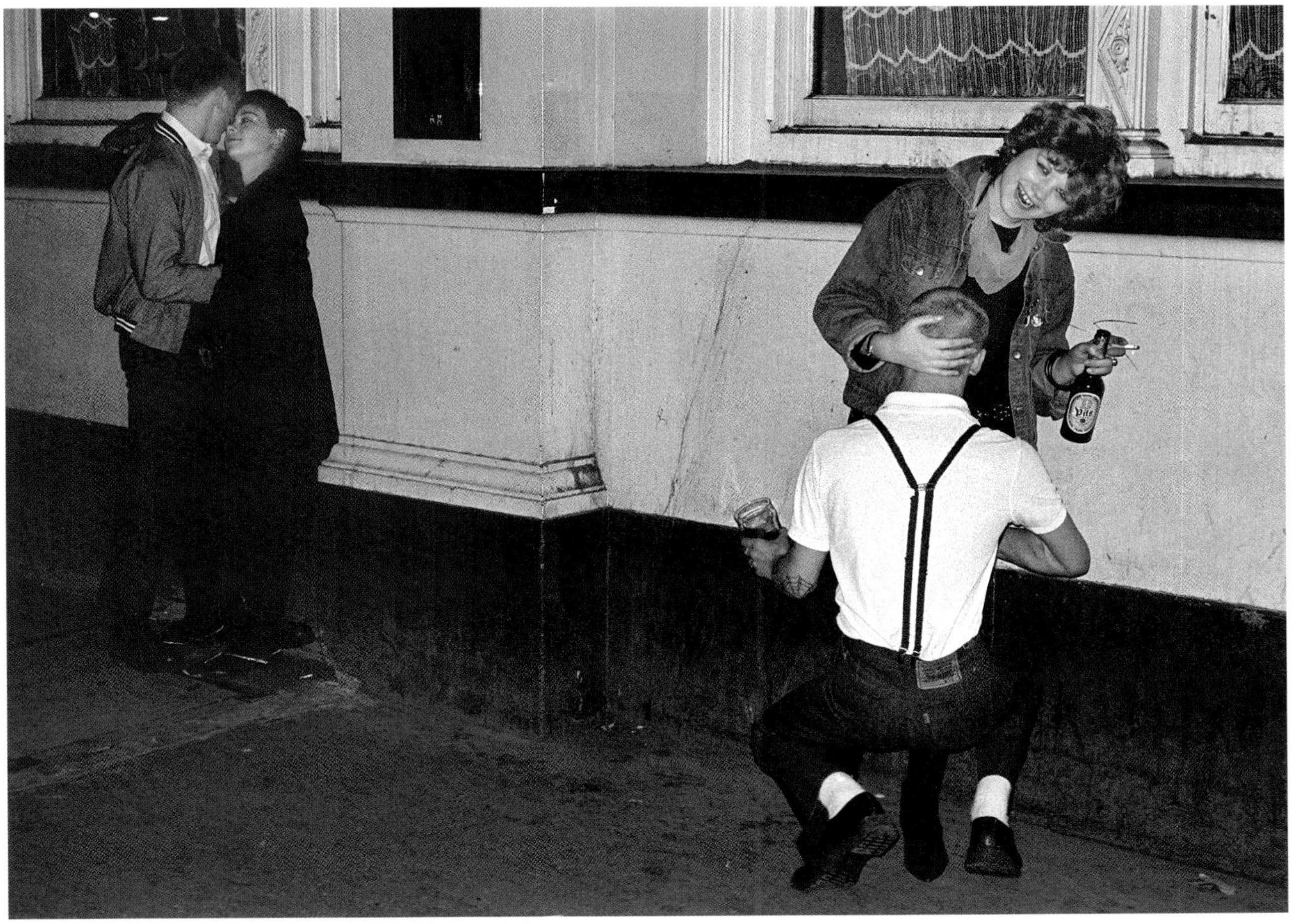

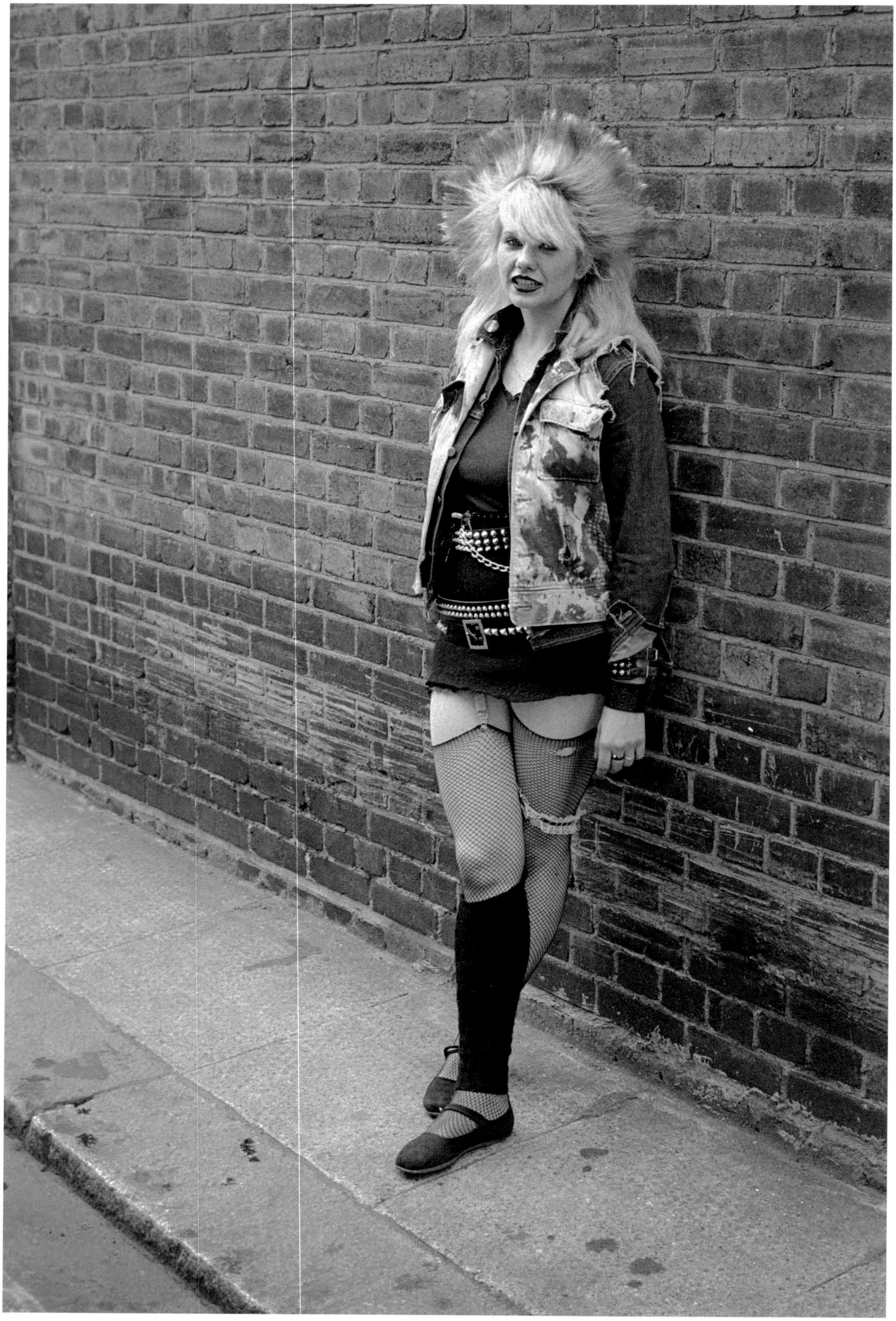

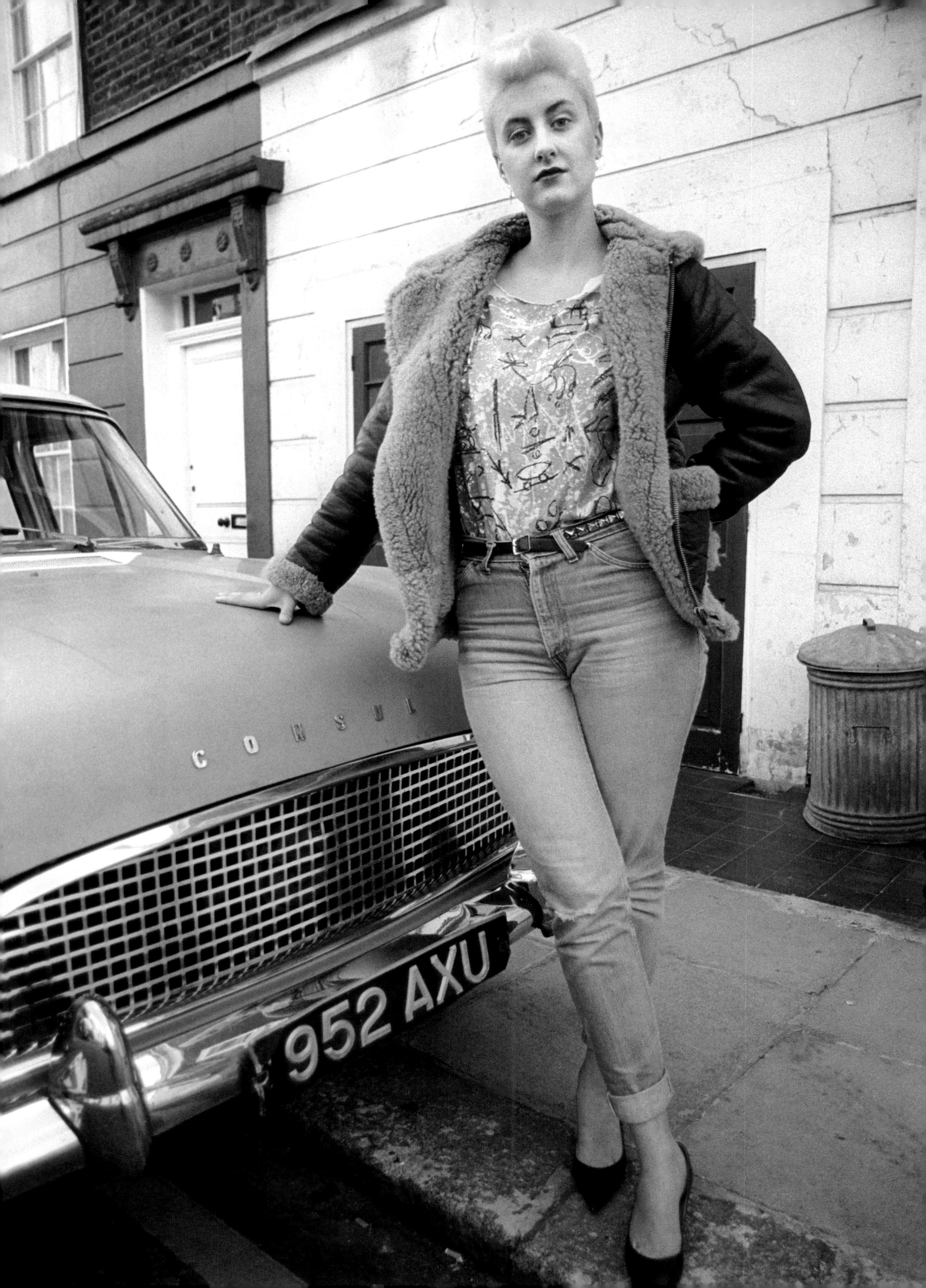
CONSUL
952 AXU

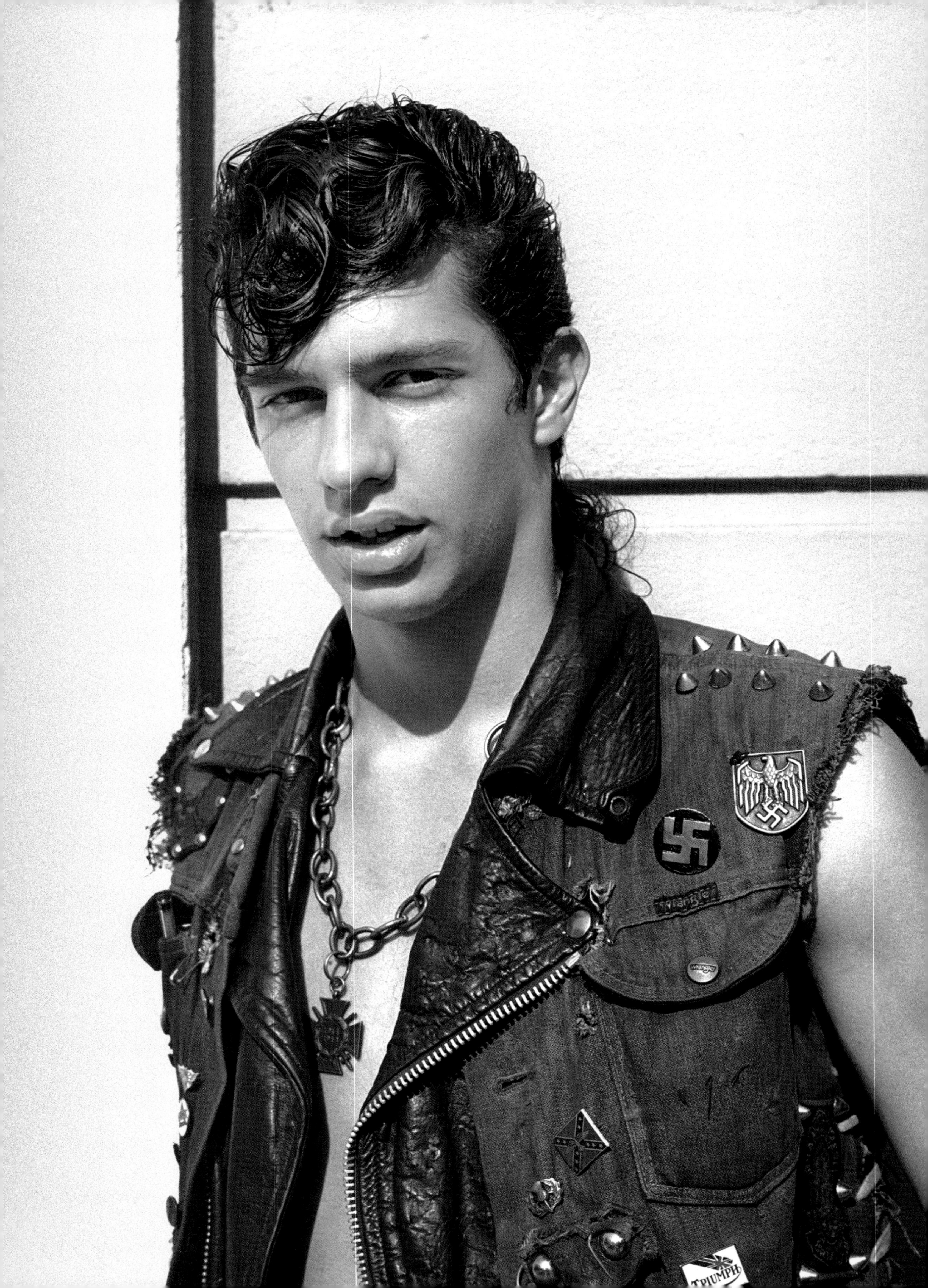
TRIUMPH

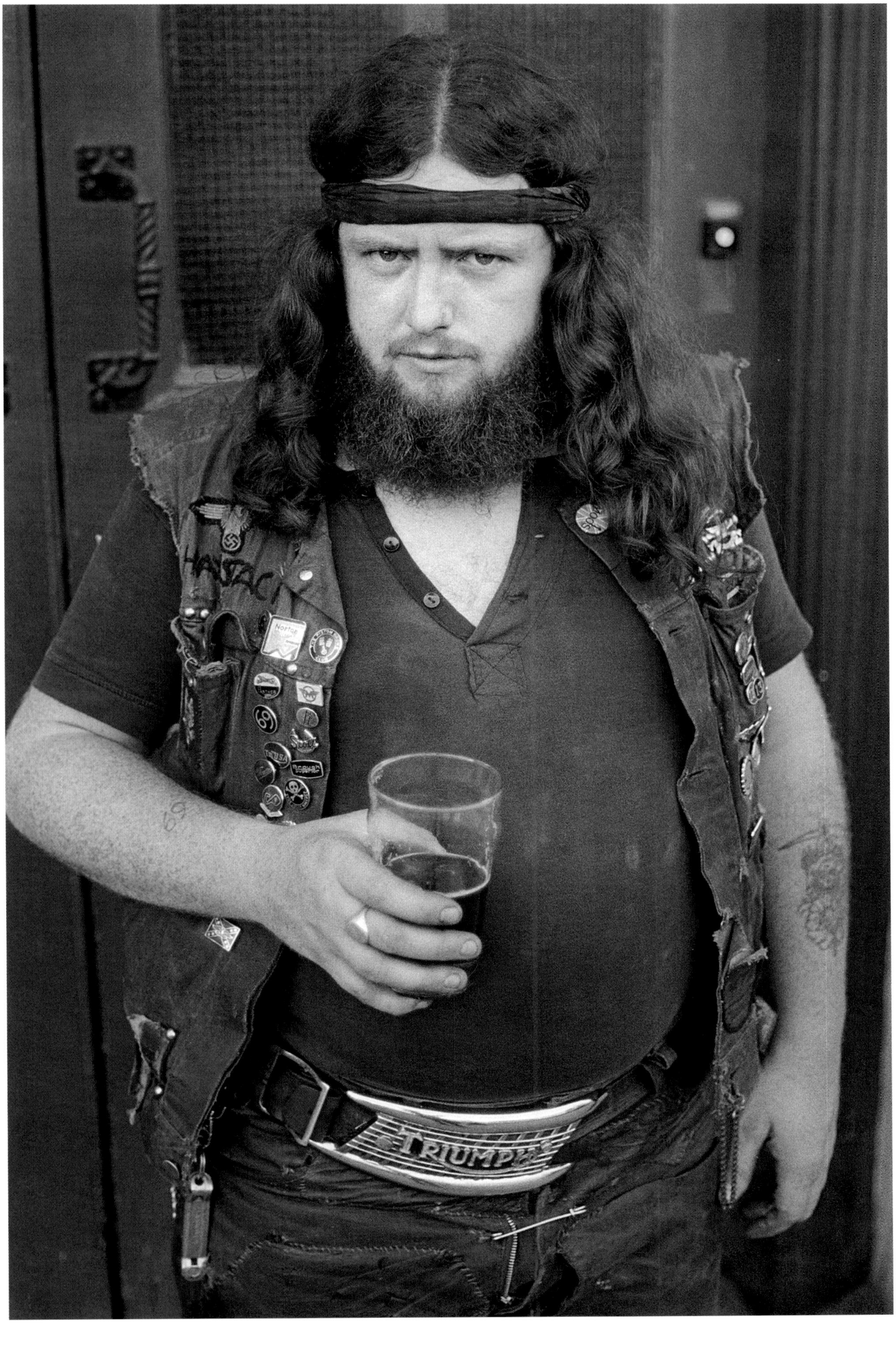
TRIUMP

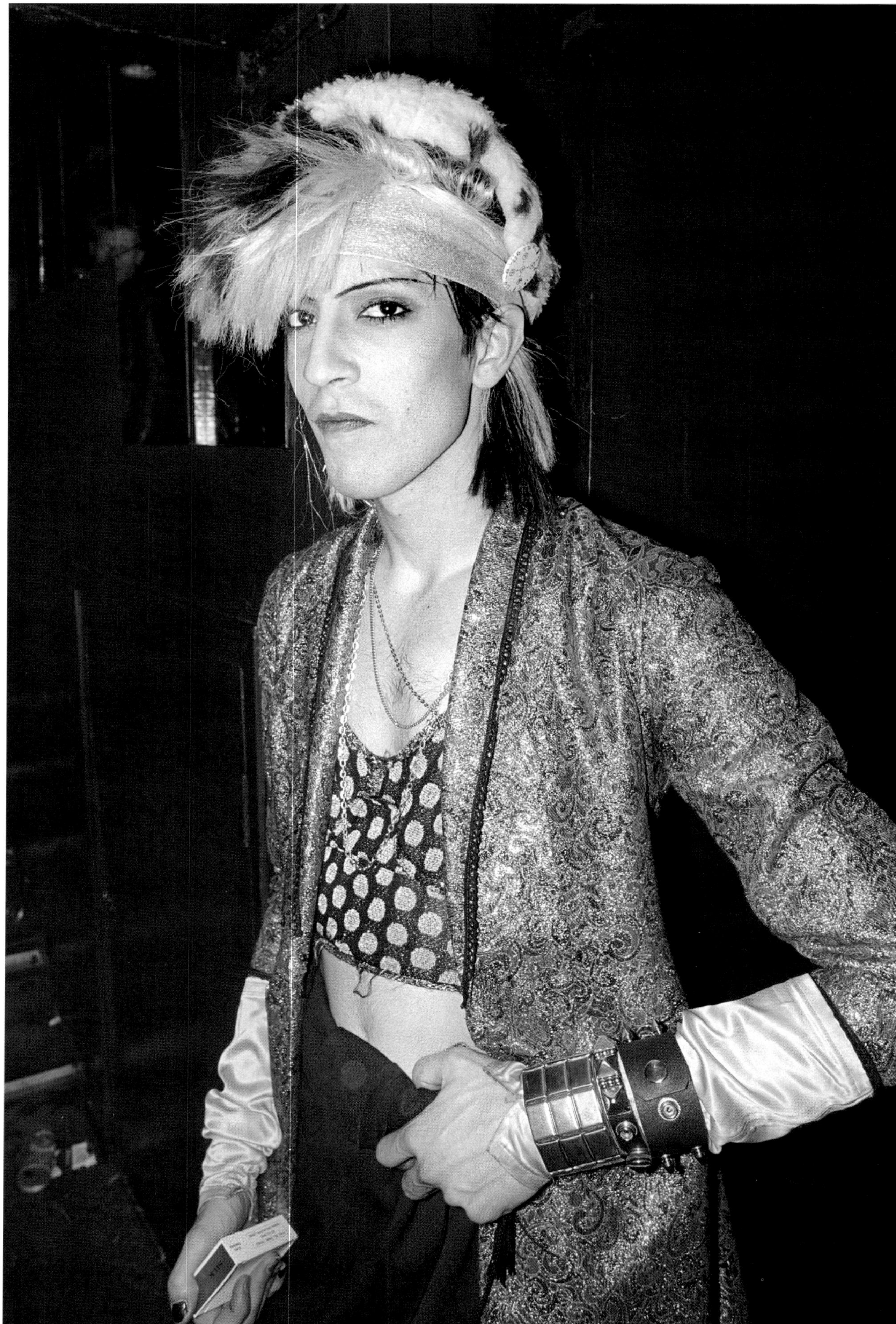

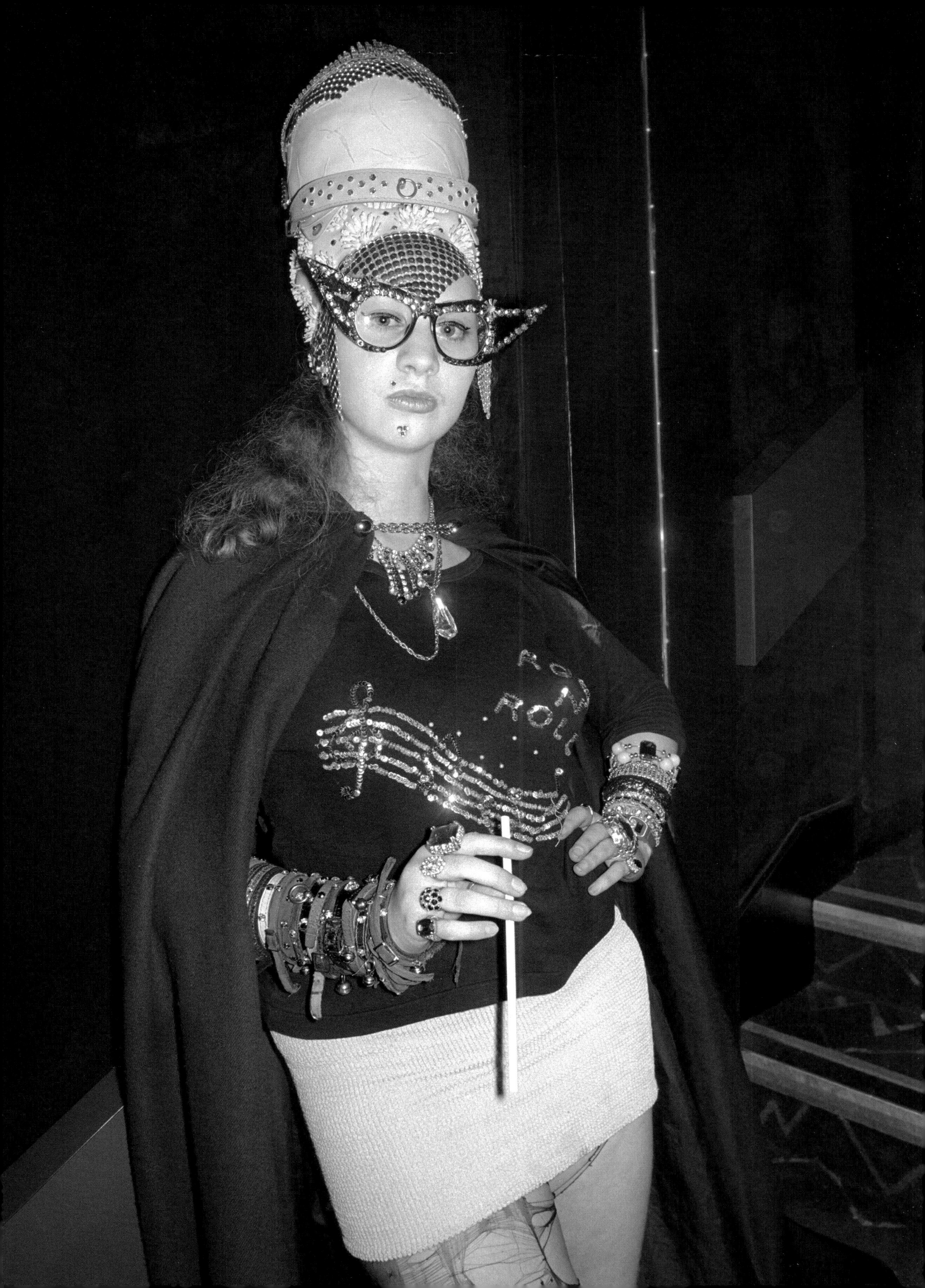

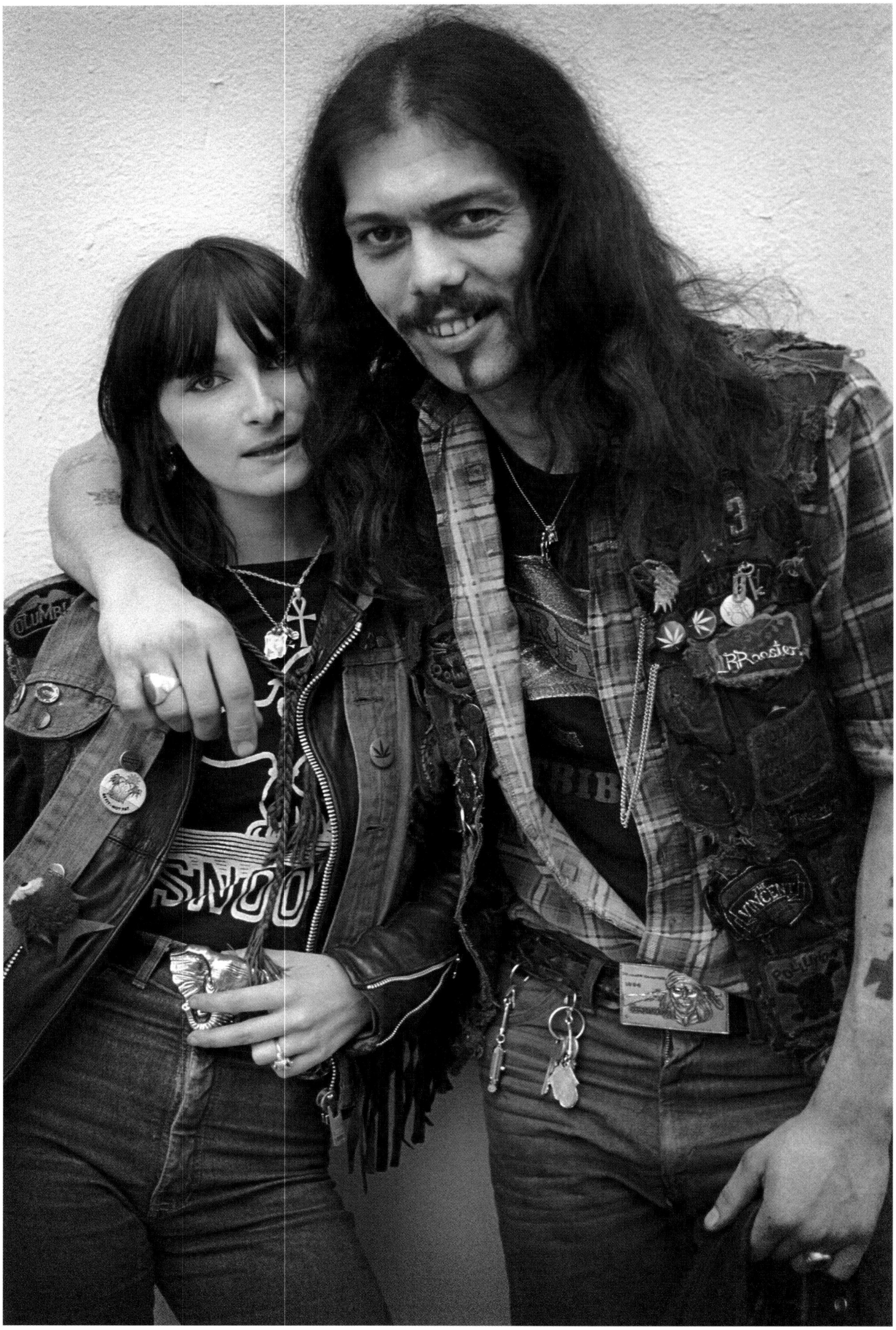
RRooster
VINCENT

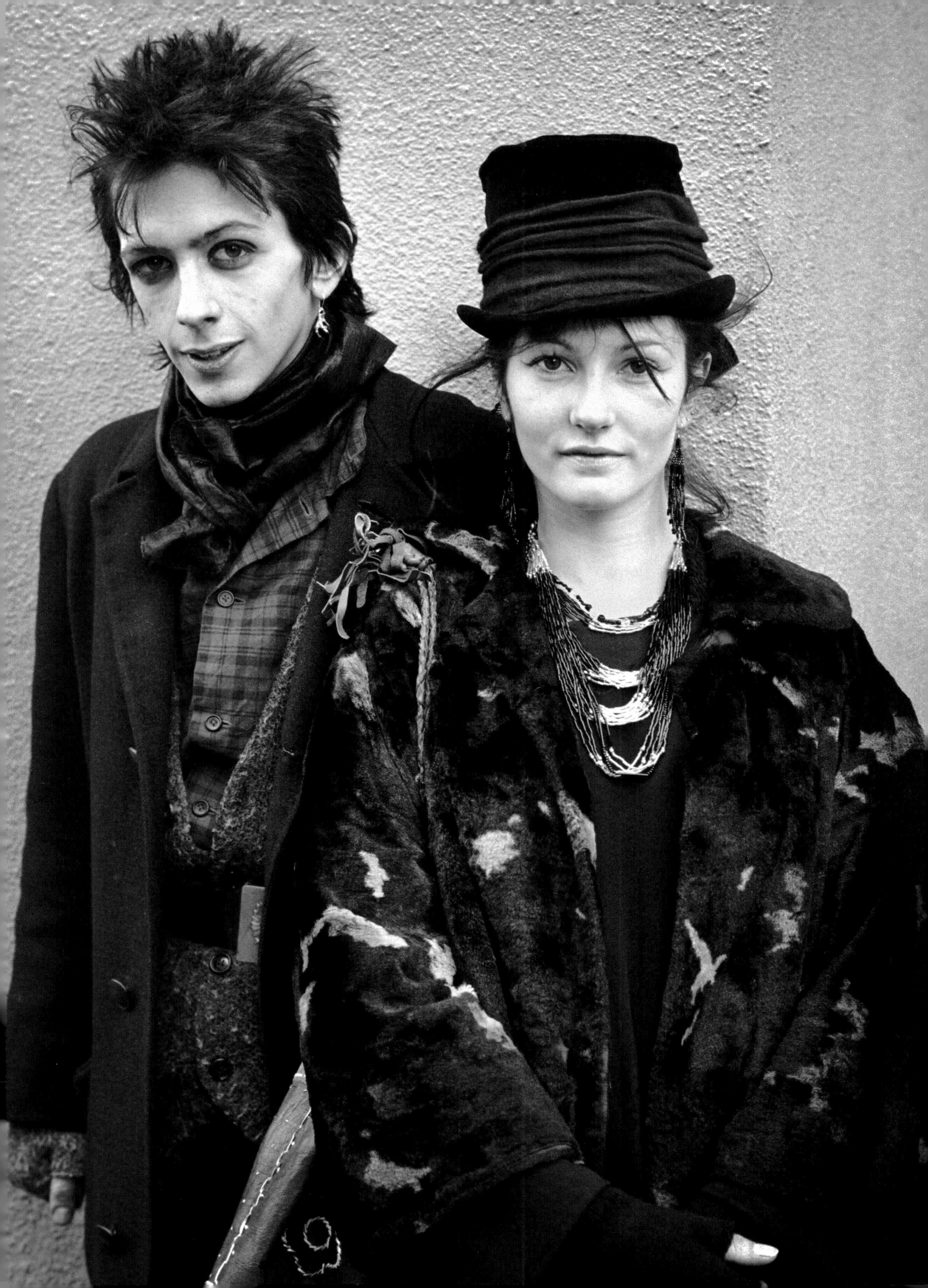

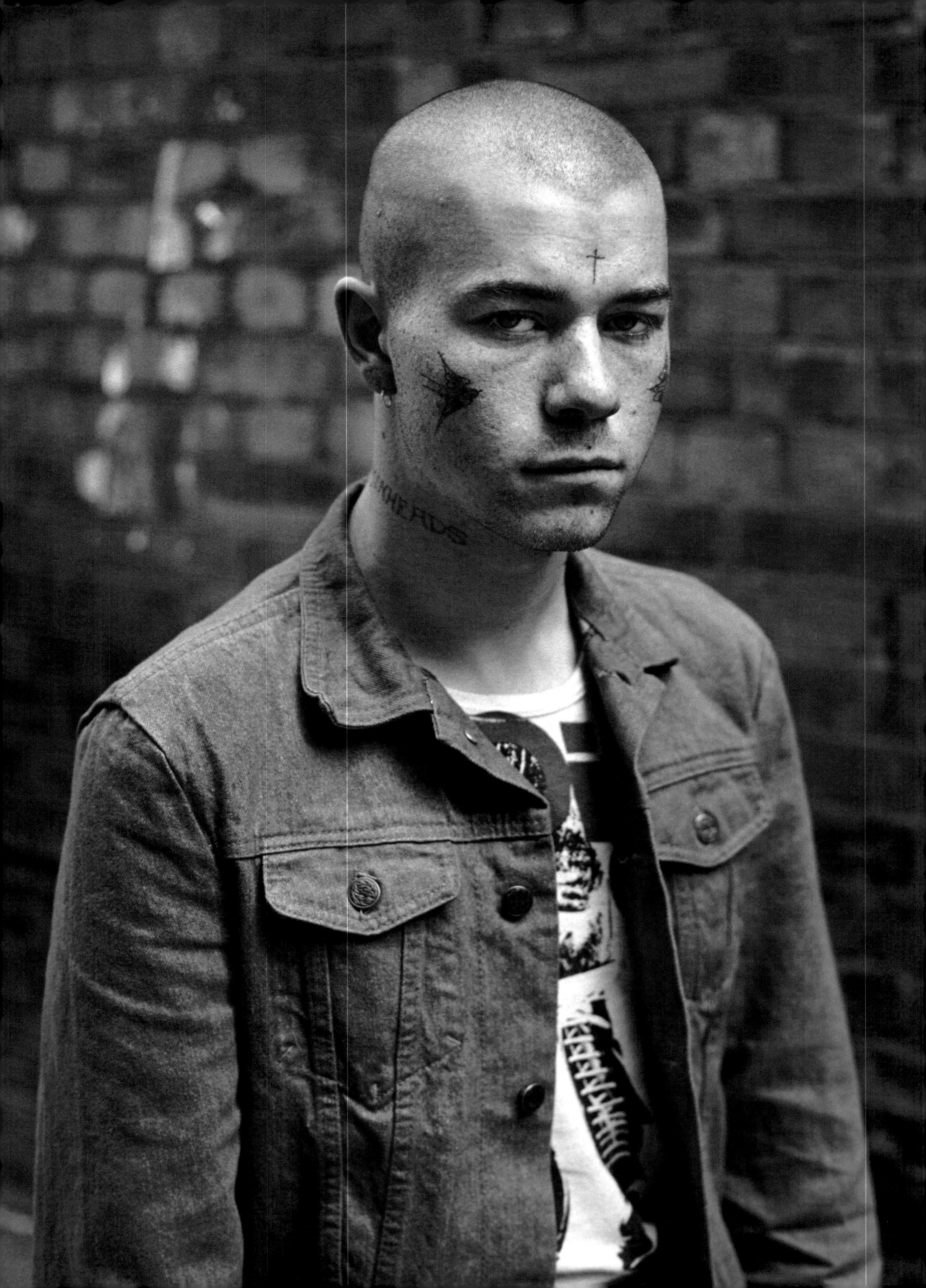

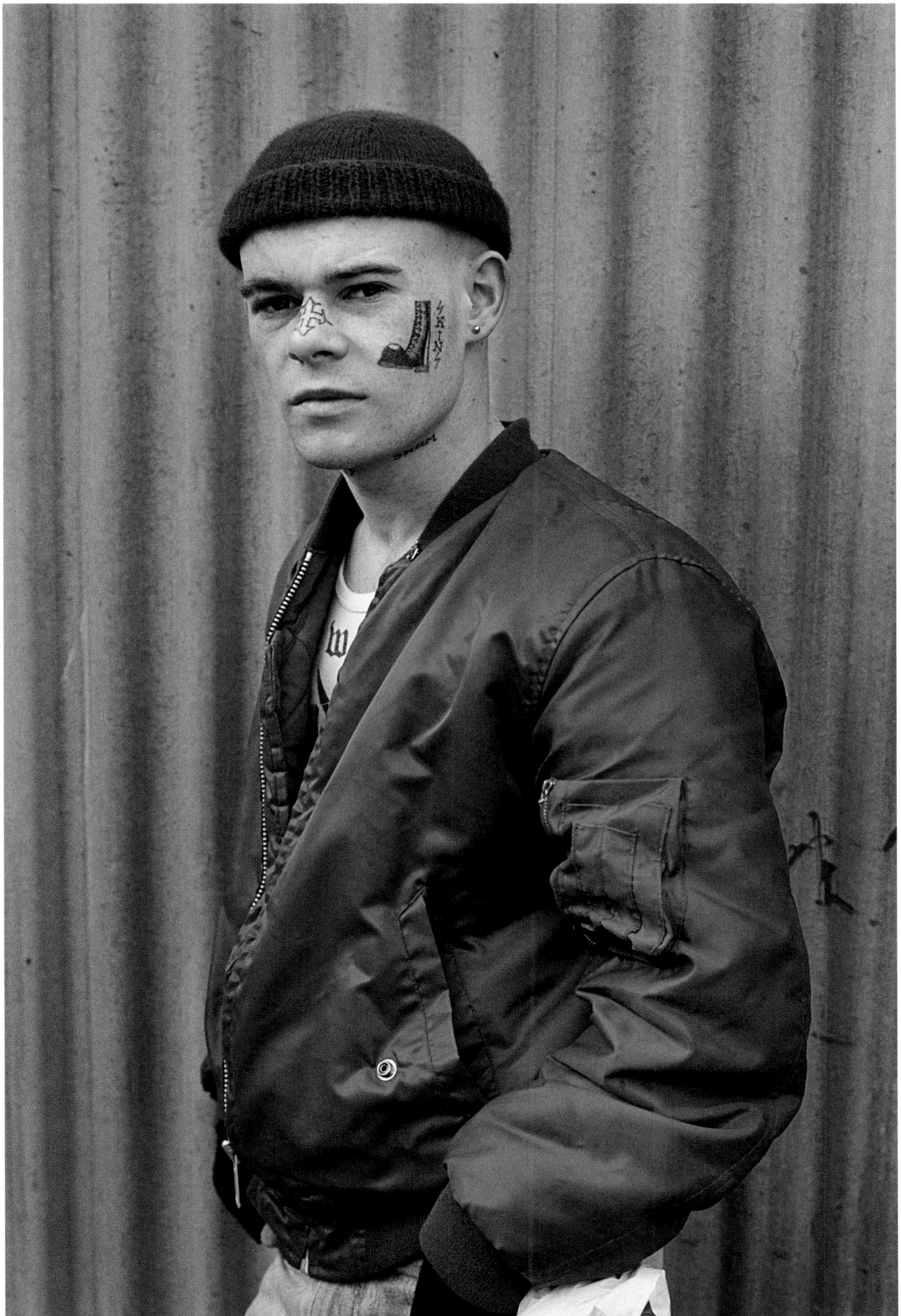

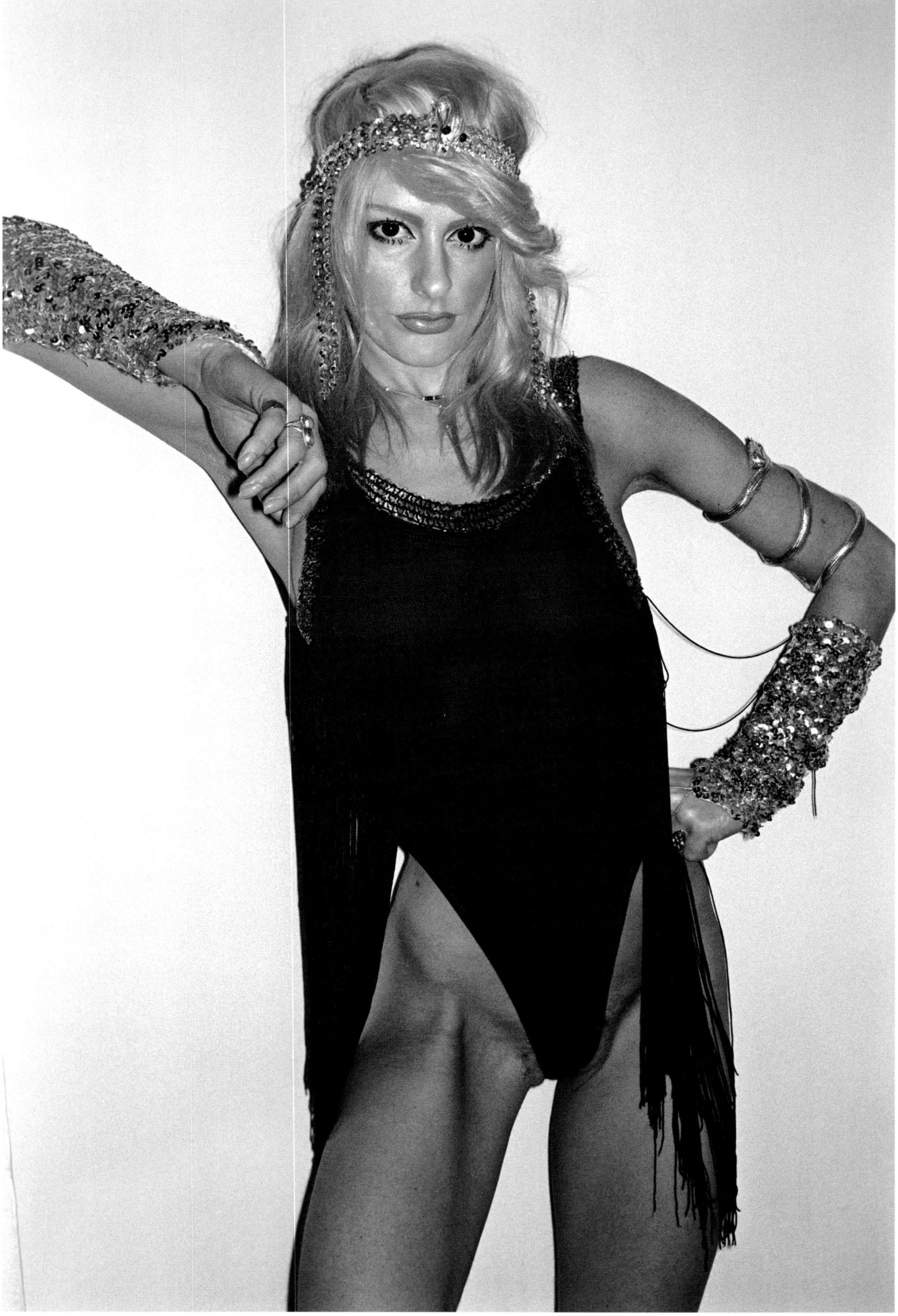

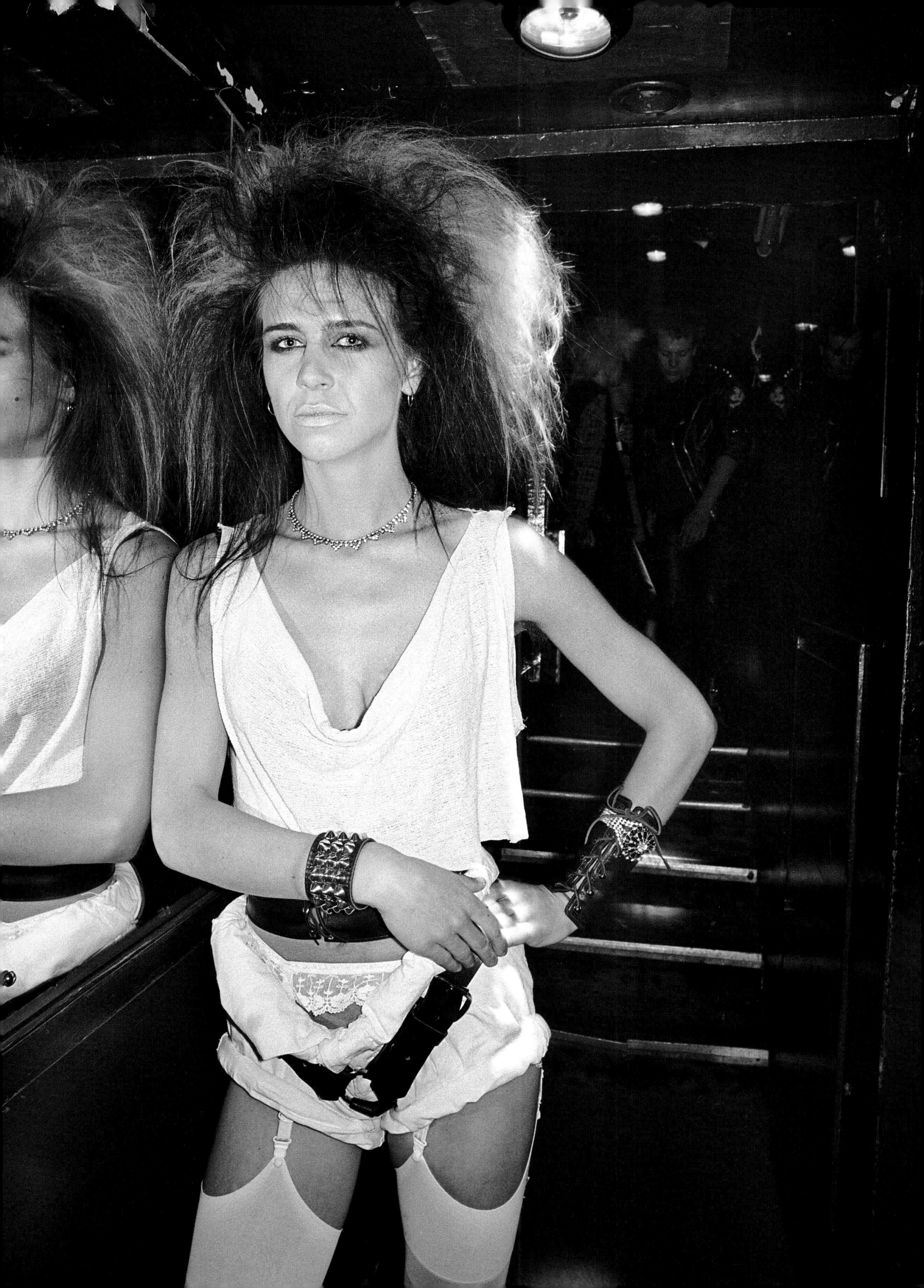

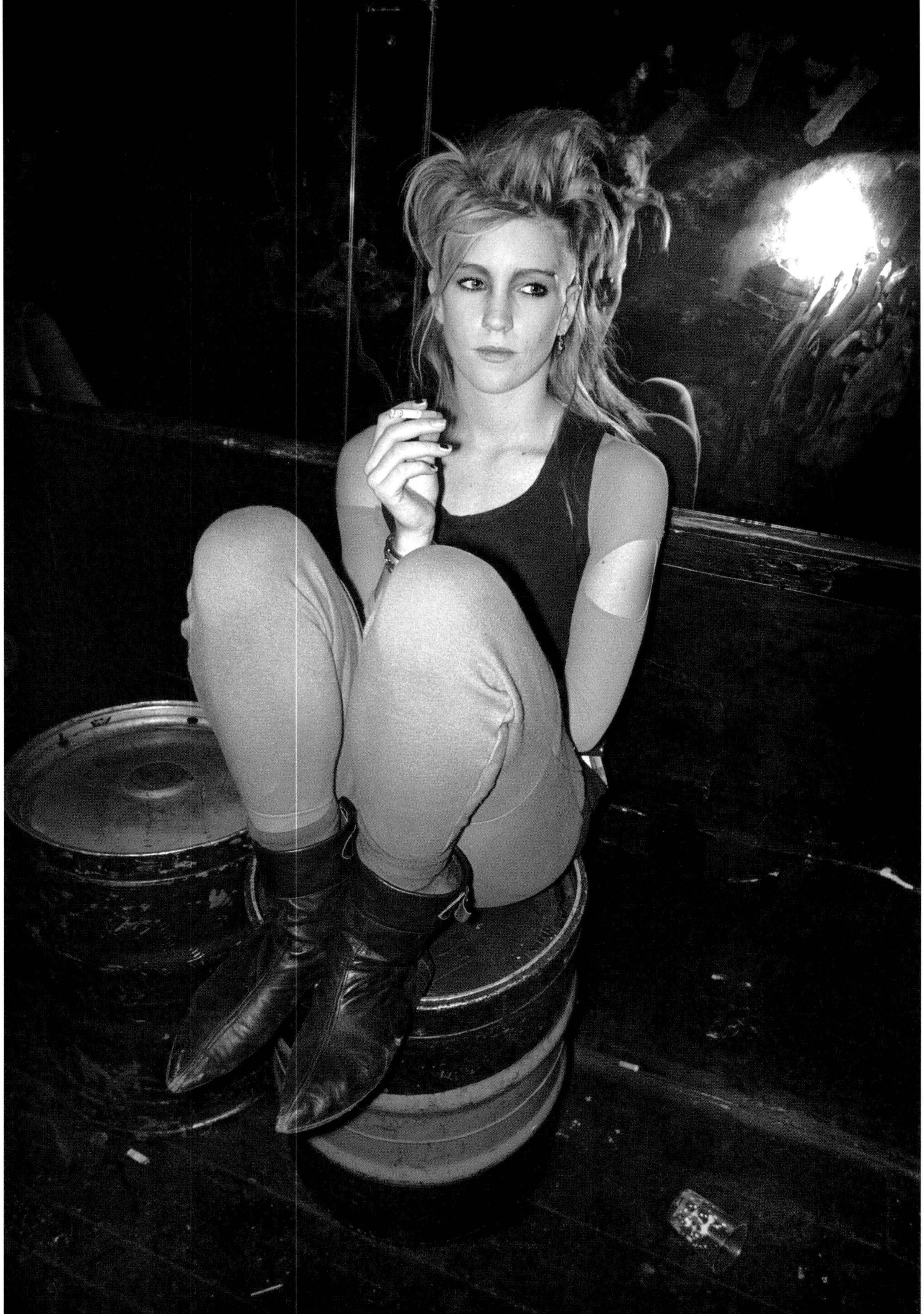

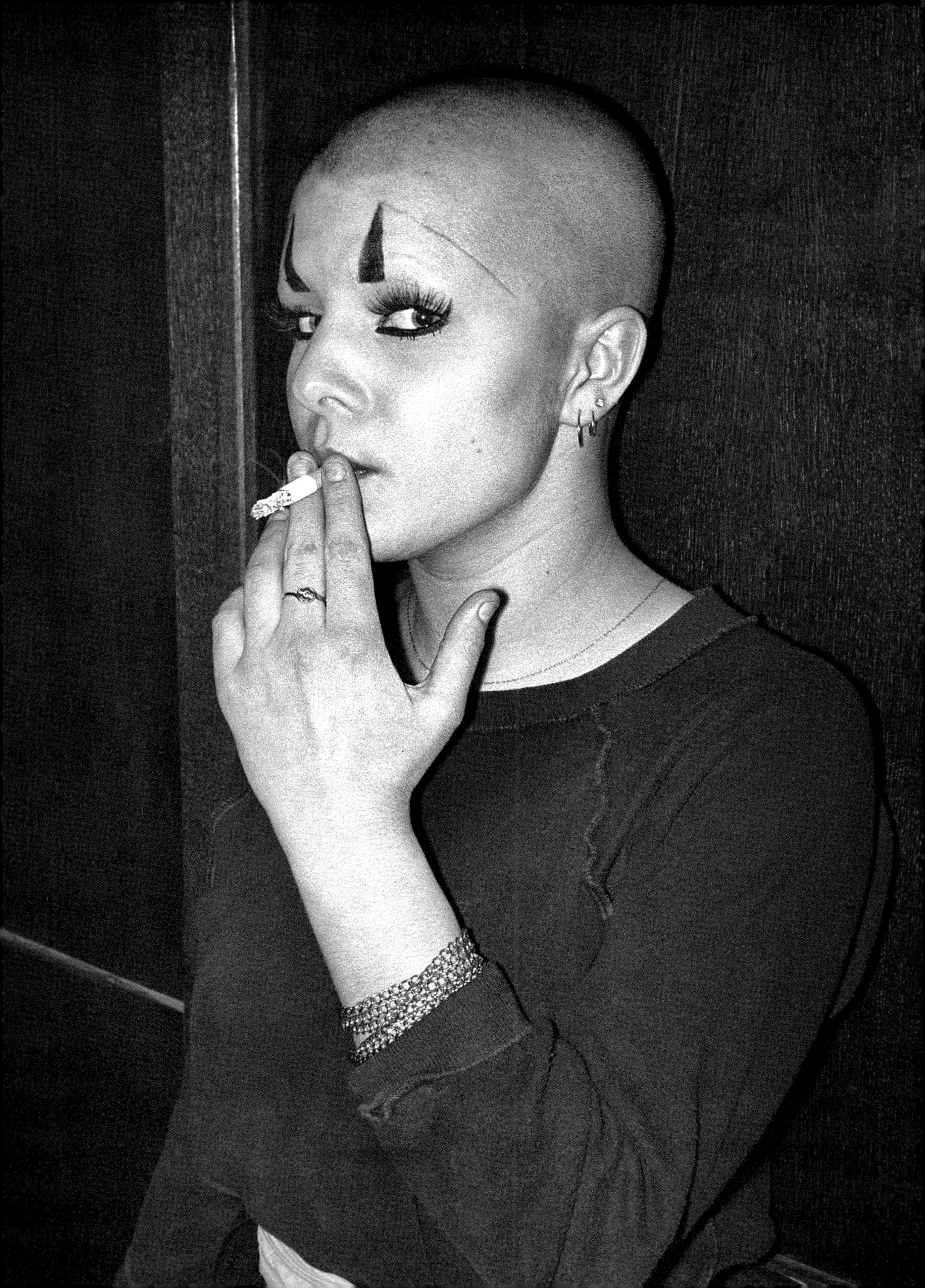

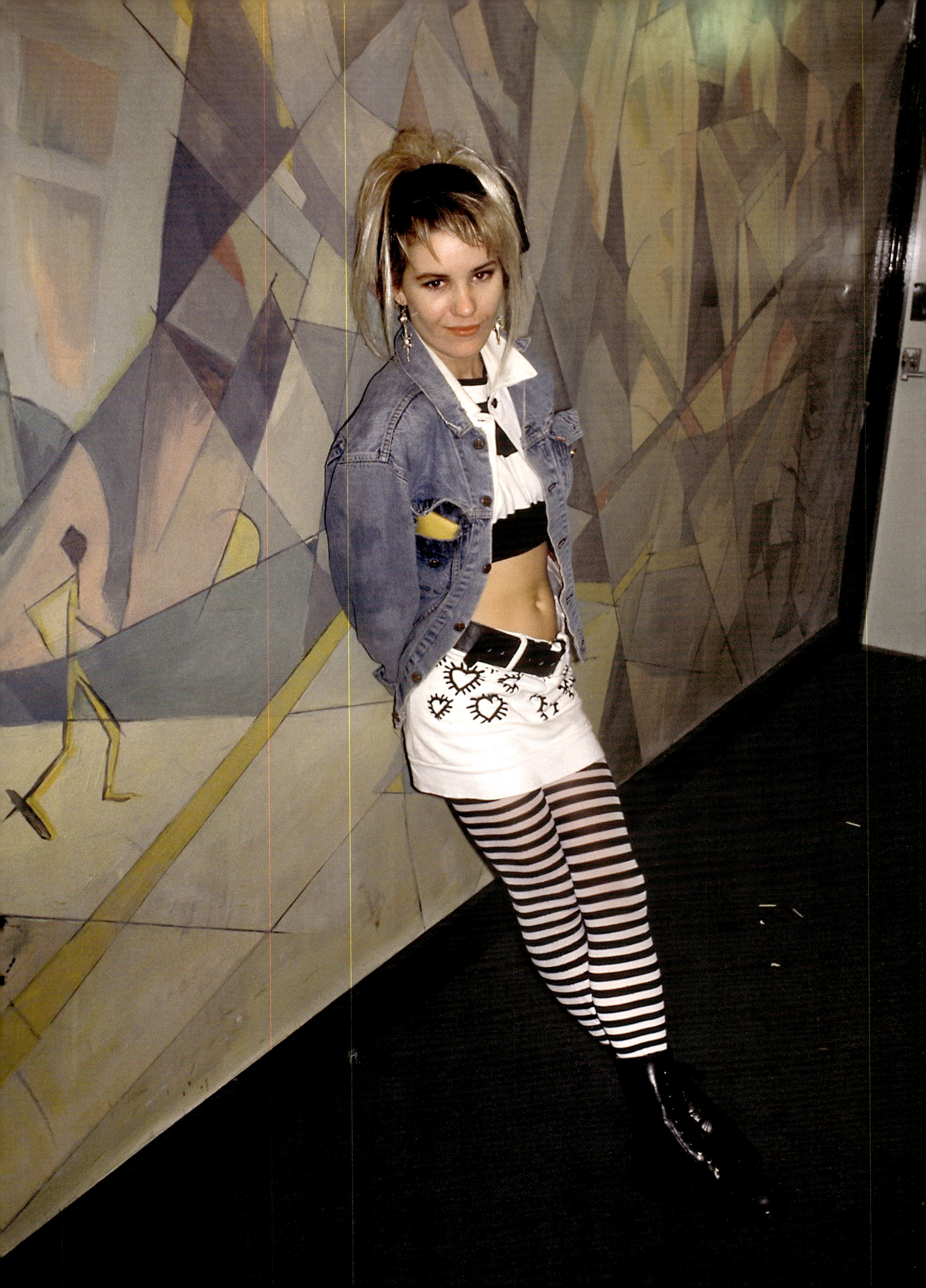

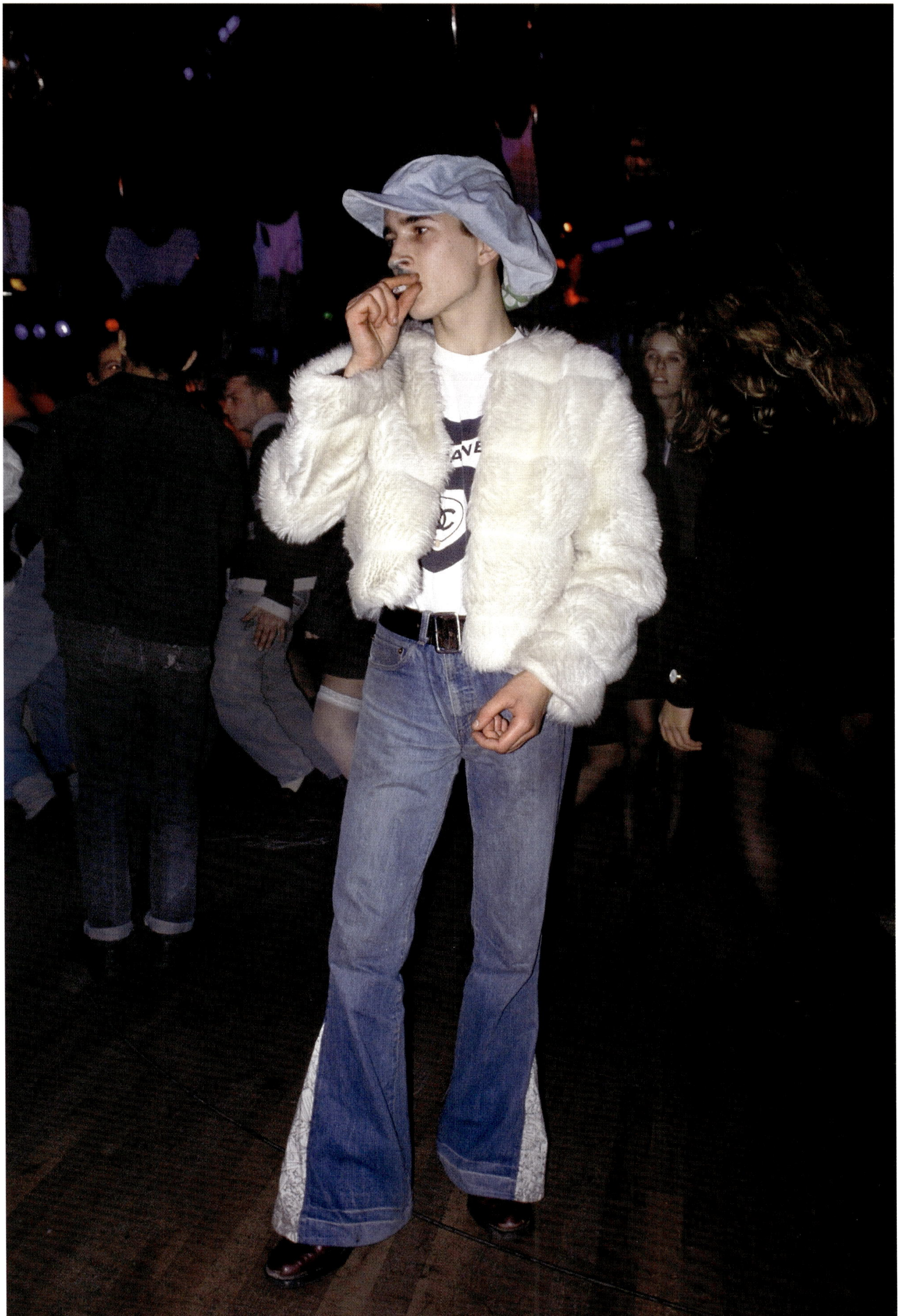

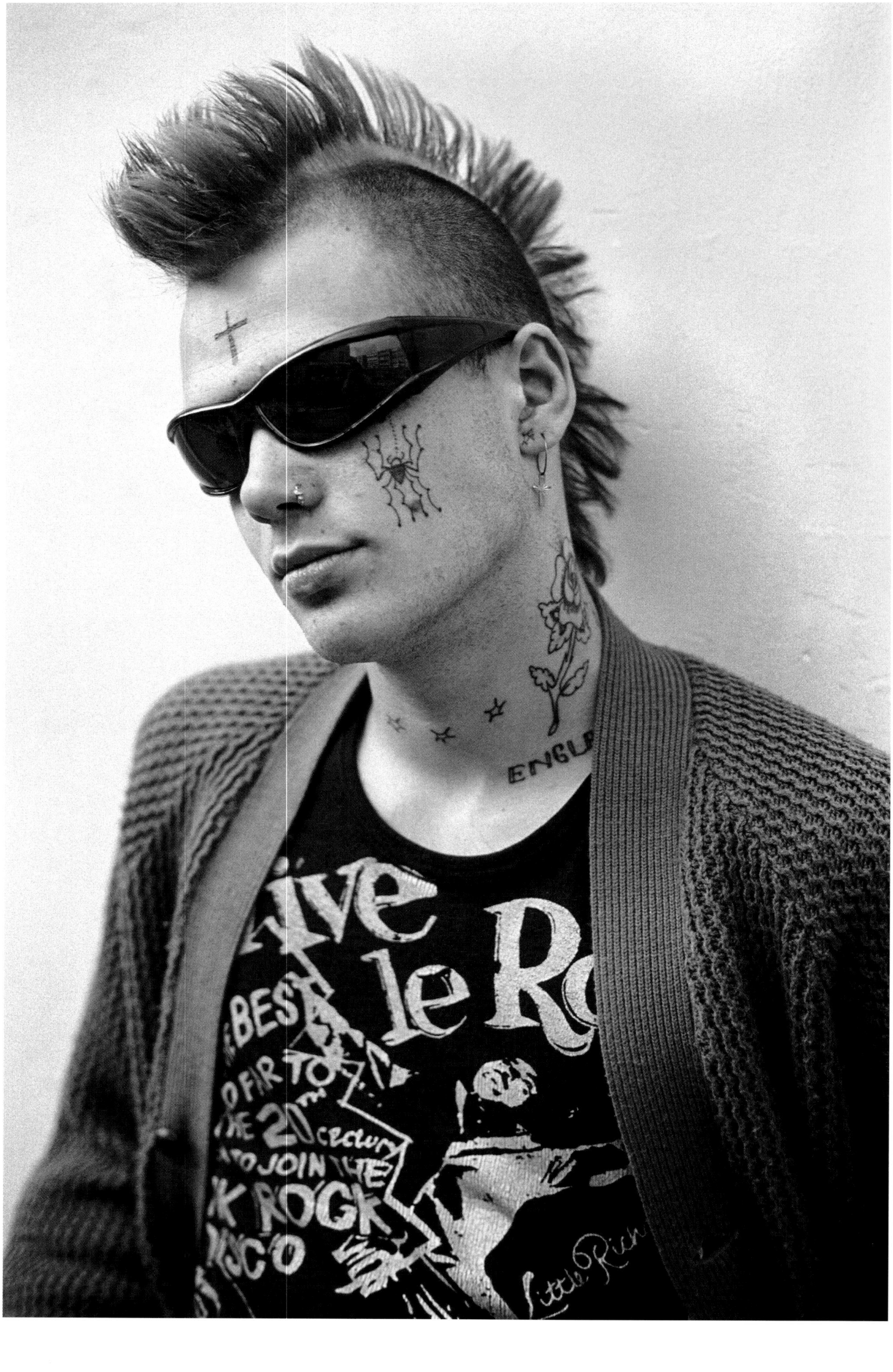
BEST
le
JOIN THE
ROCK

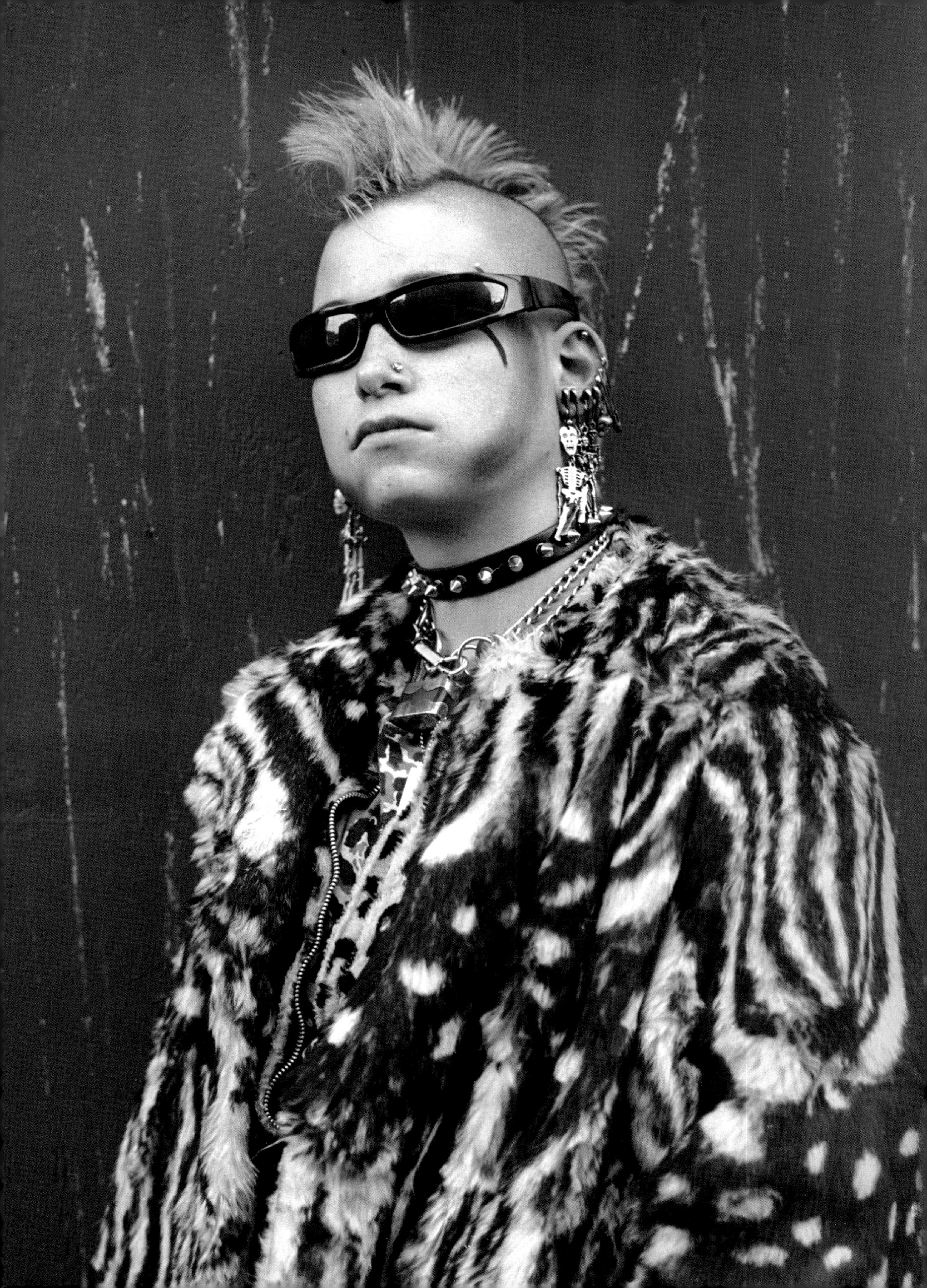

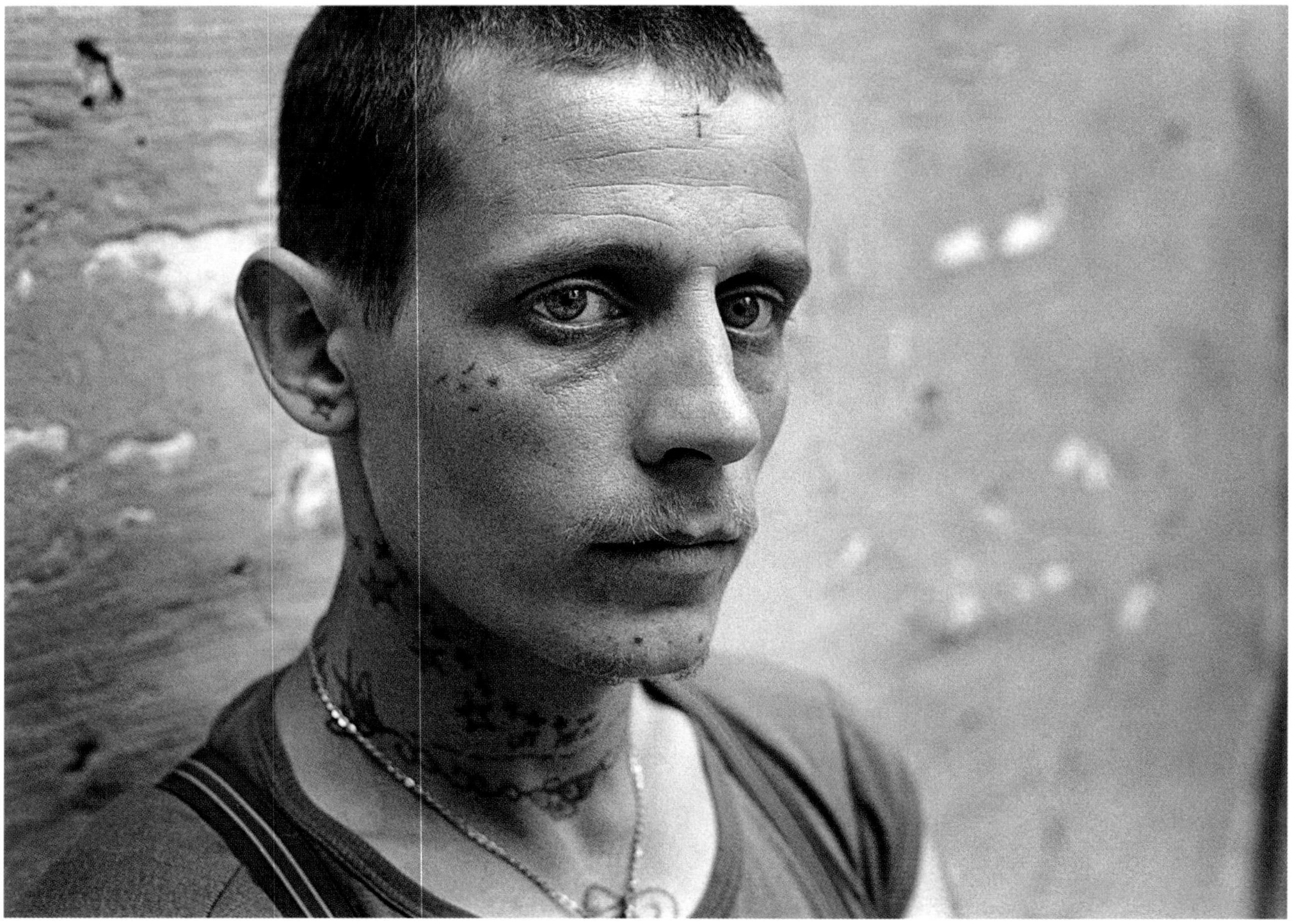

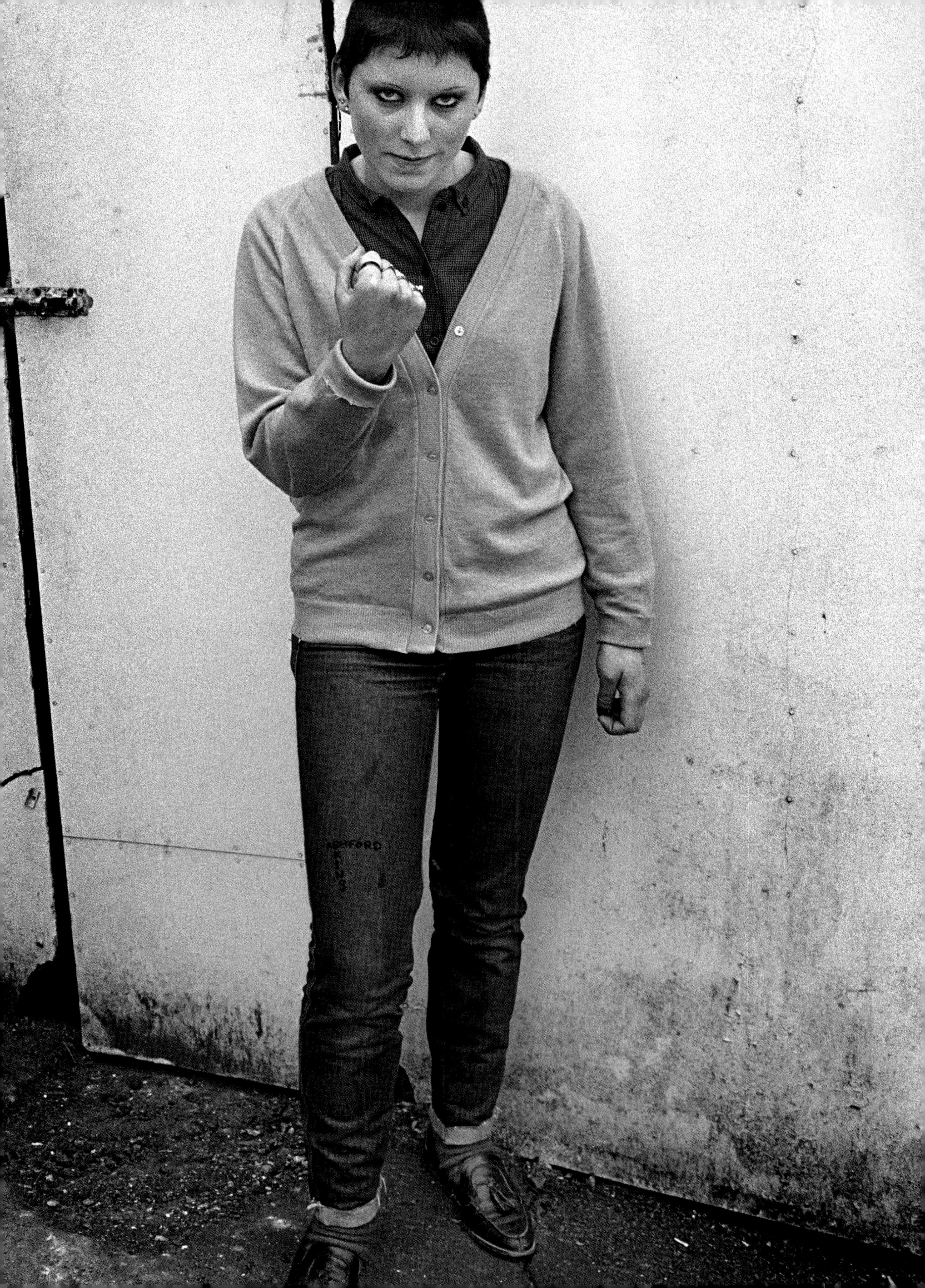
ASHFORD

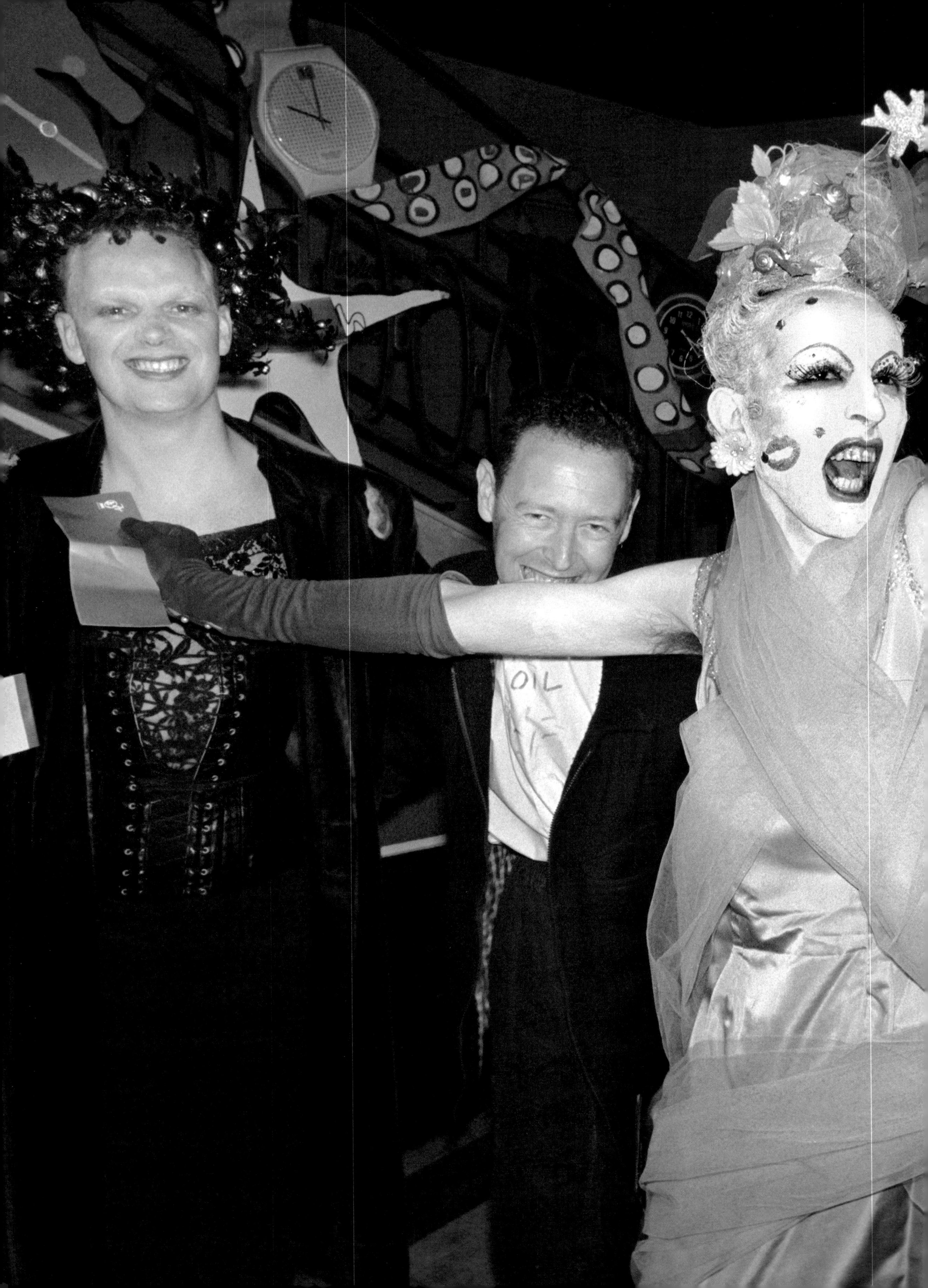

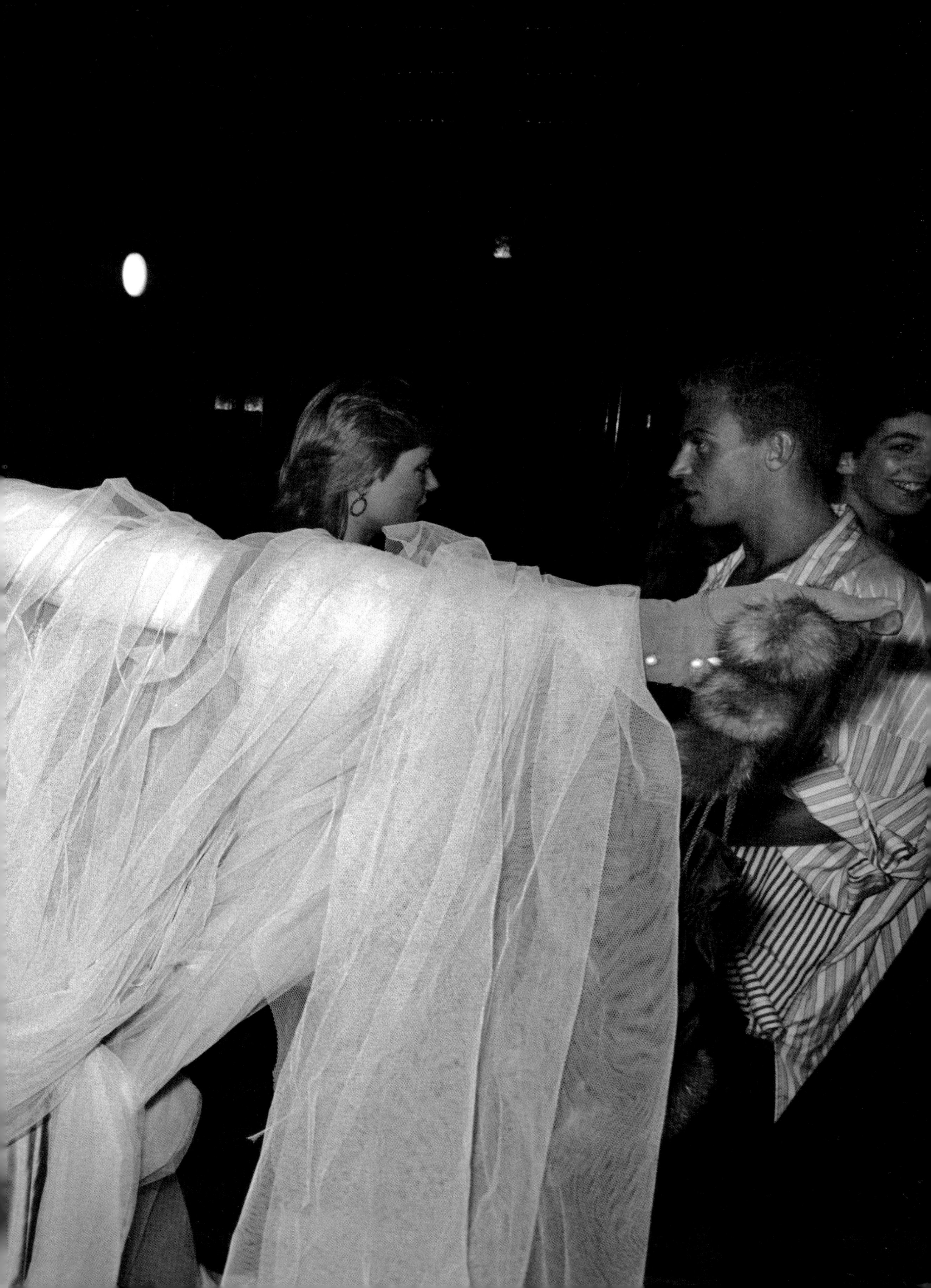

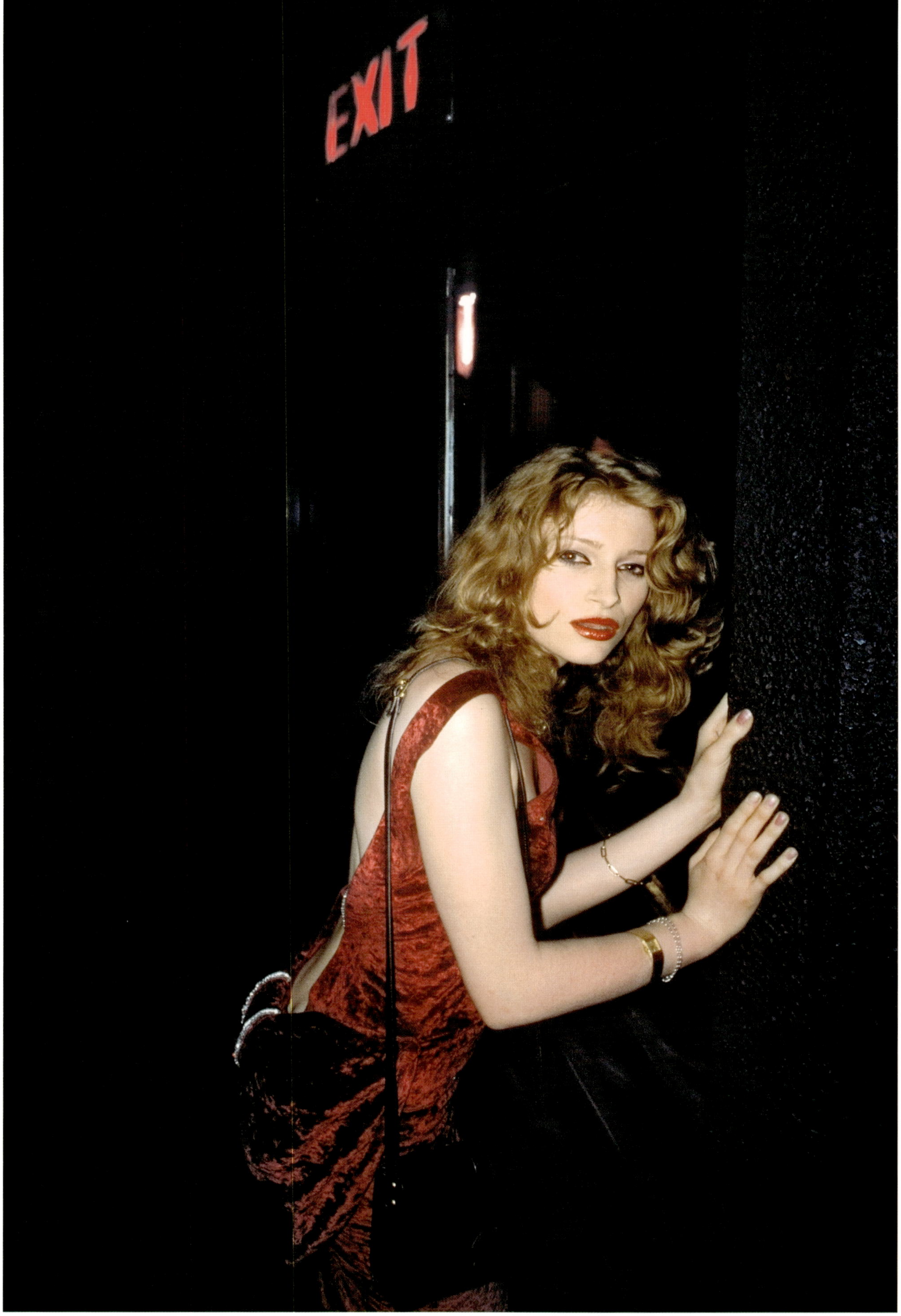
EXIT

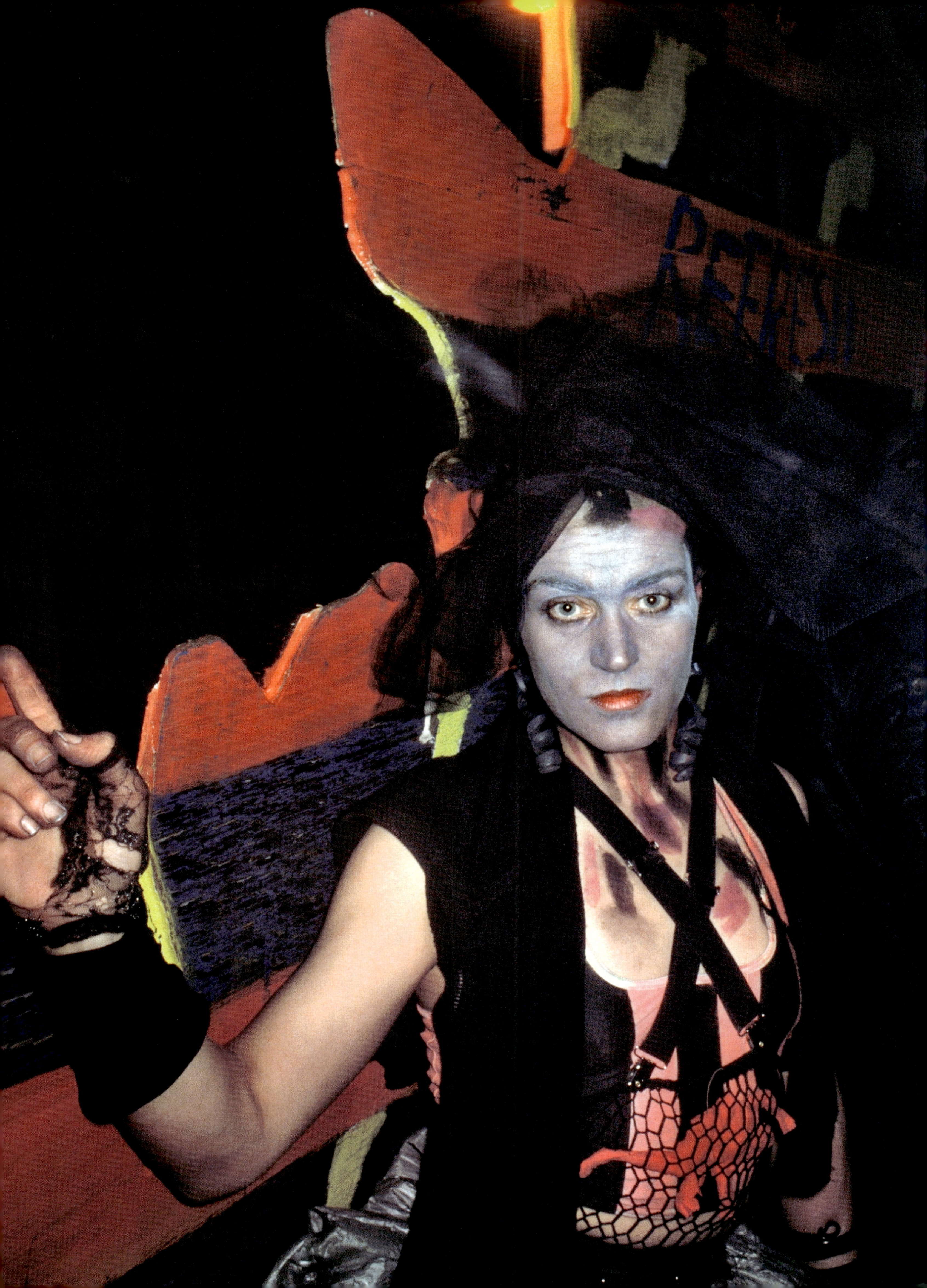

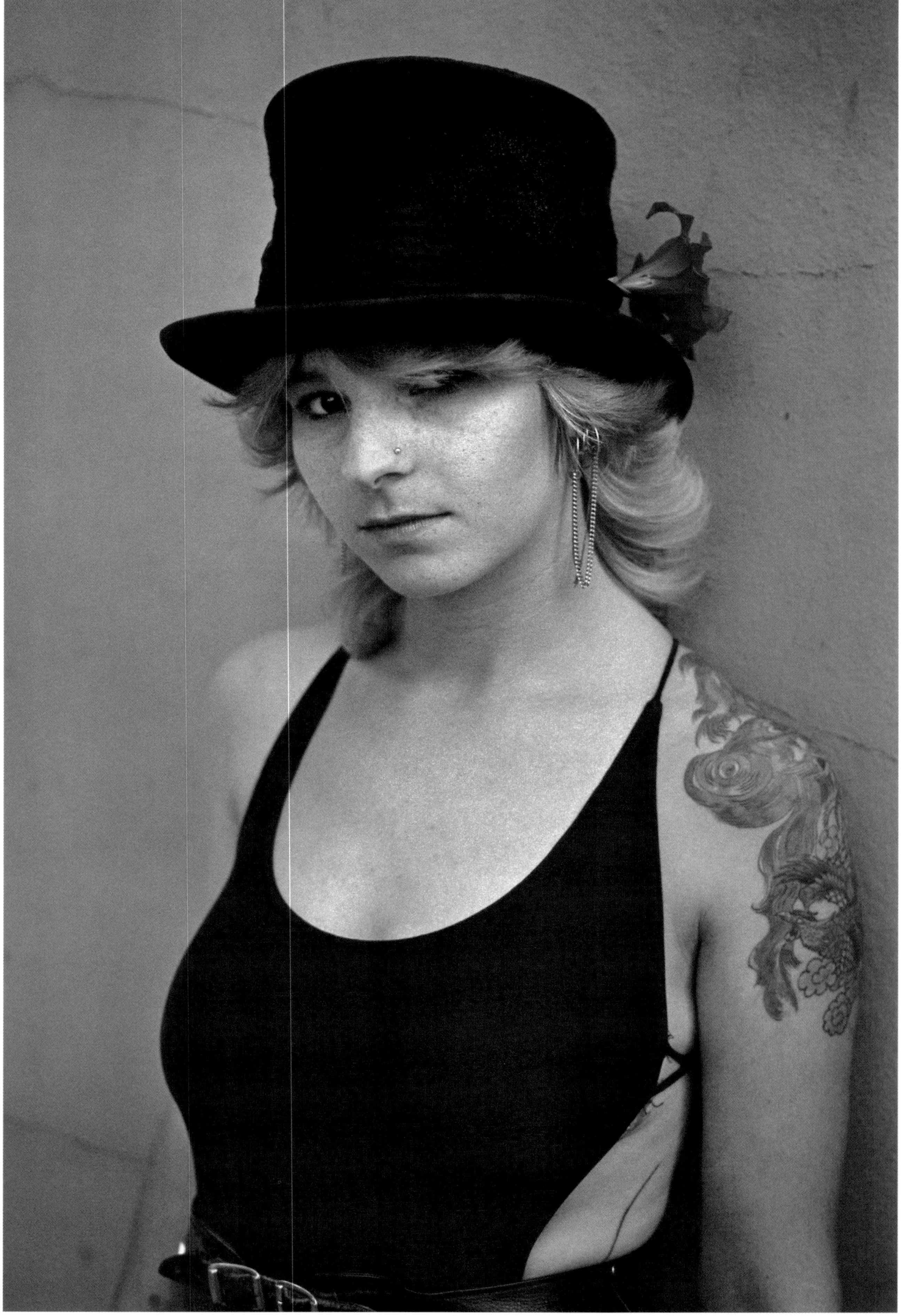

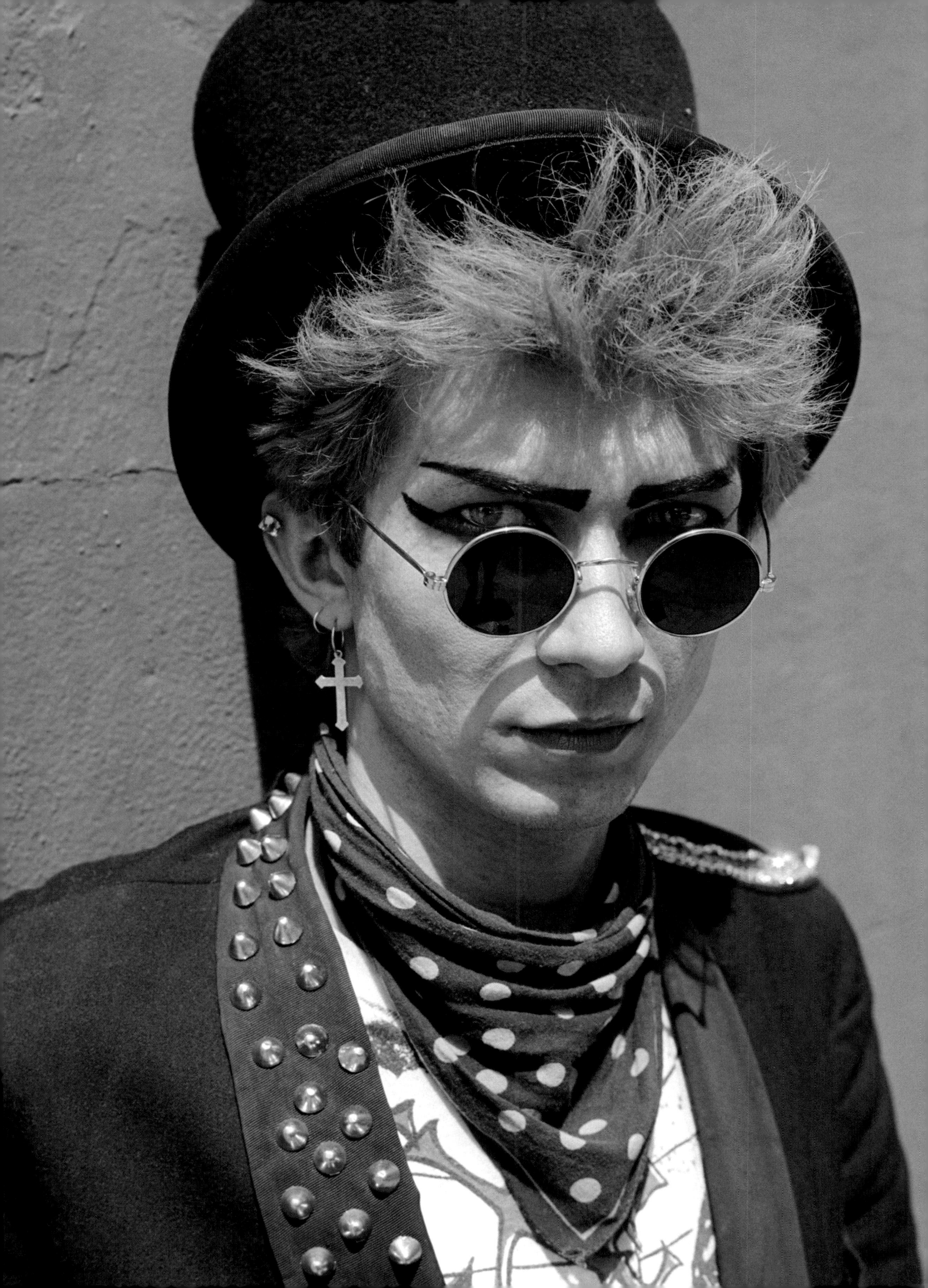

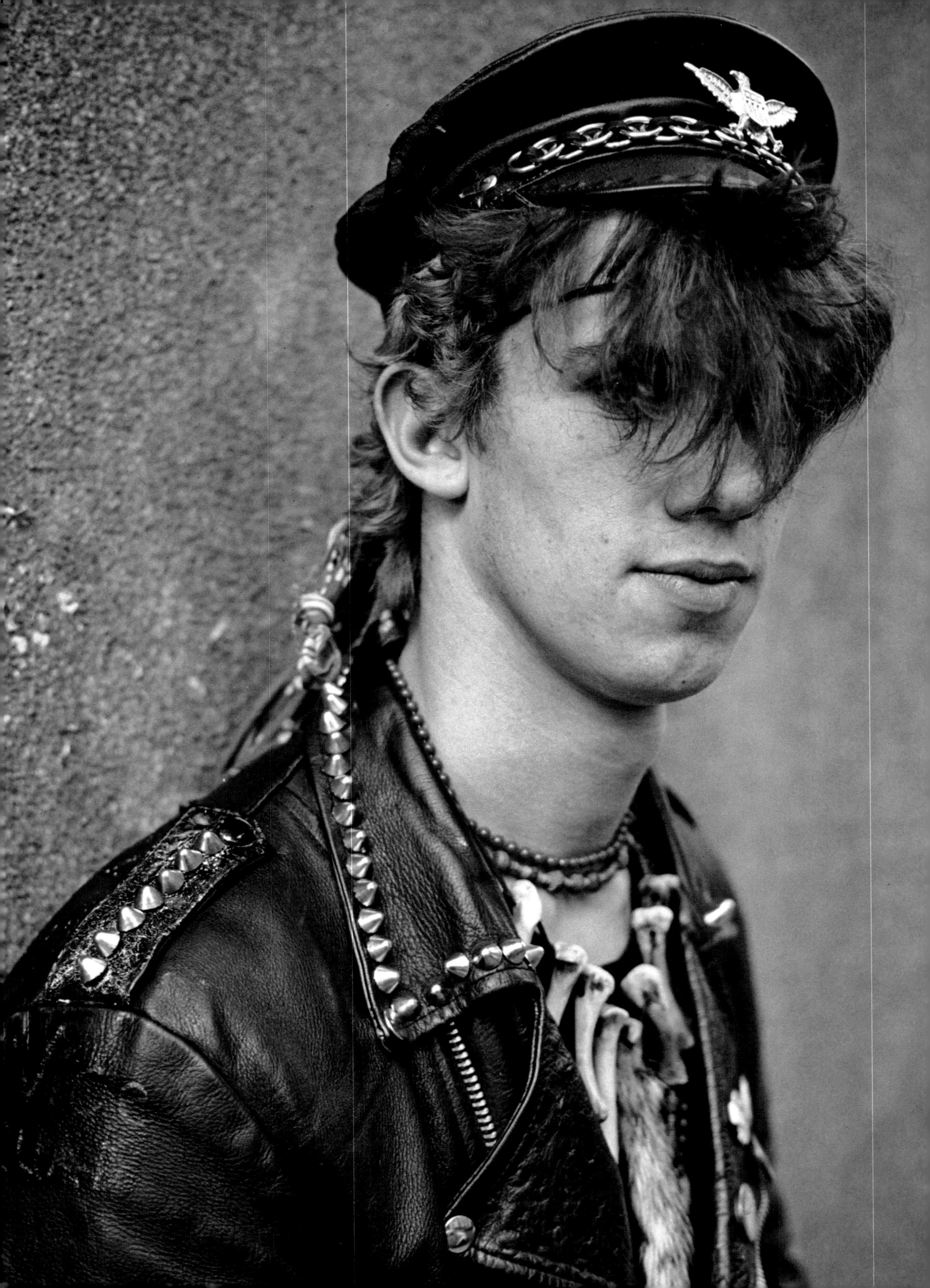

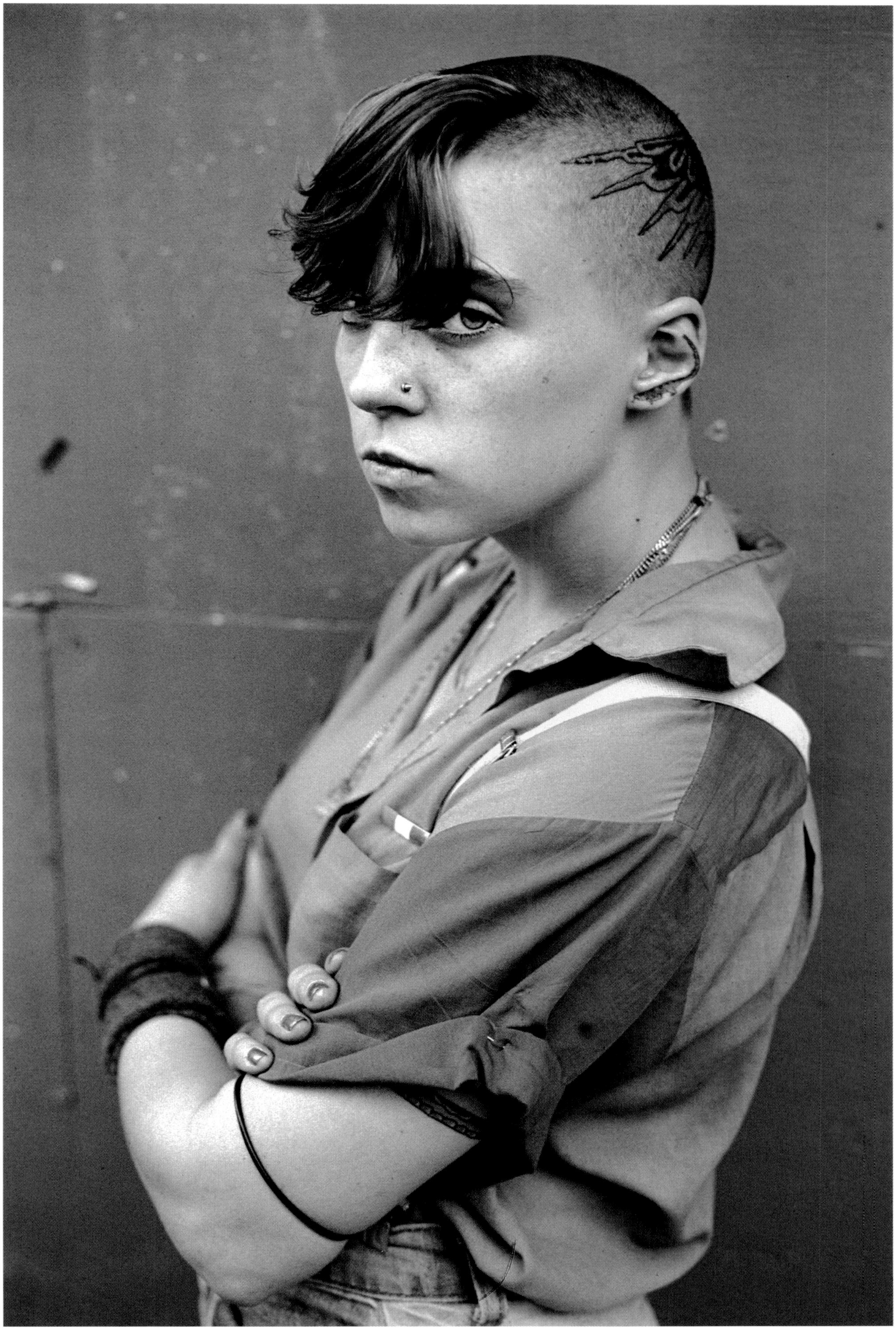

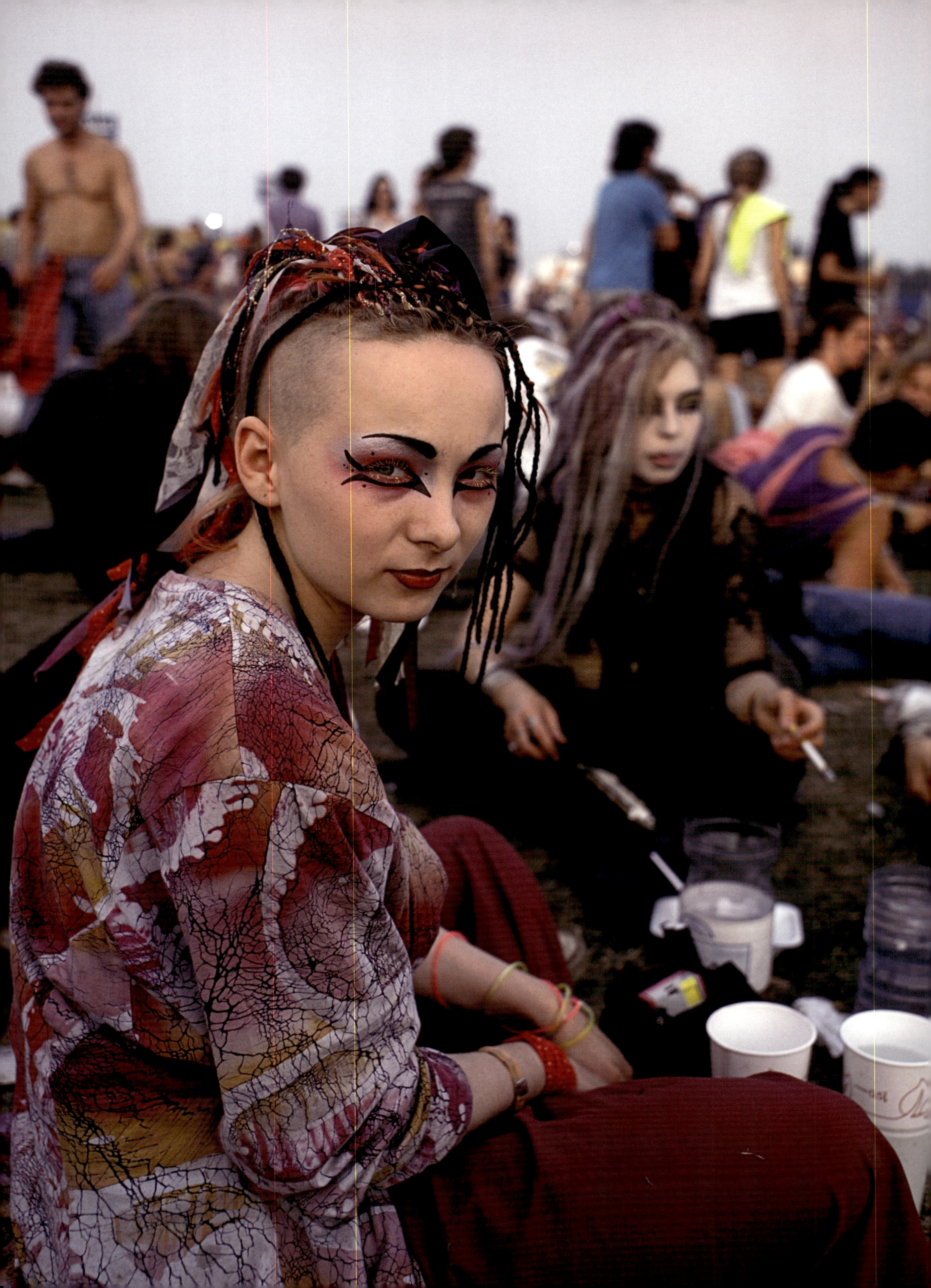

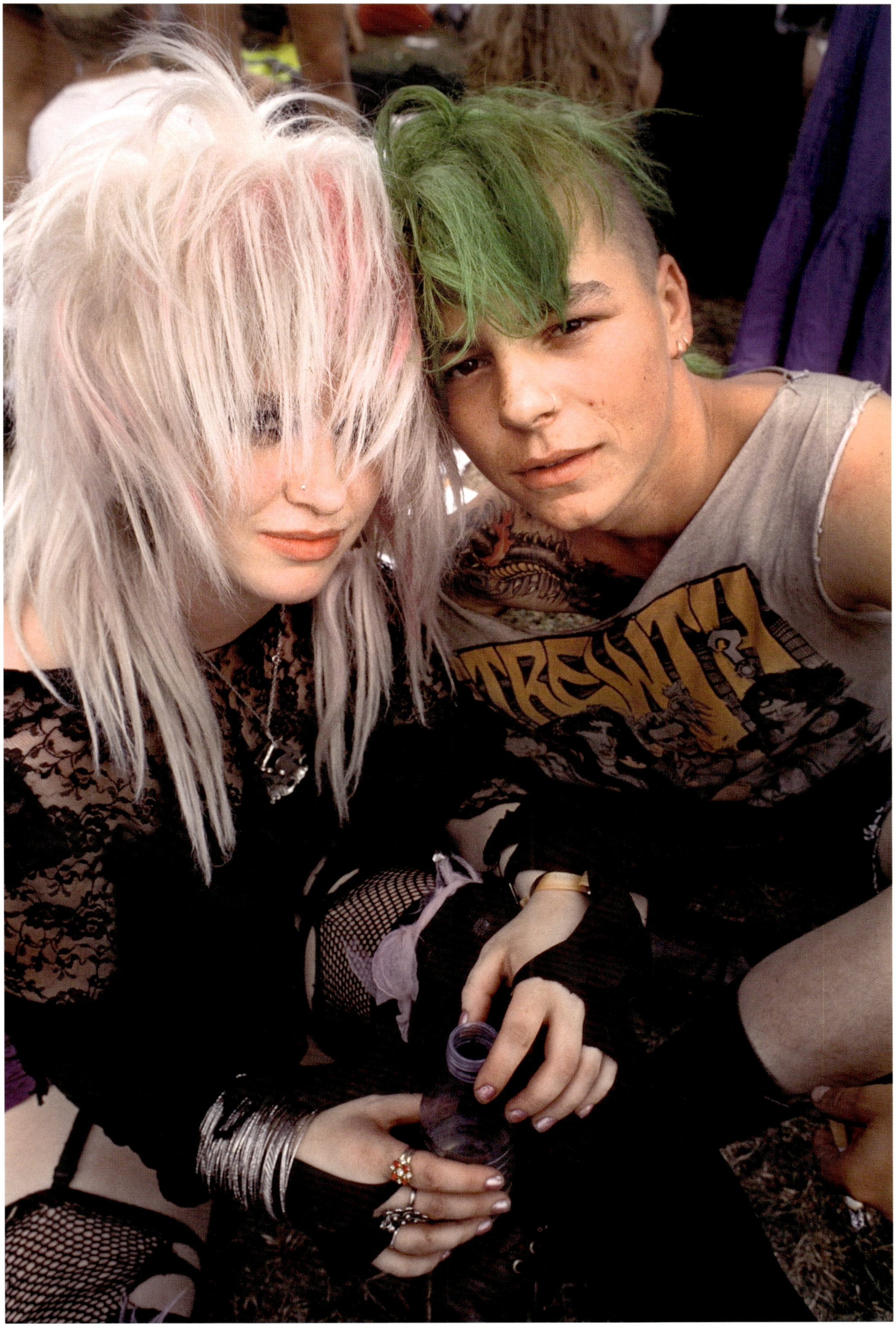

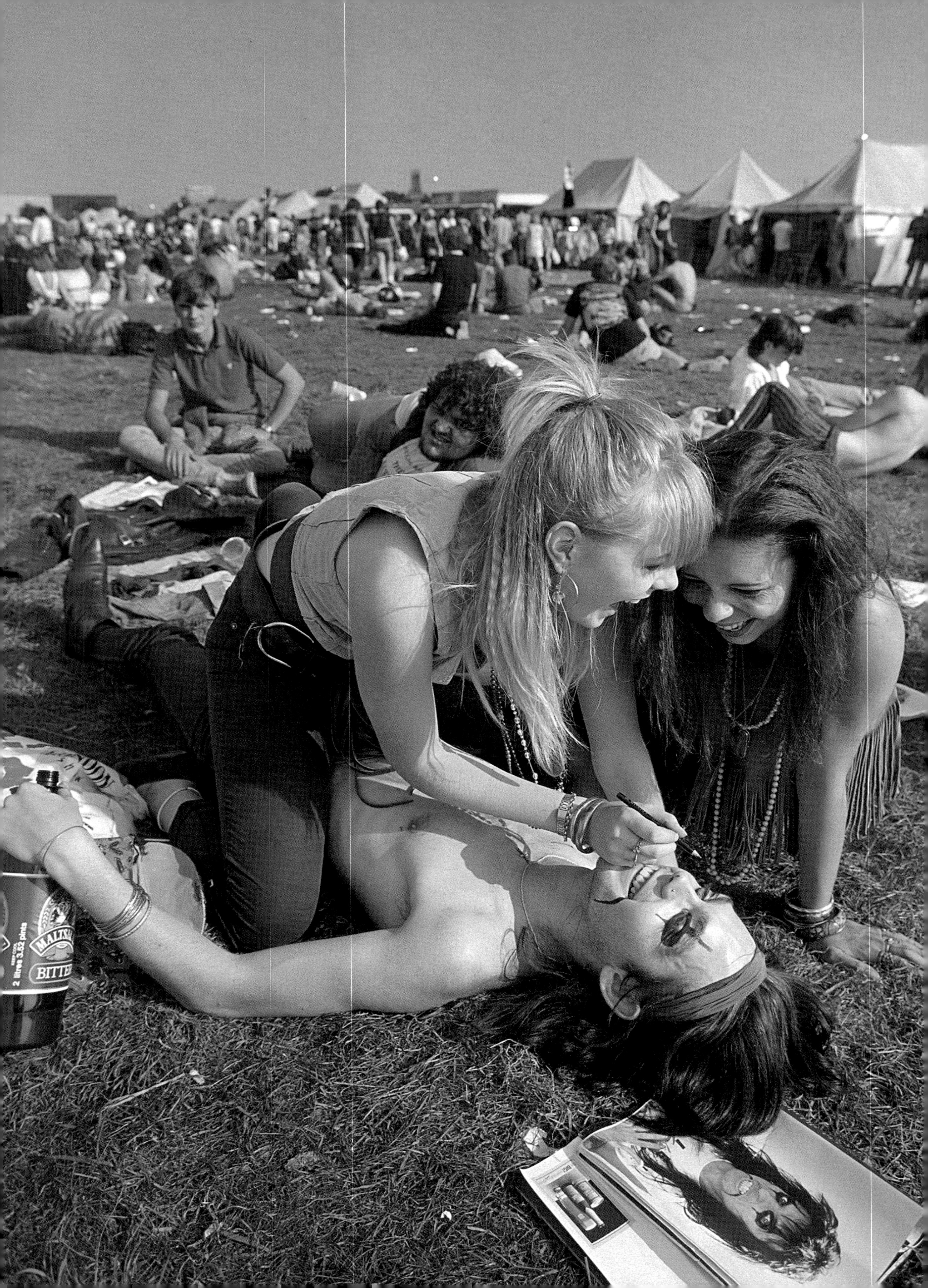
2 litres 3.52 pints
BITTER

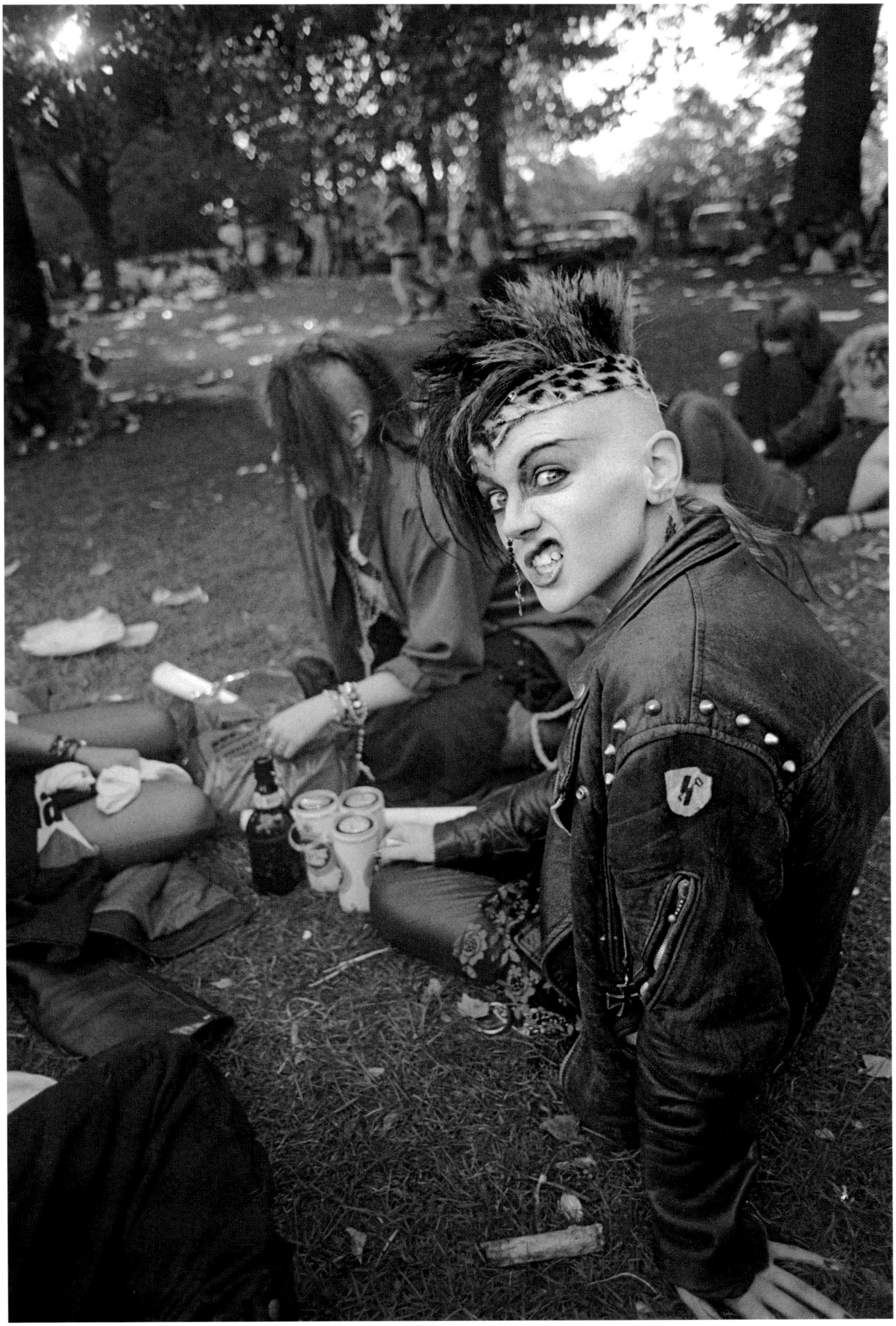

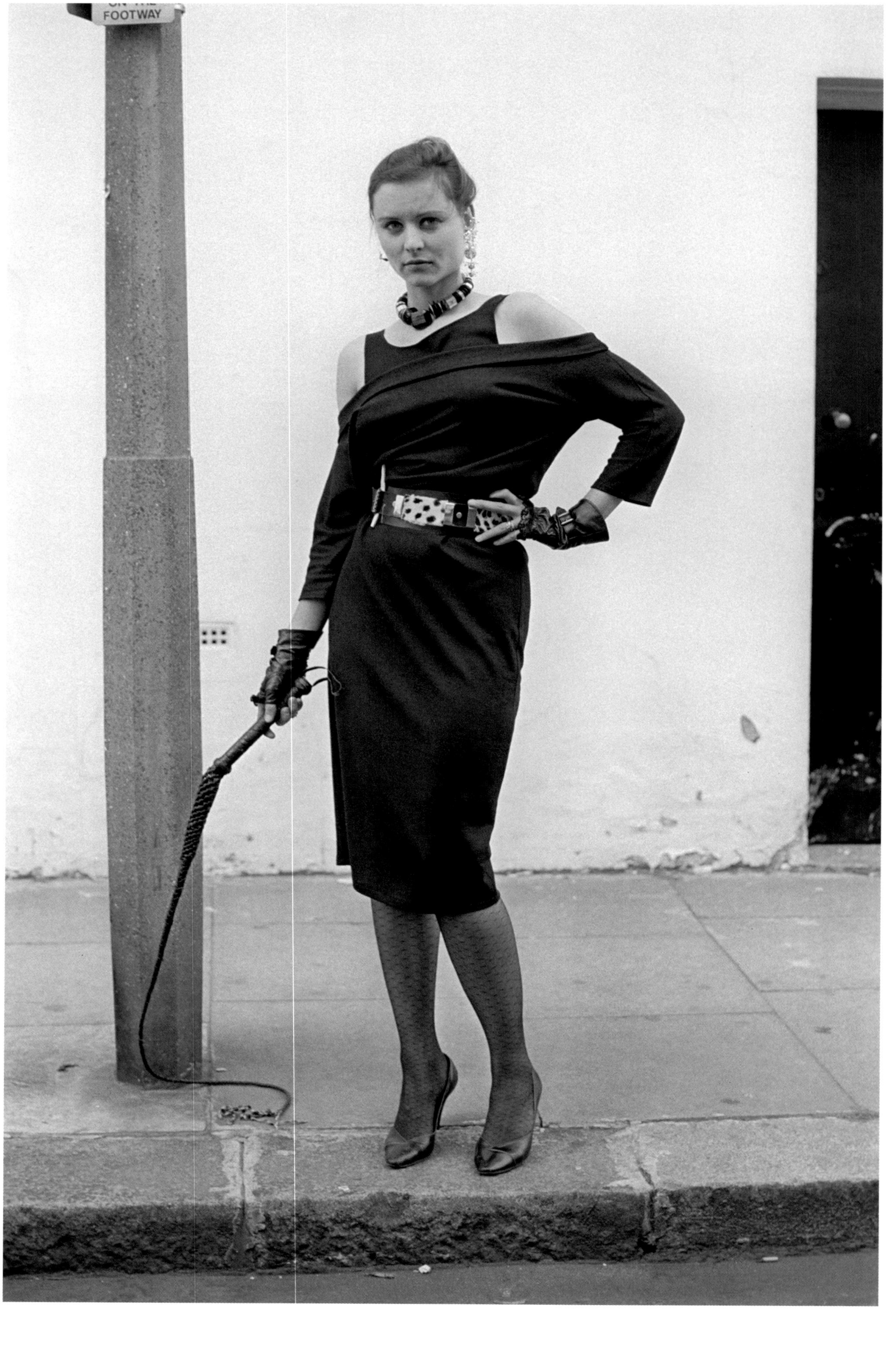
FOOTWAY

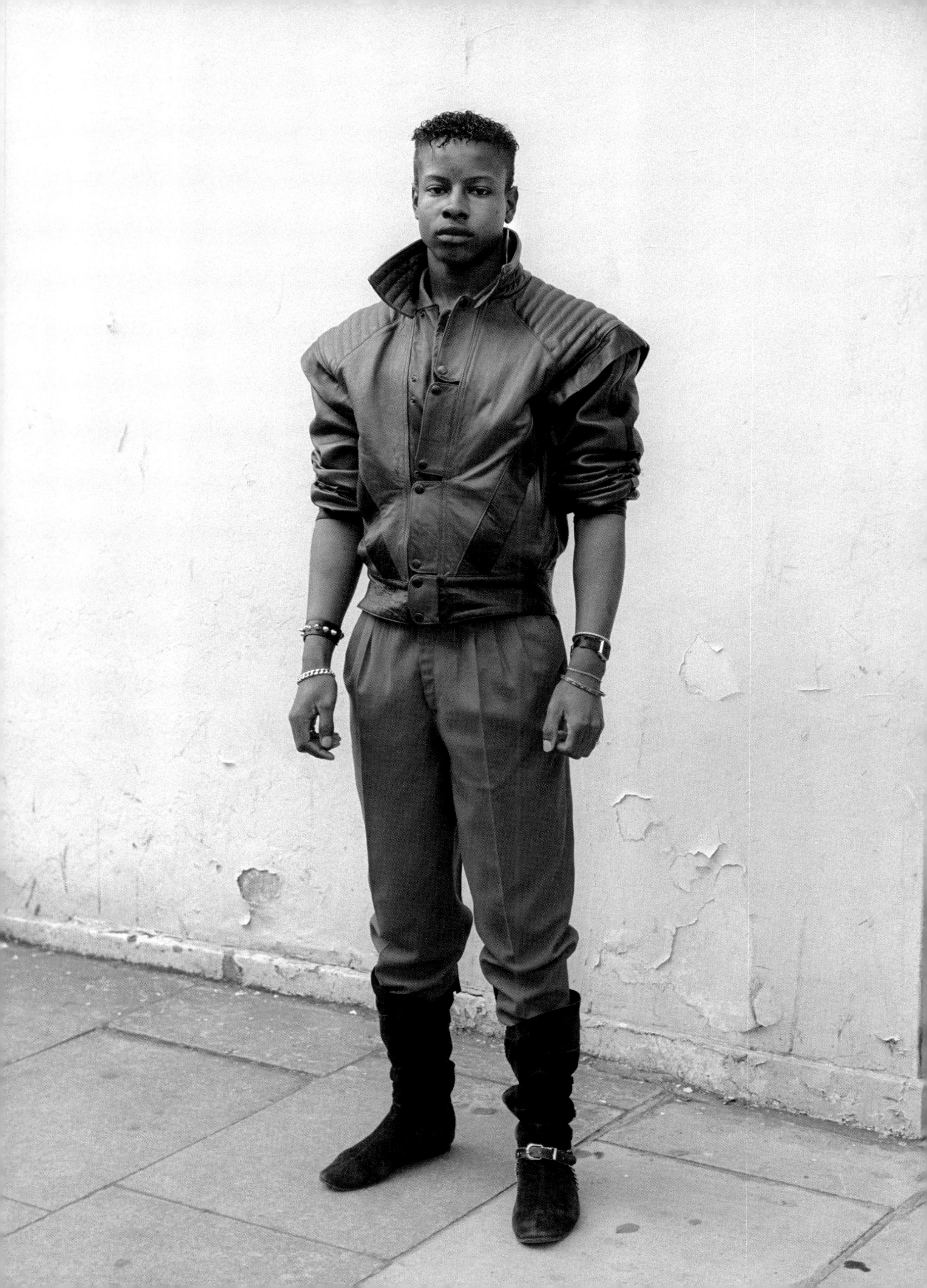

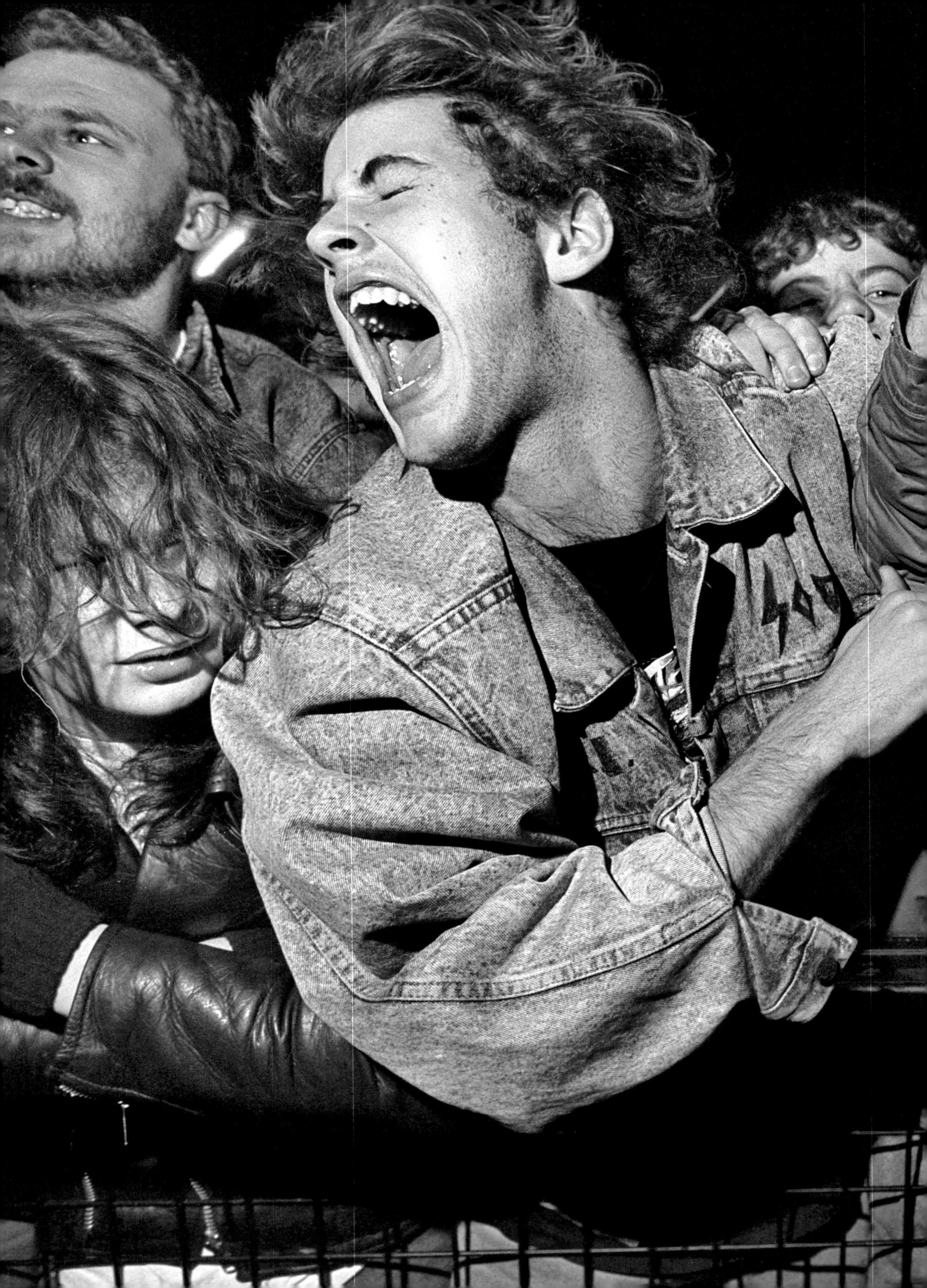

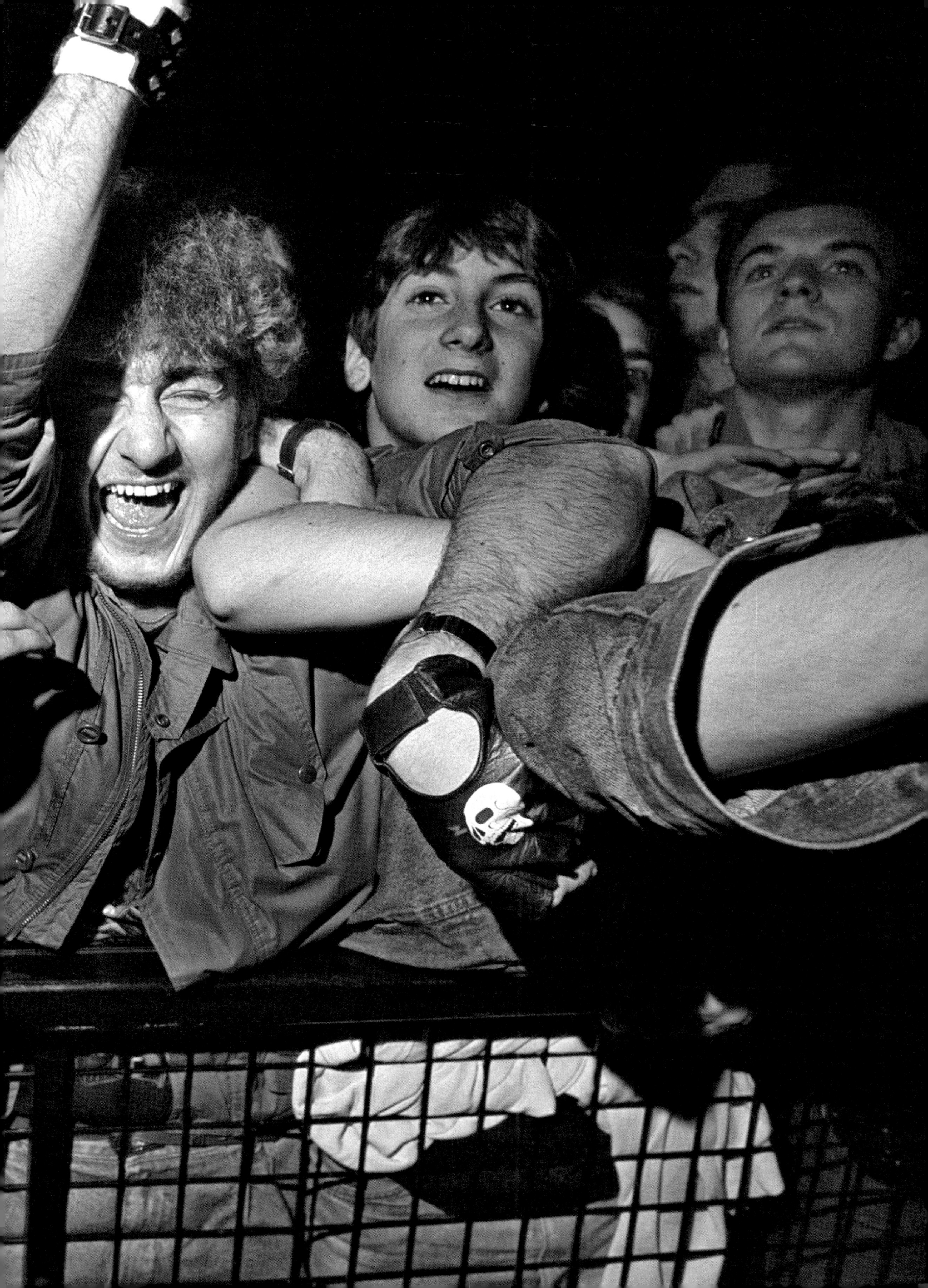

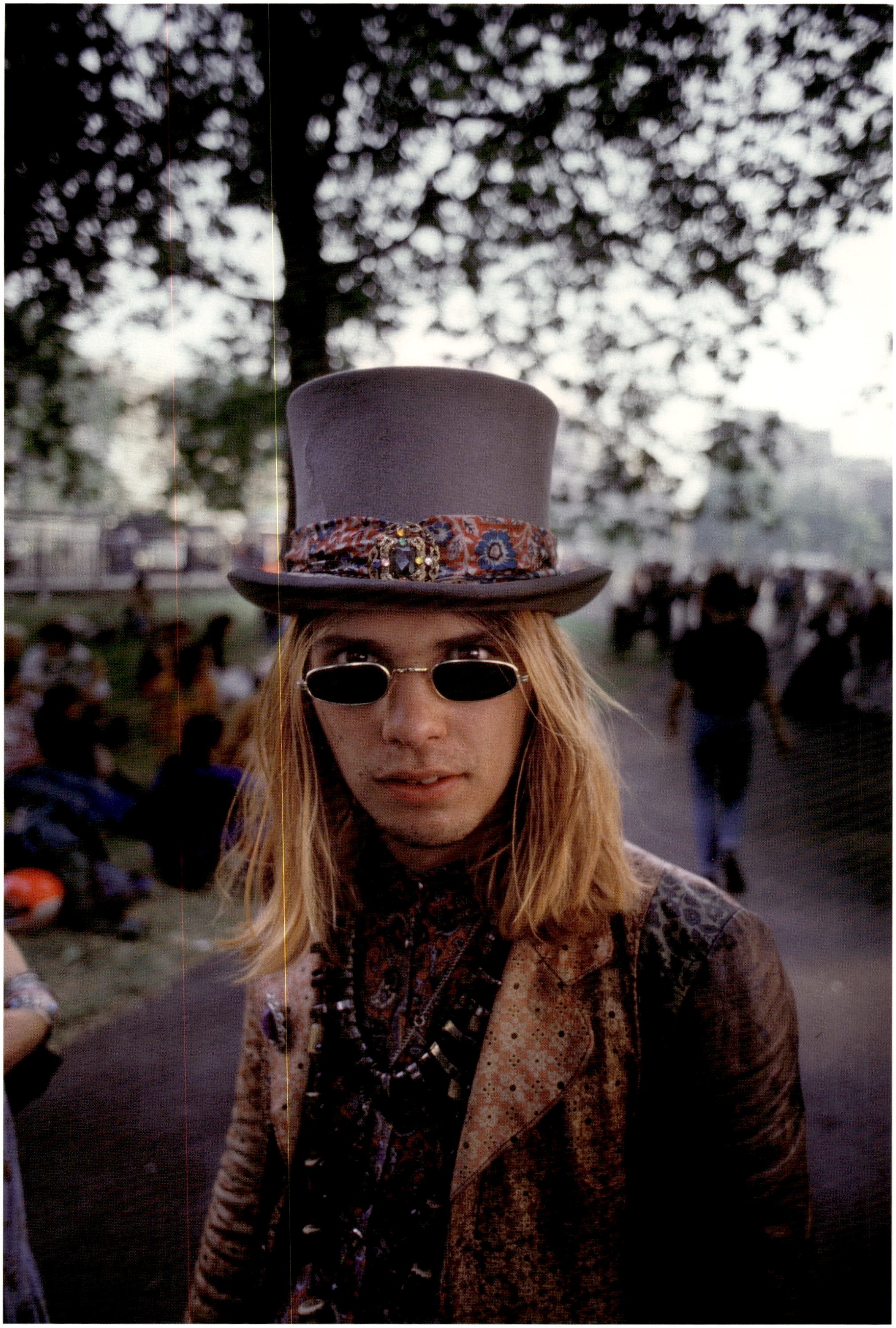

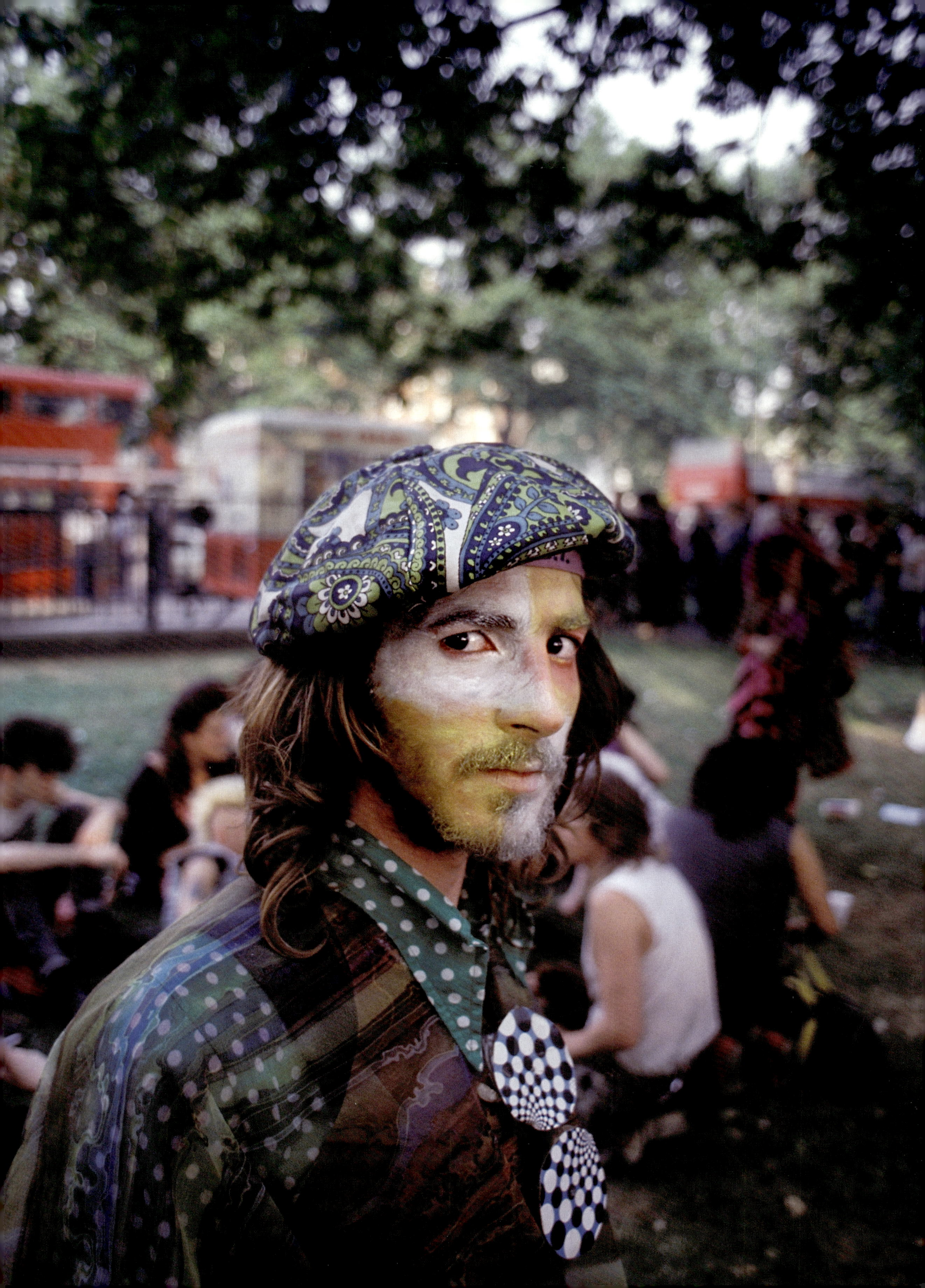

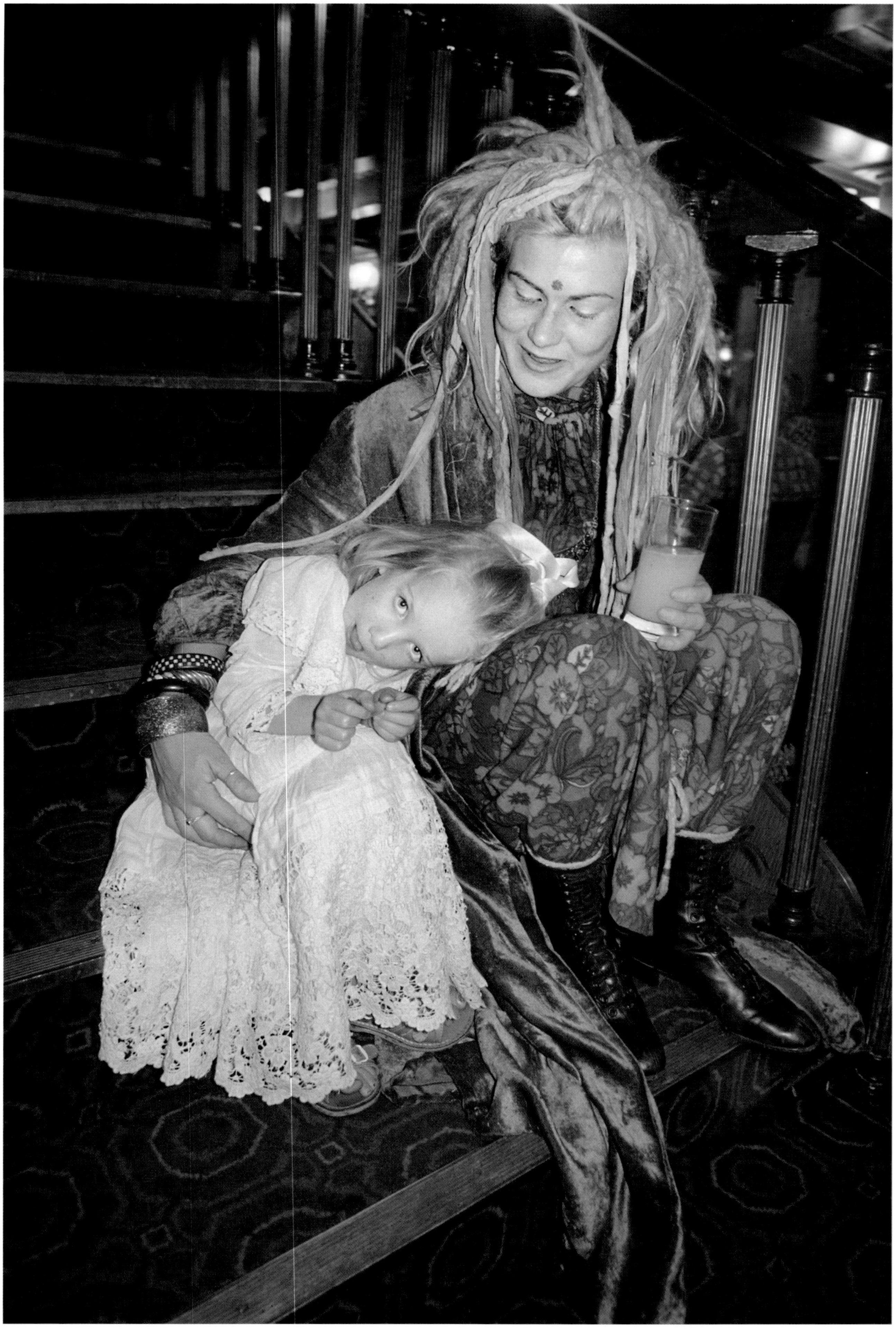

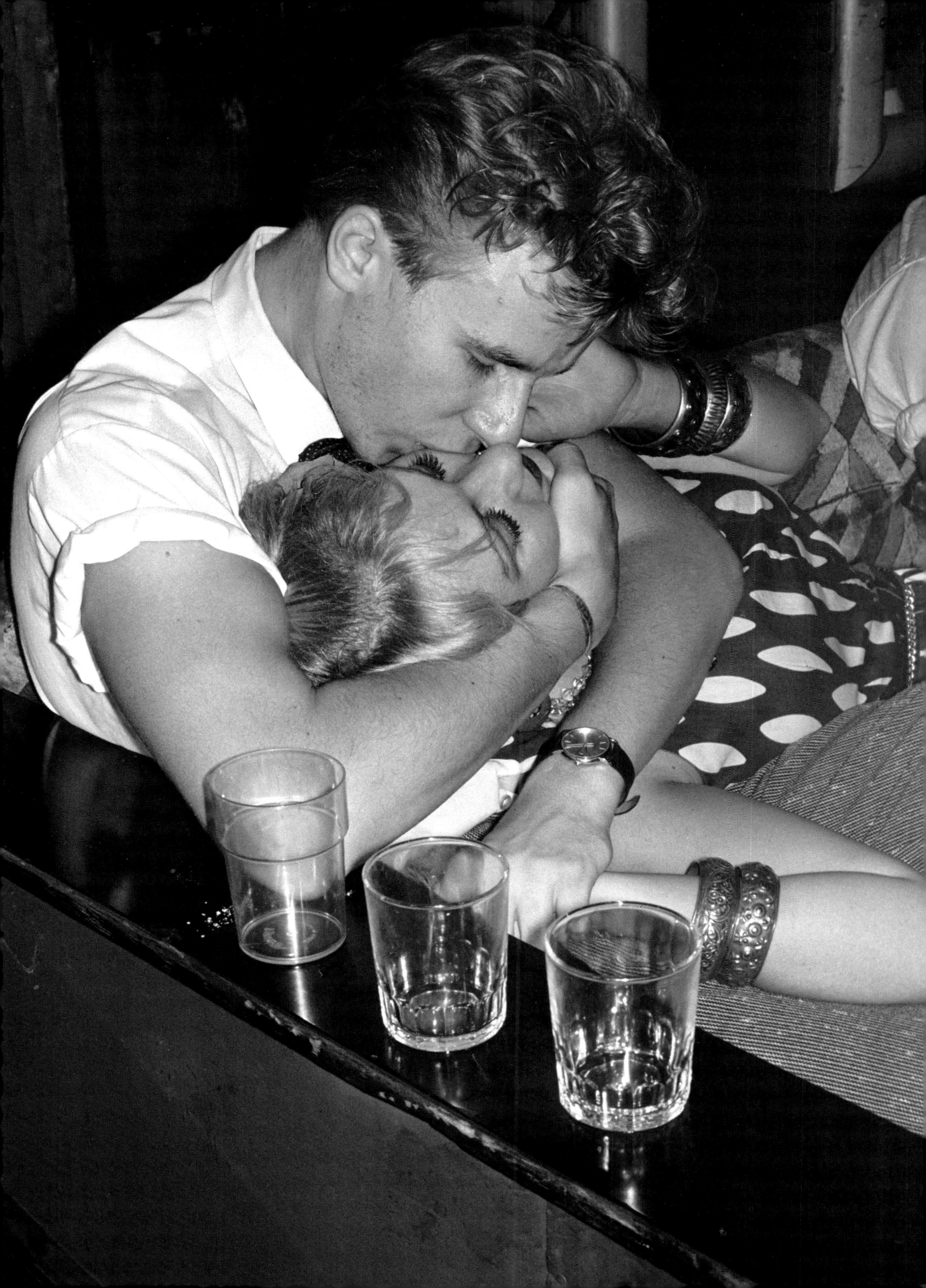

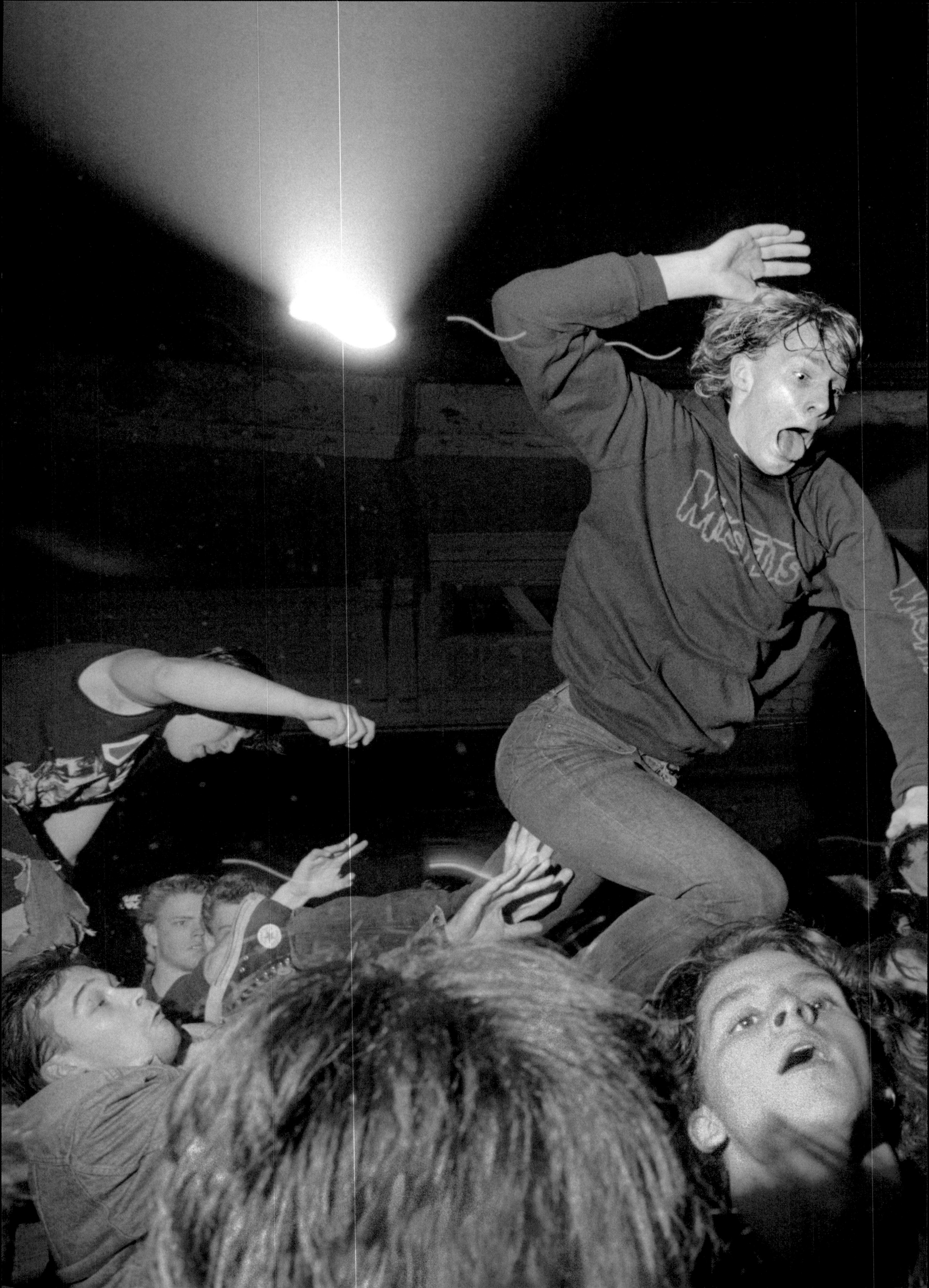

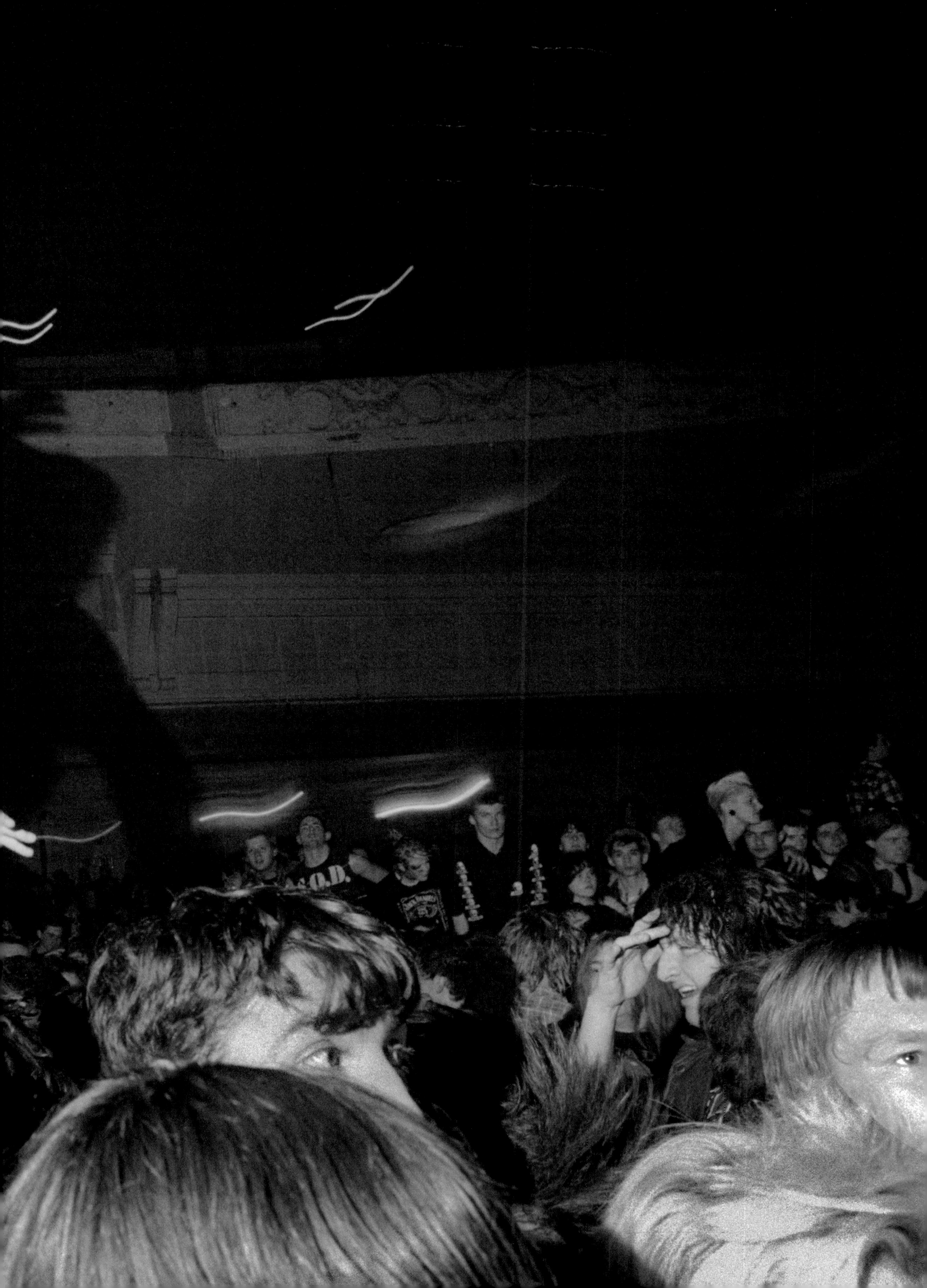

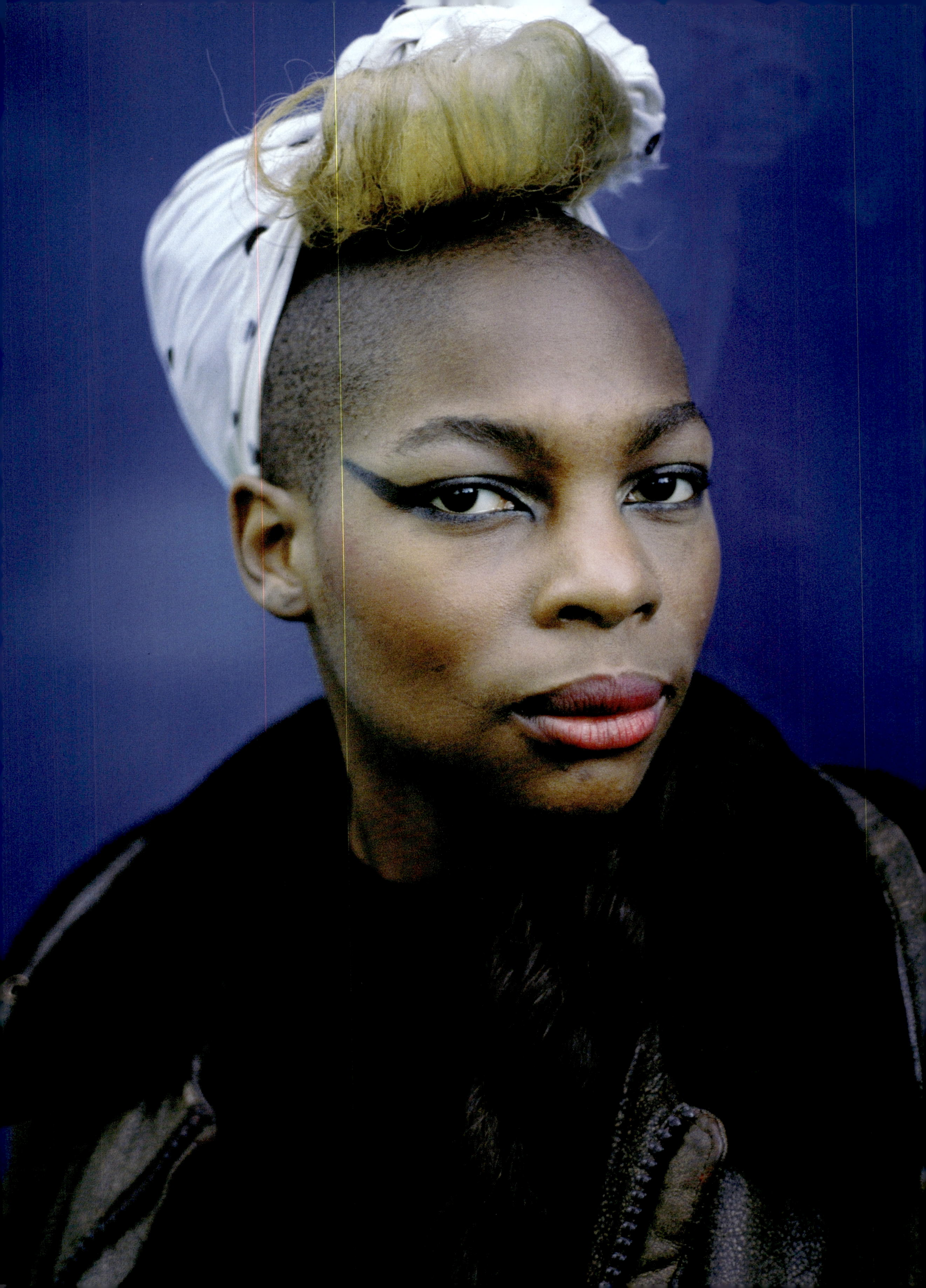

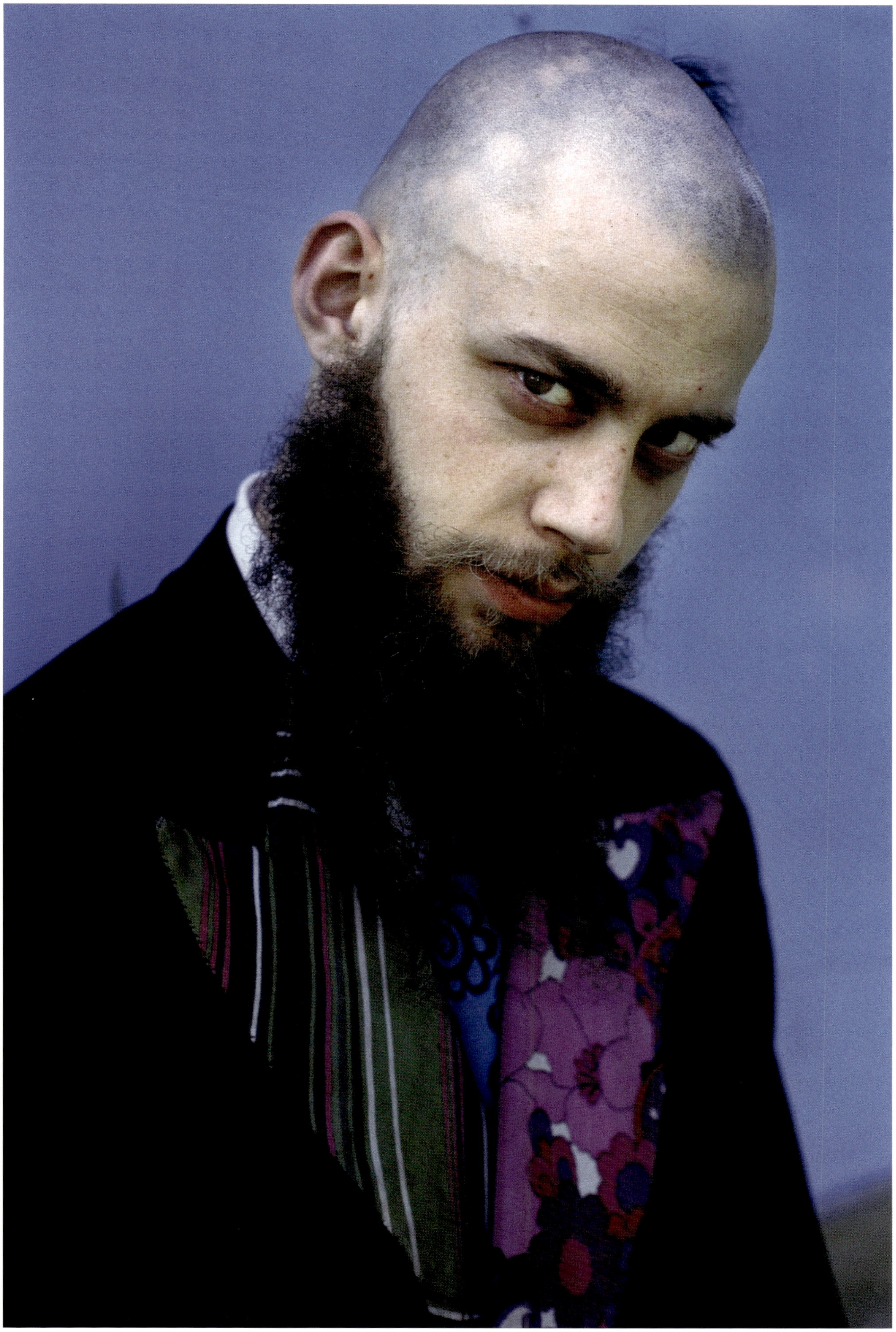

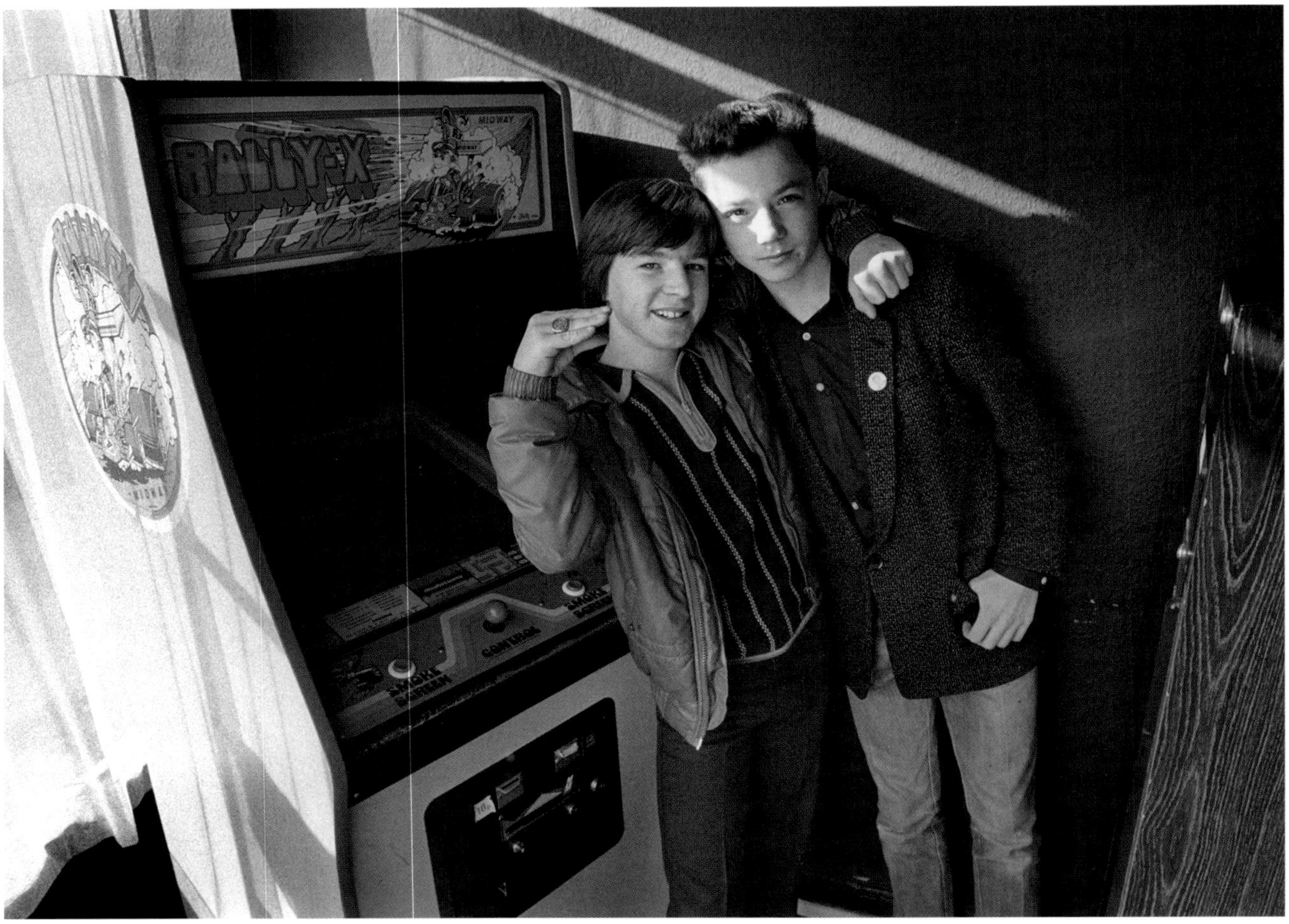
RALLY-X
MIDWAY

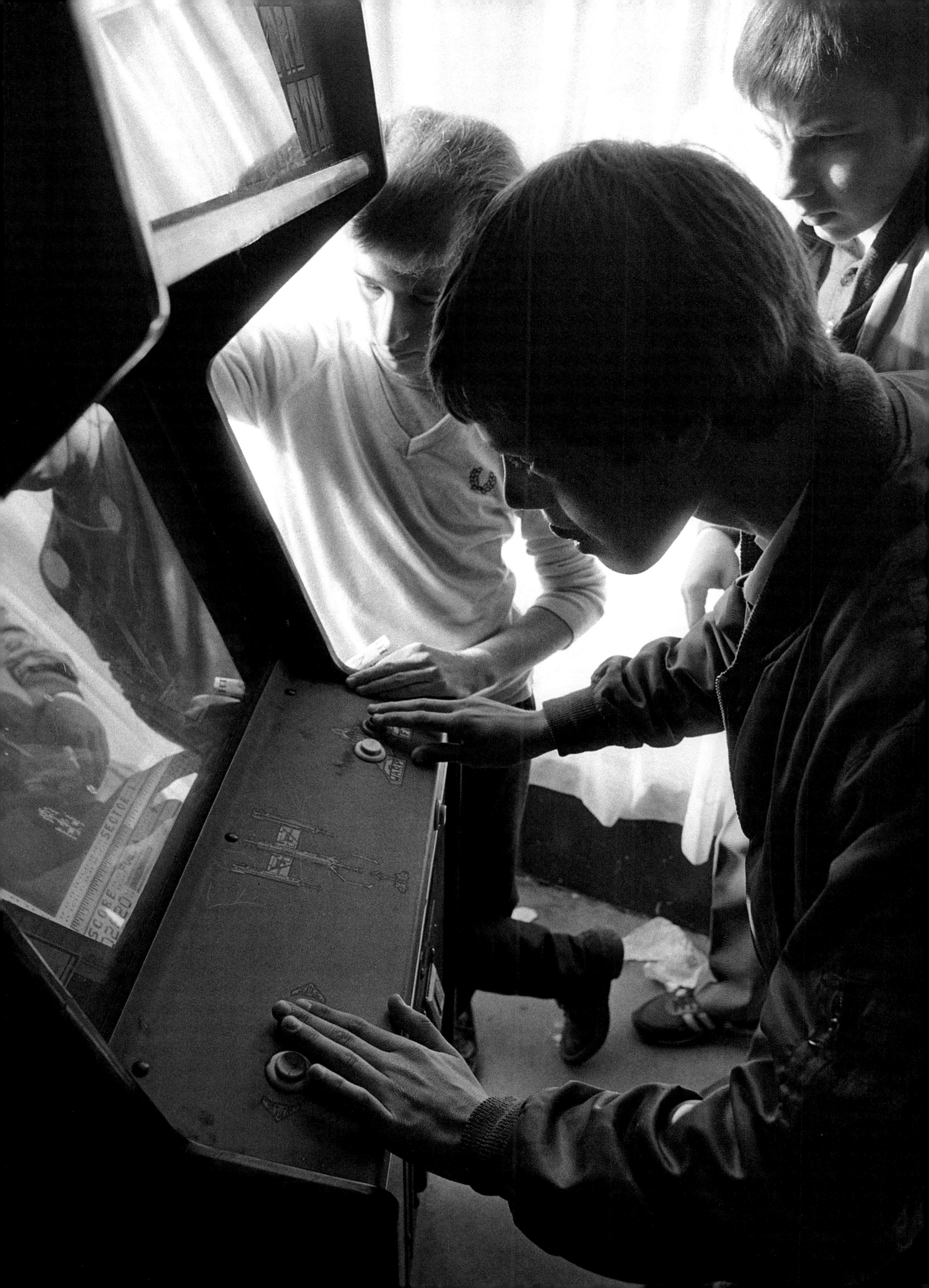

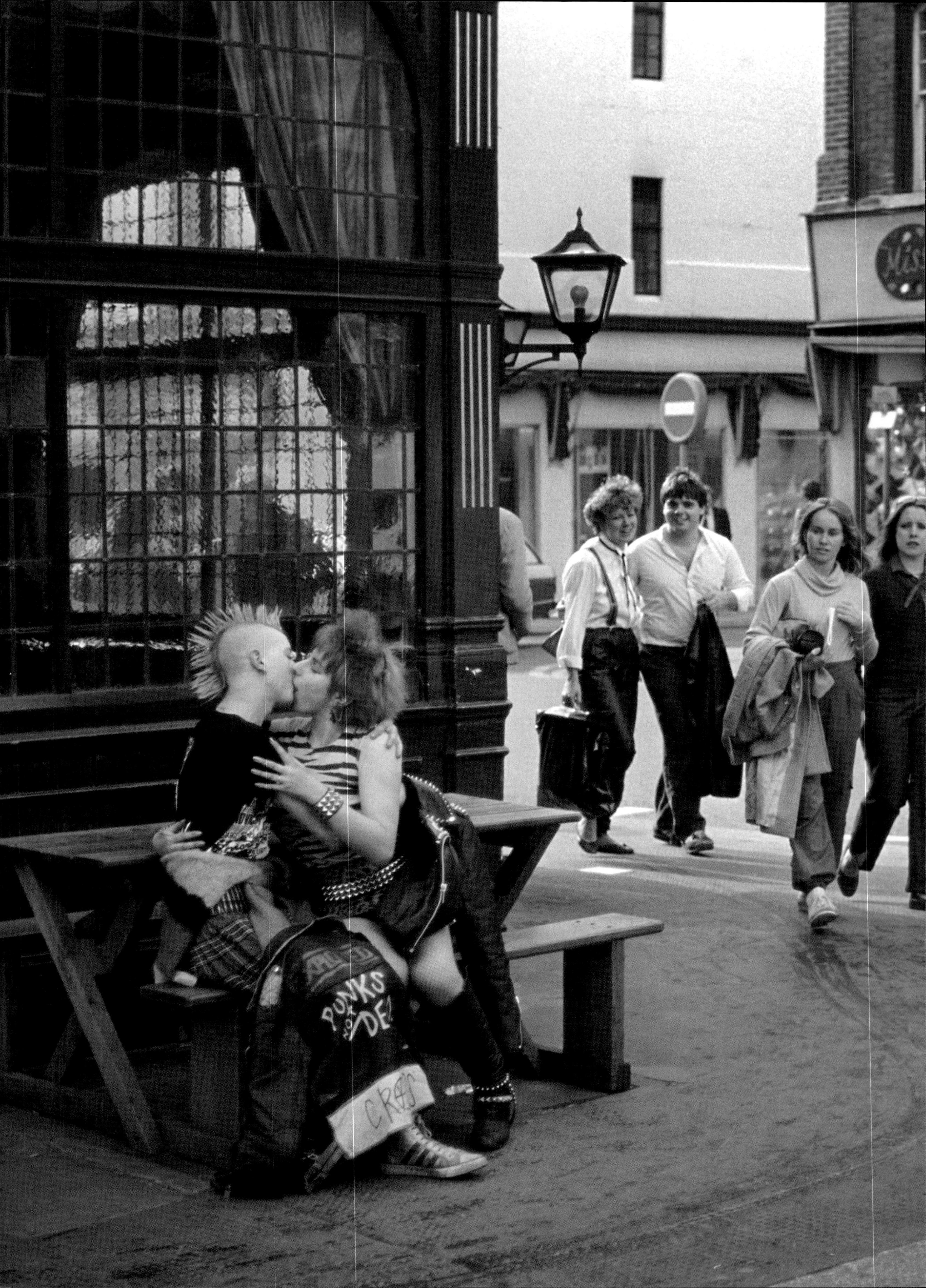
PUNKS

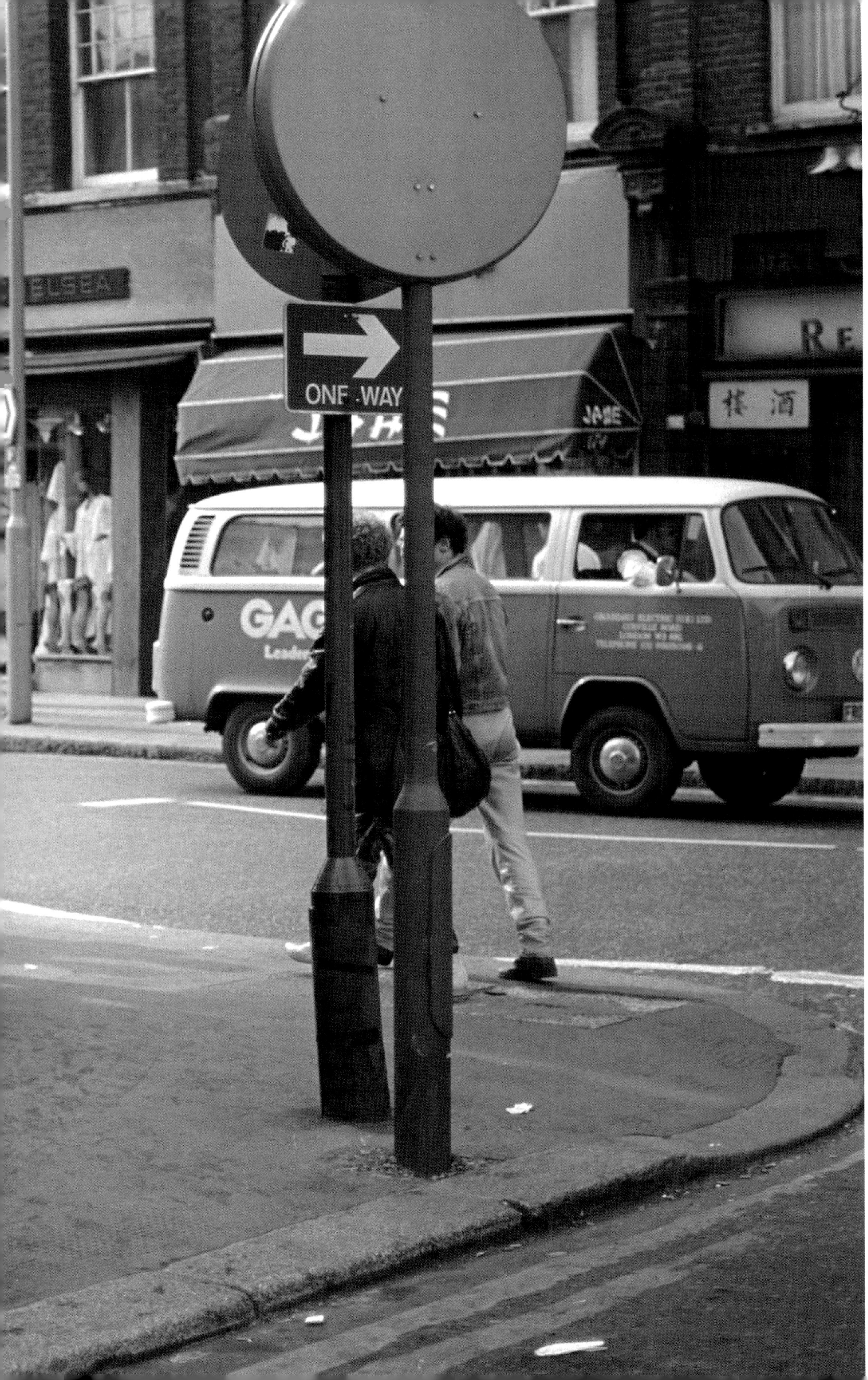
ONE WAY

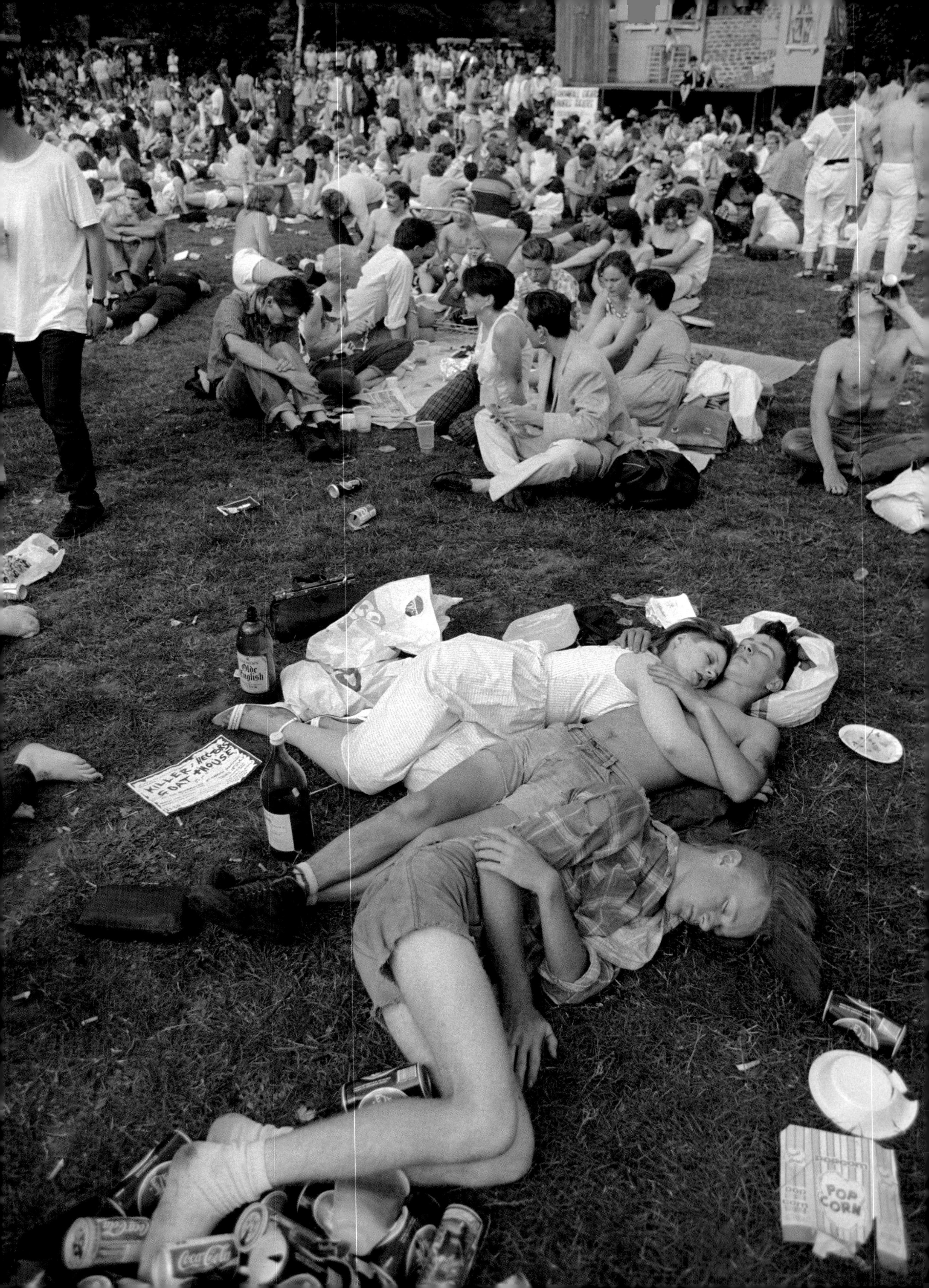
Olde English
KILLER HECTORS
GOAT HOUSE
POP CORN
Coca-Cola

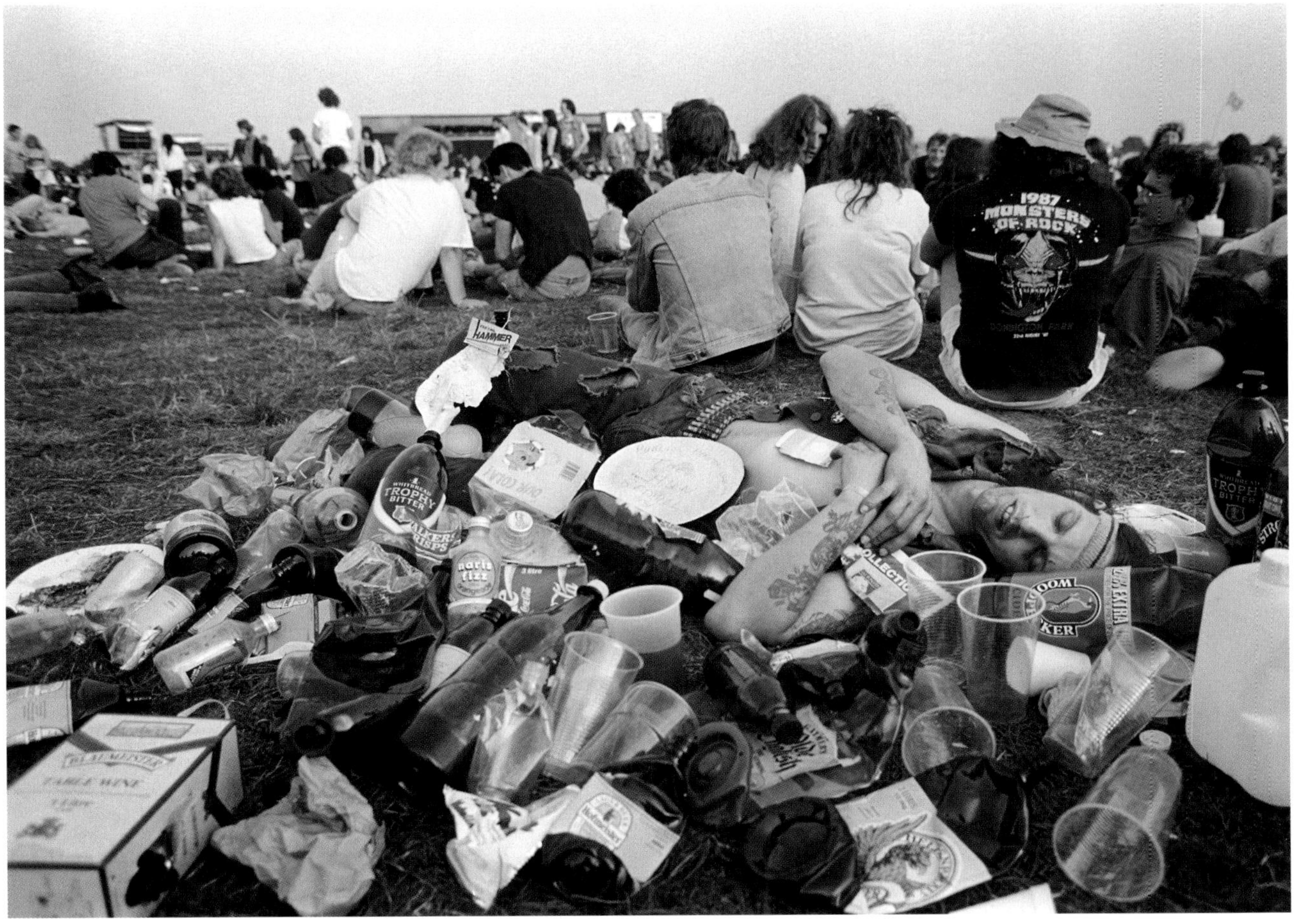
1987
MONSTERS
OF ROCK
HAMMER
TROPHY
BITTER
TABLE WINE

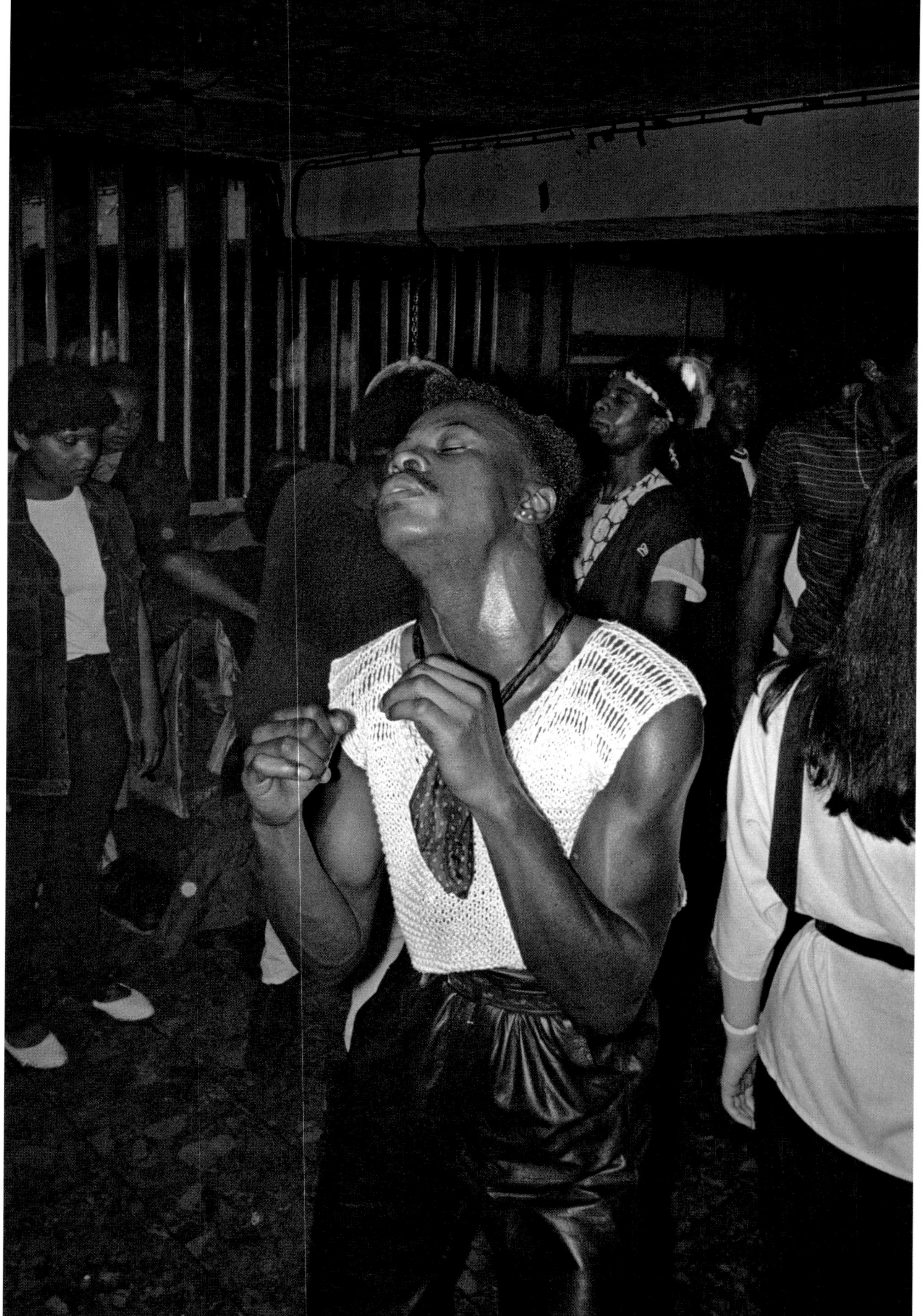

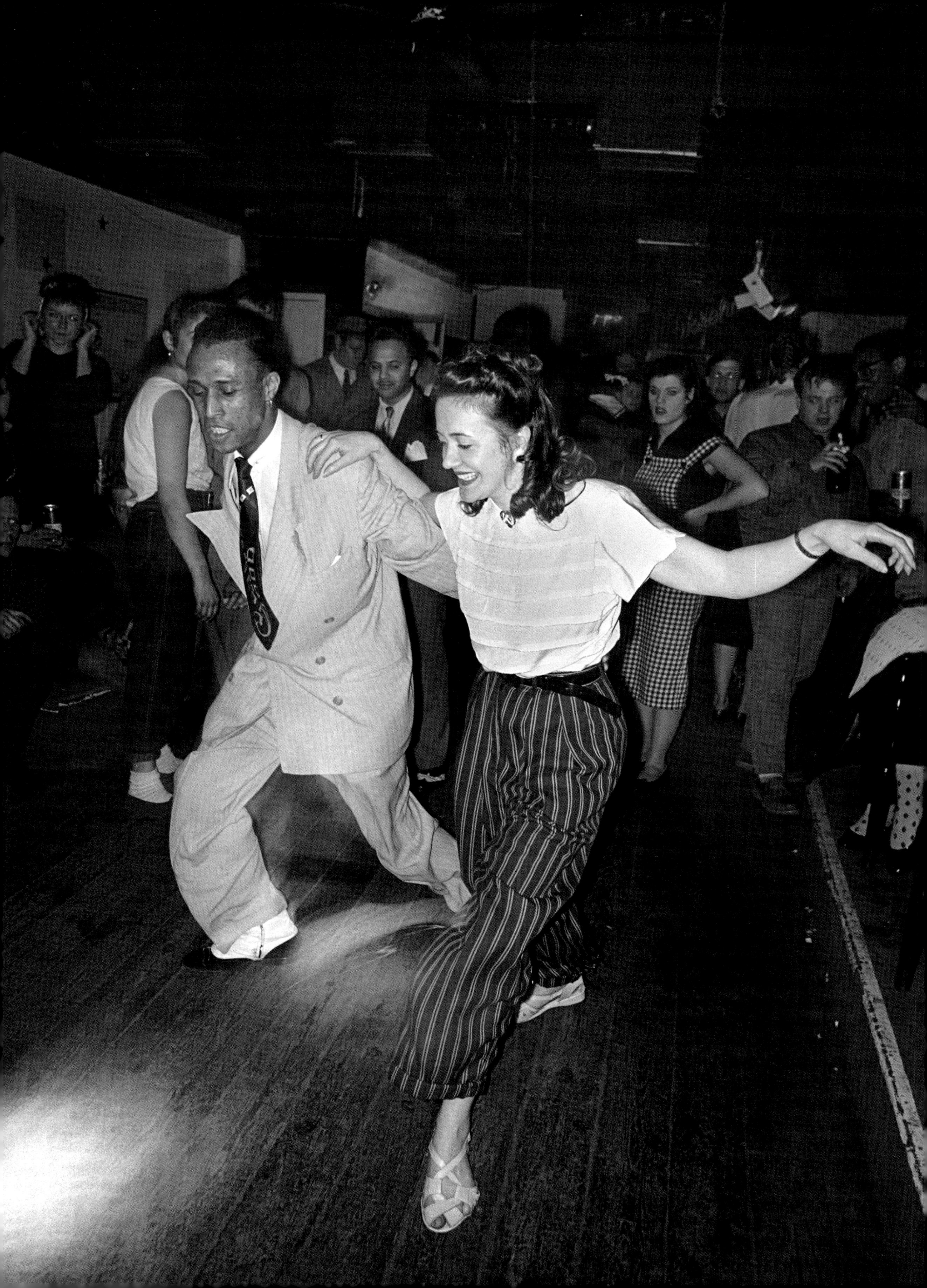

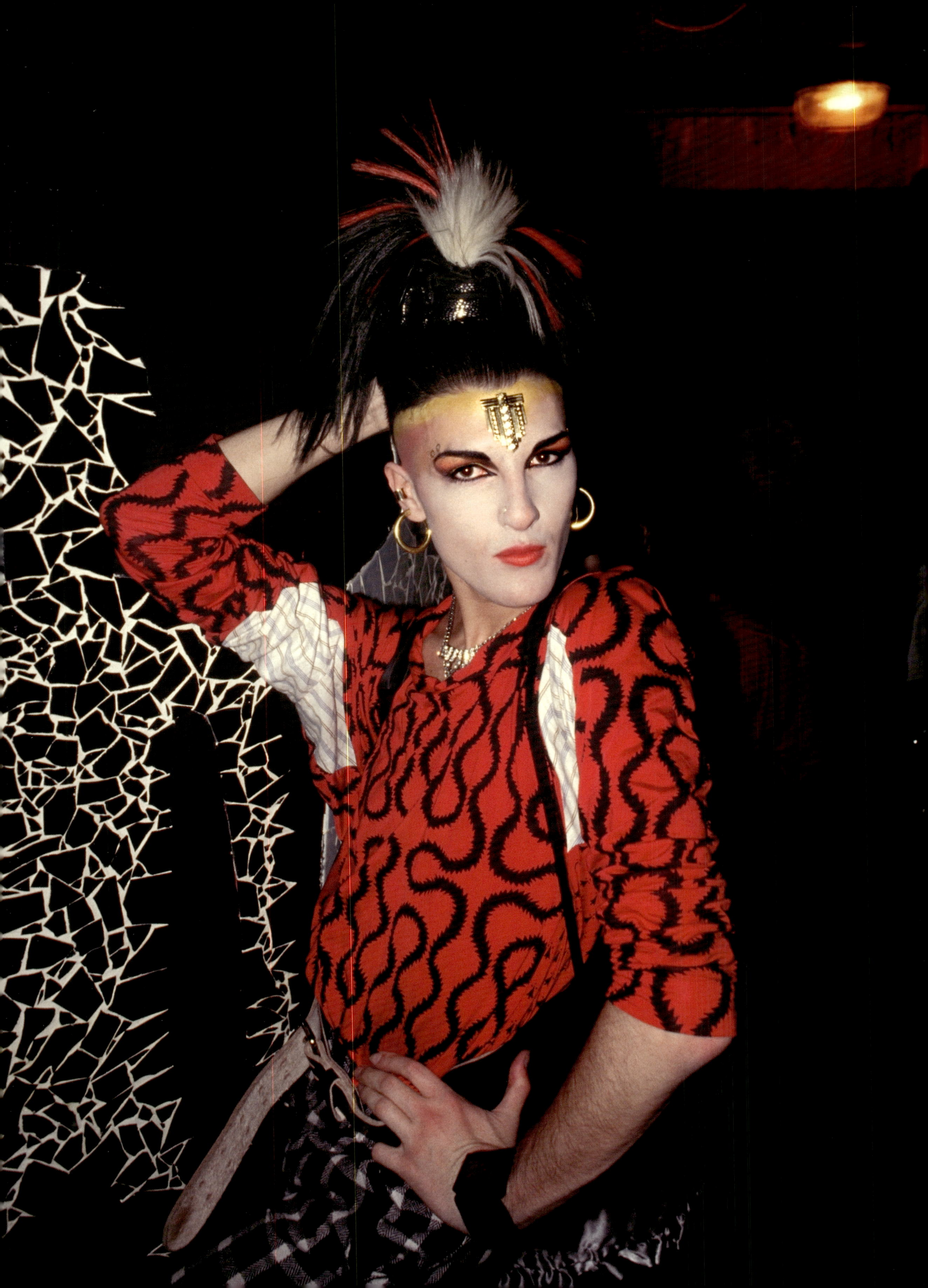

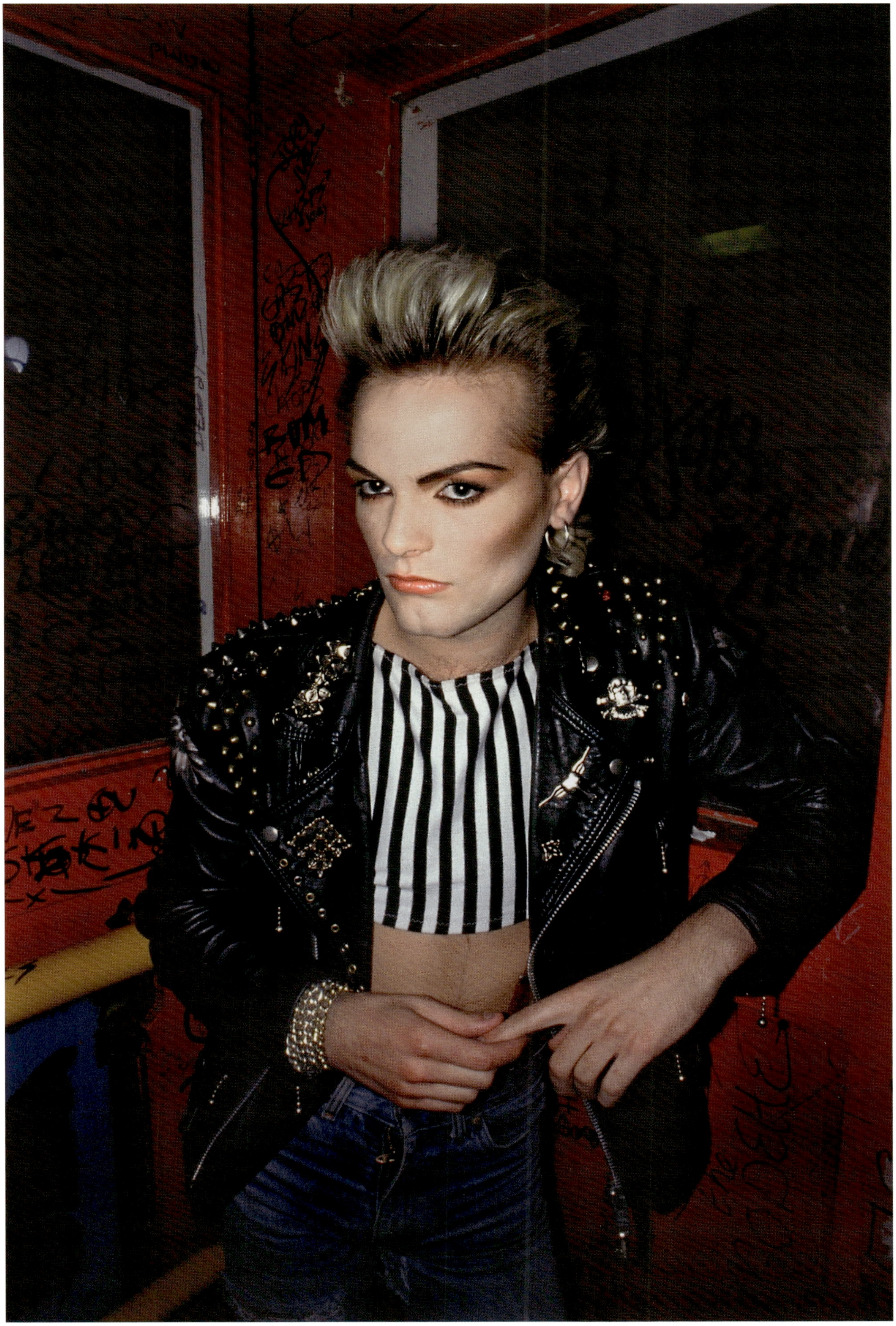

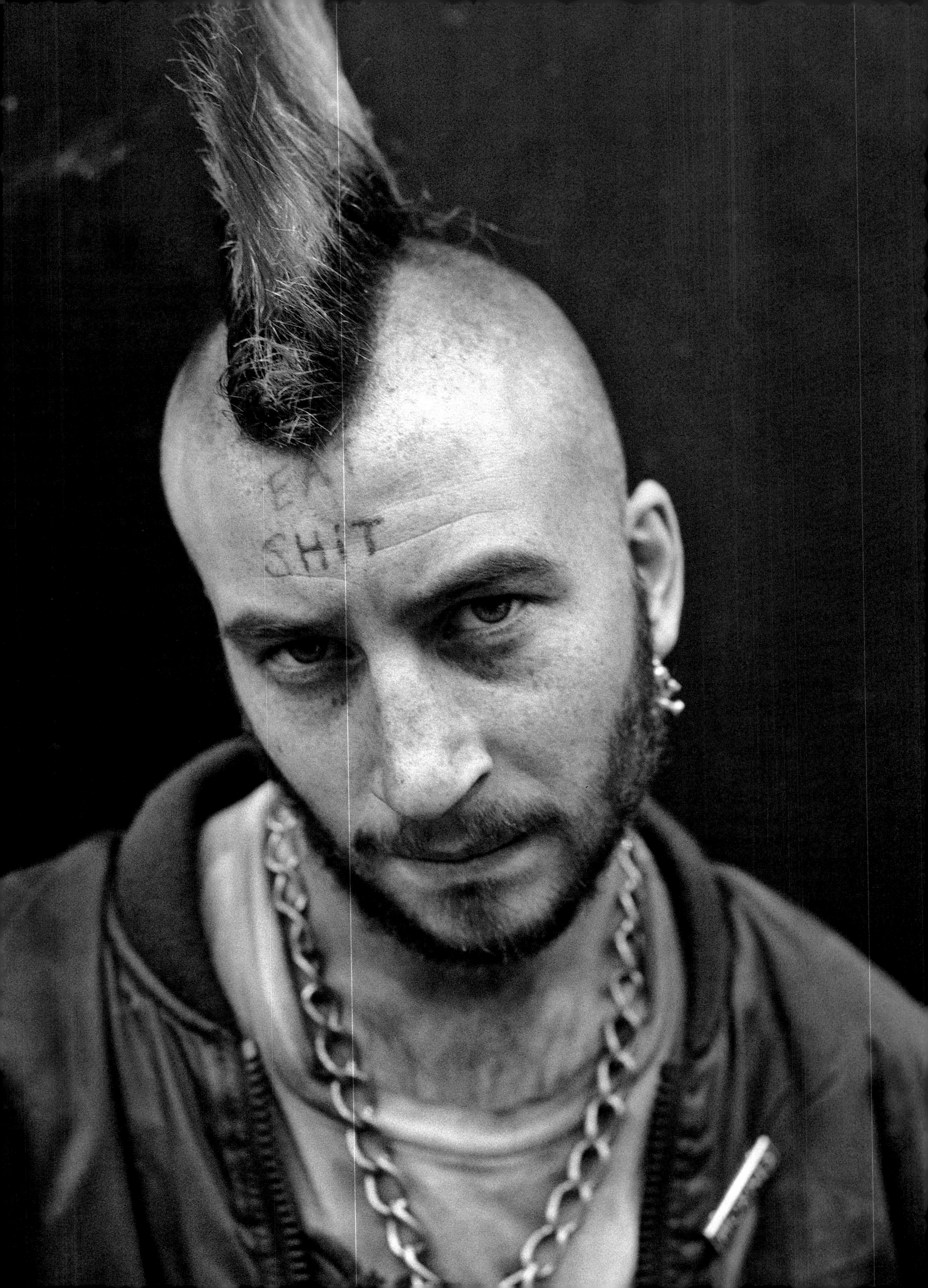
SHIT

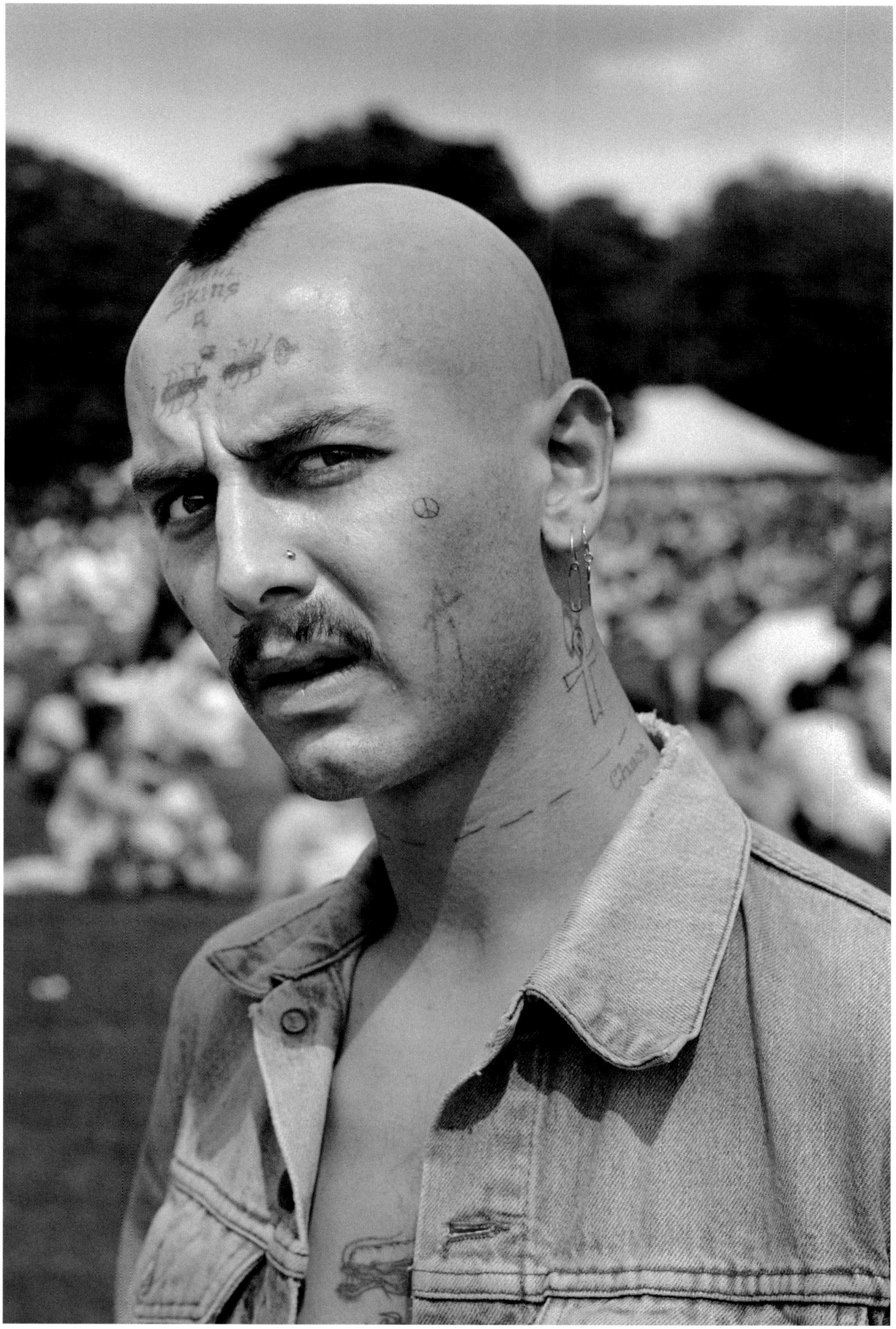
Skins

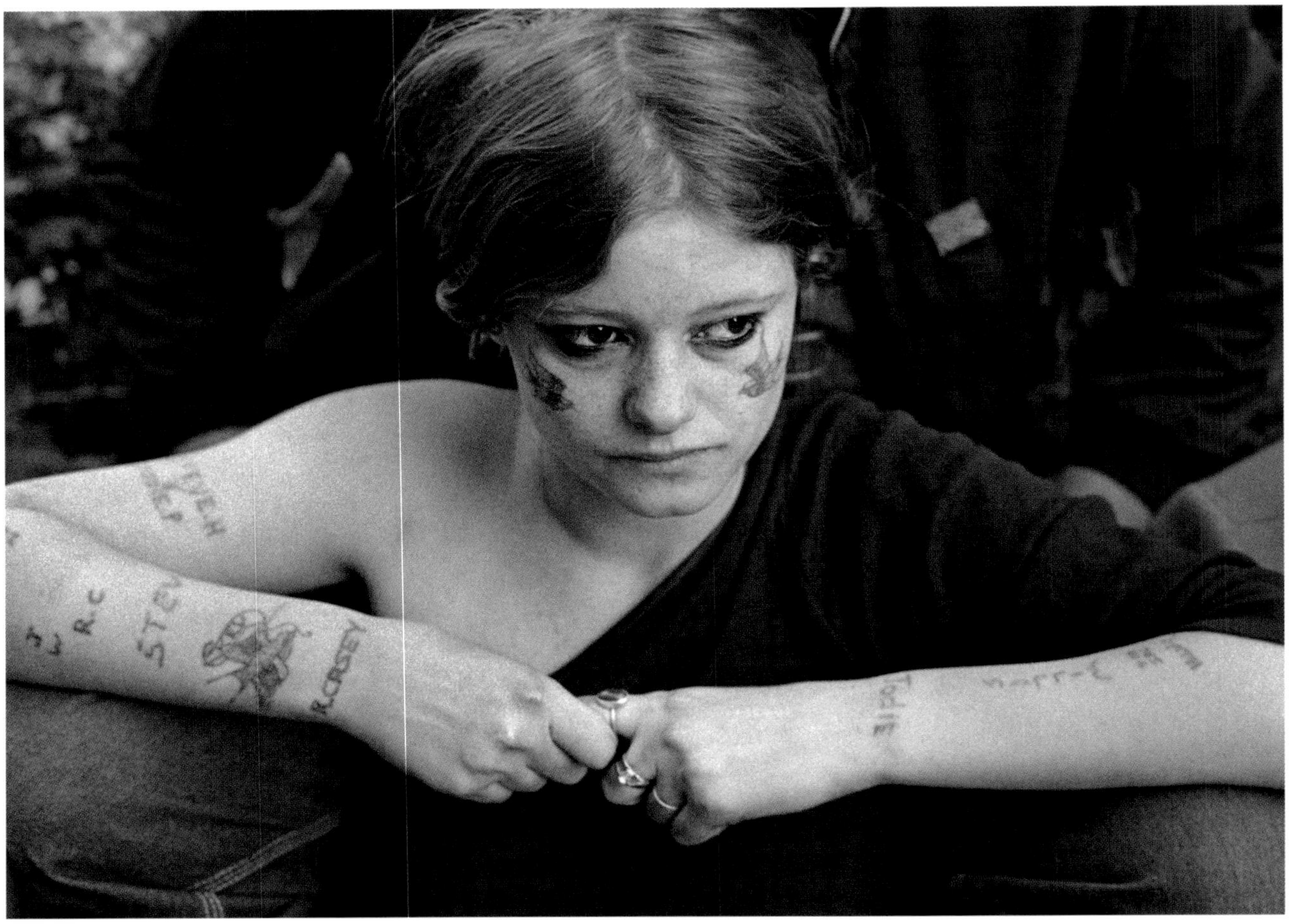
R.C
R.CASEY

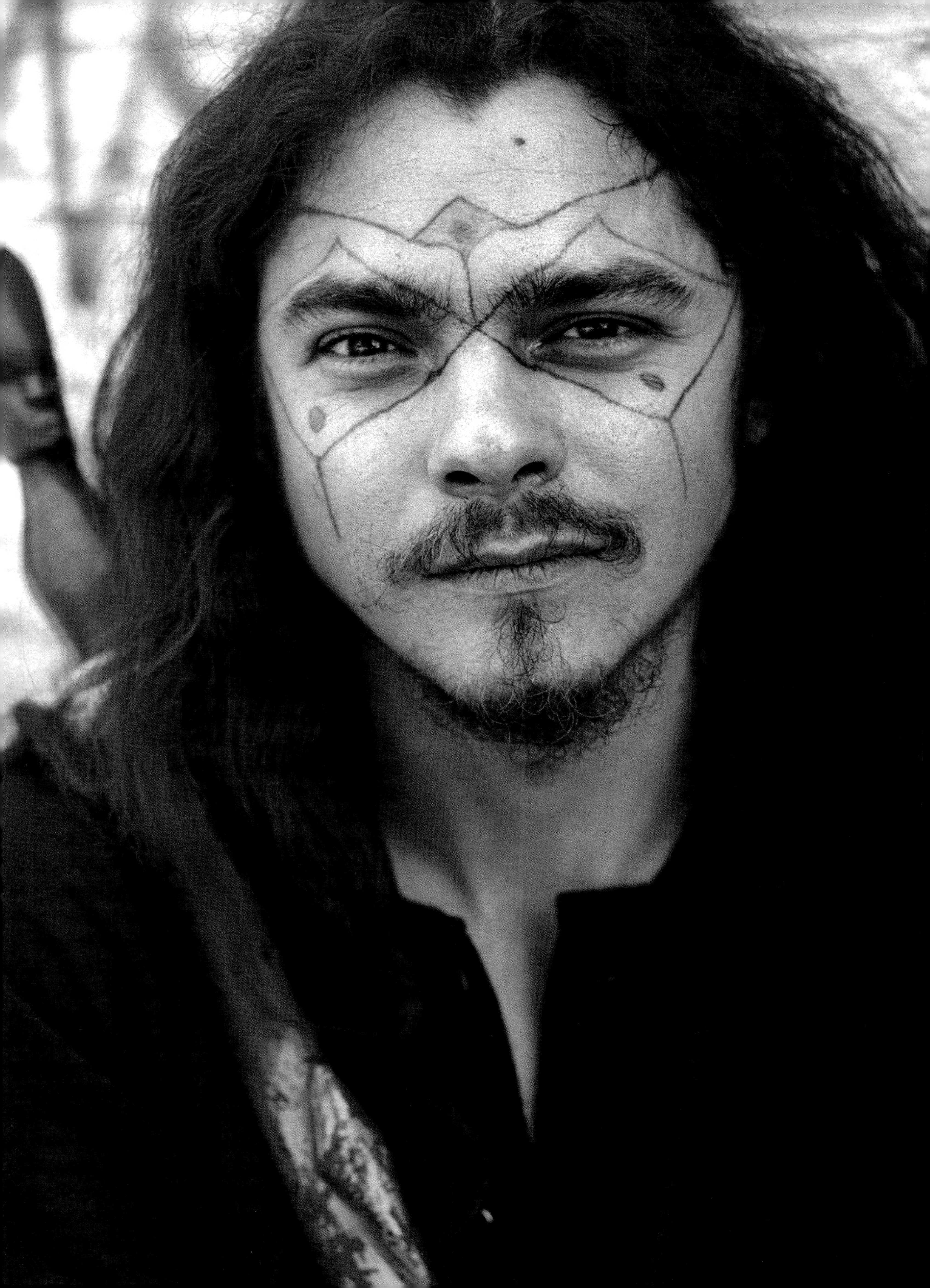

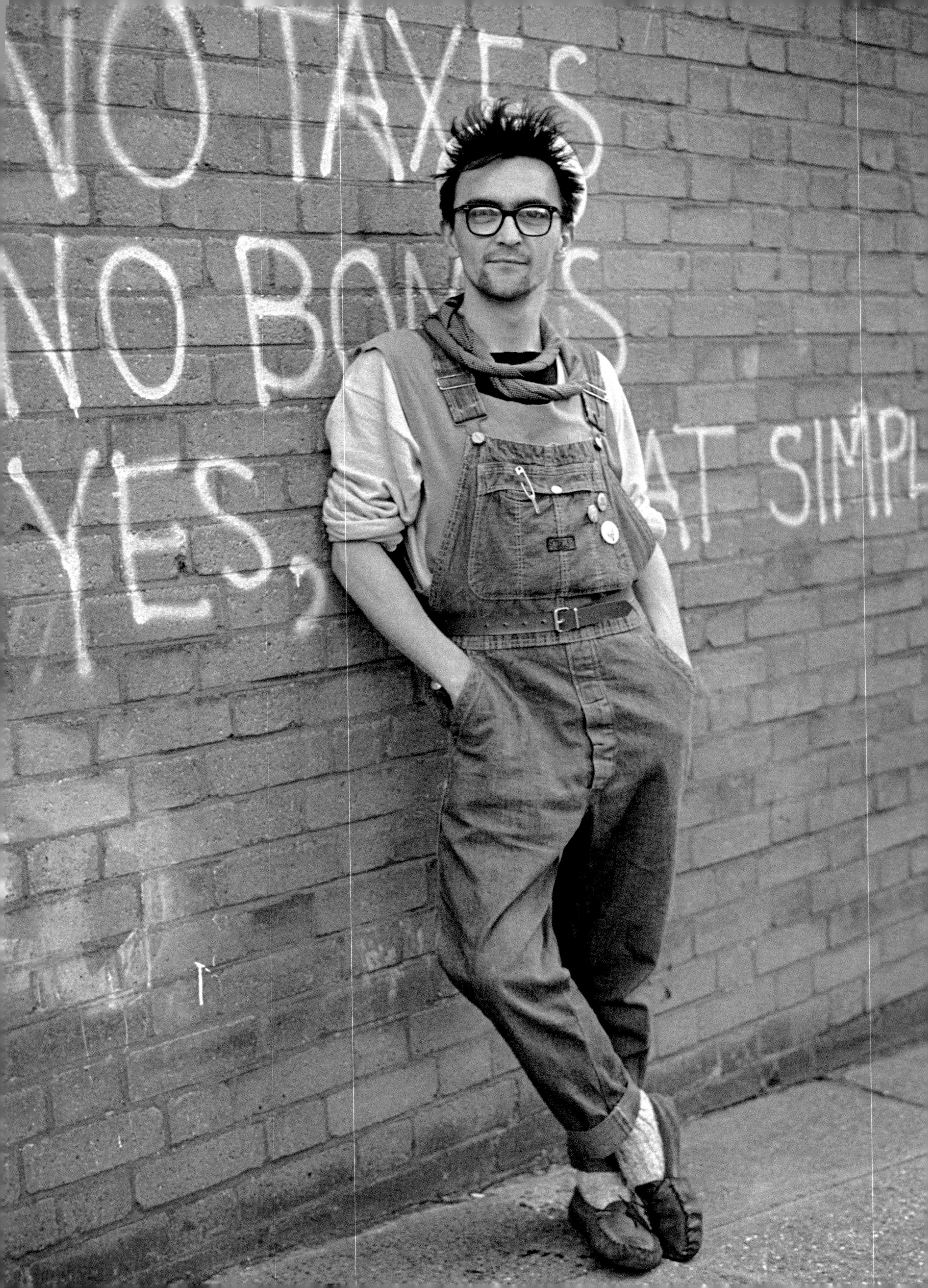
NO TAXES

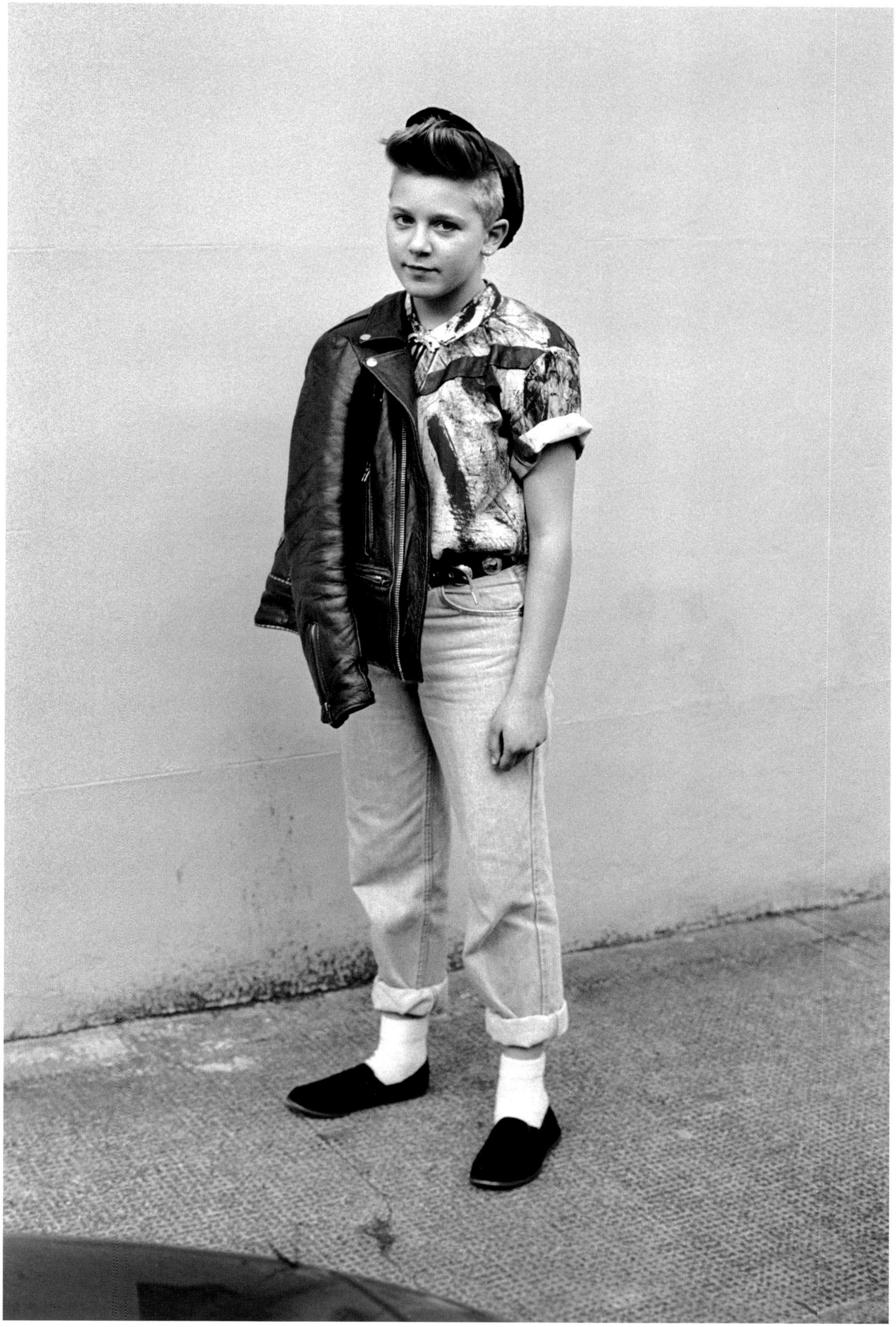

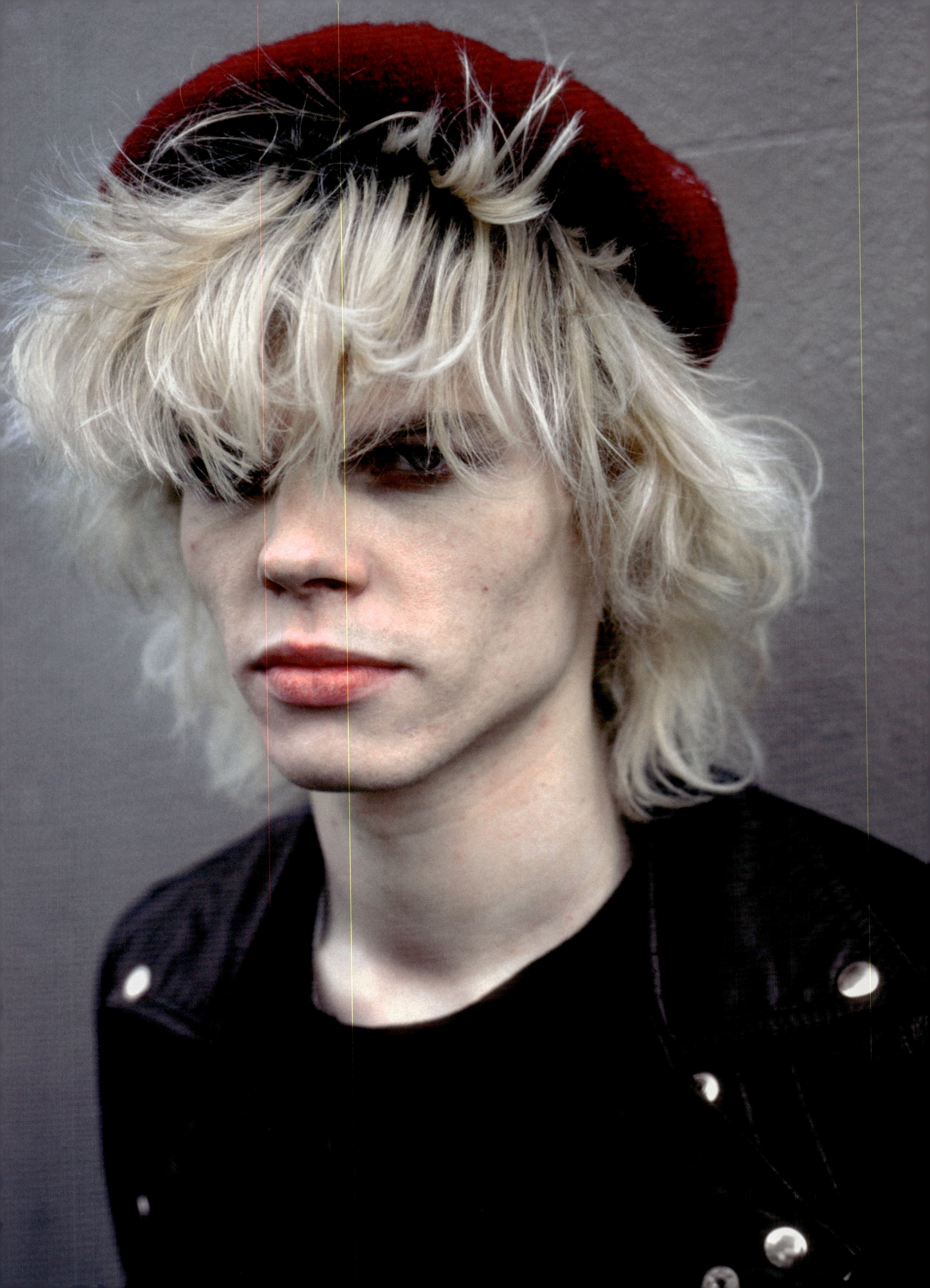

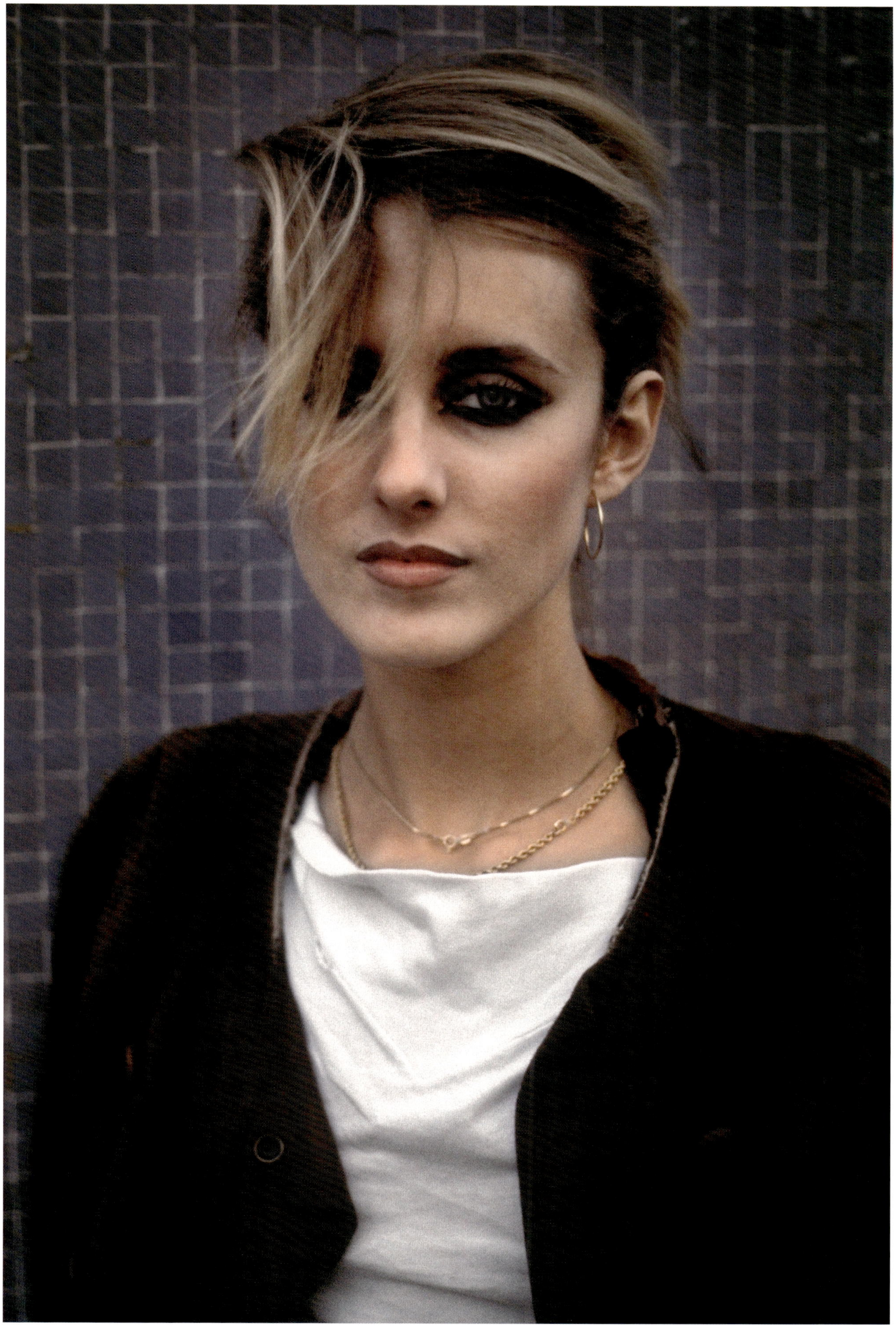

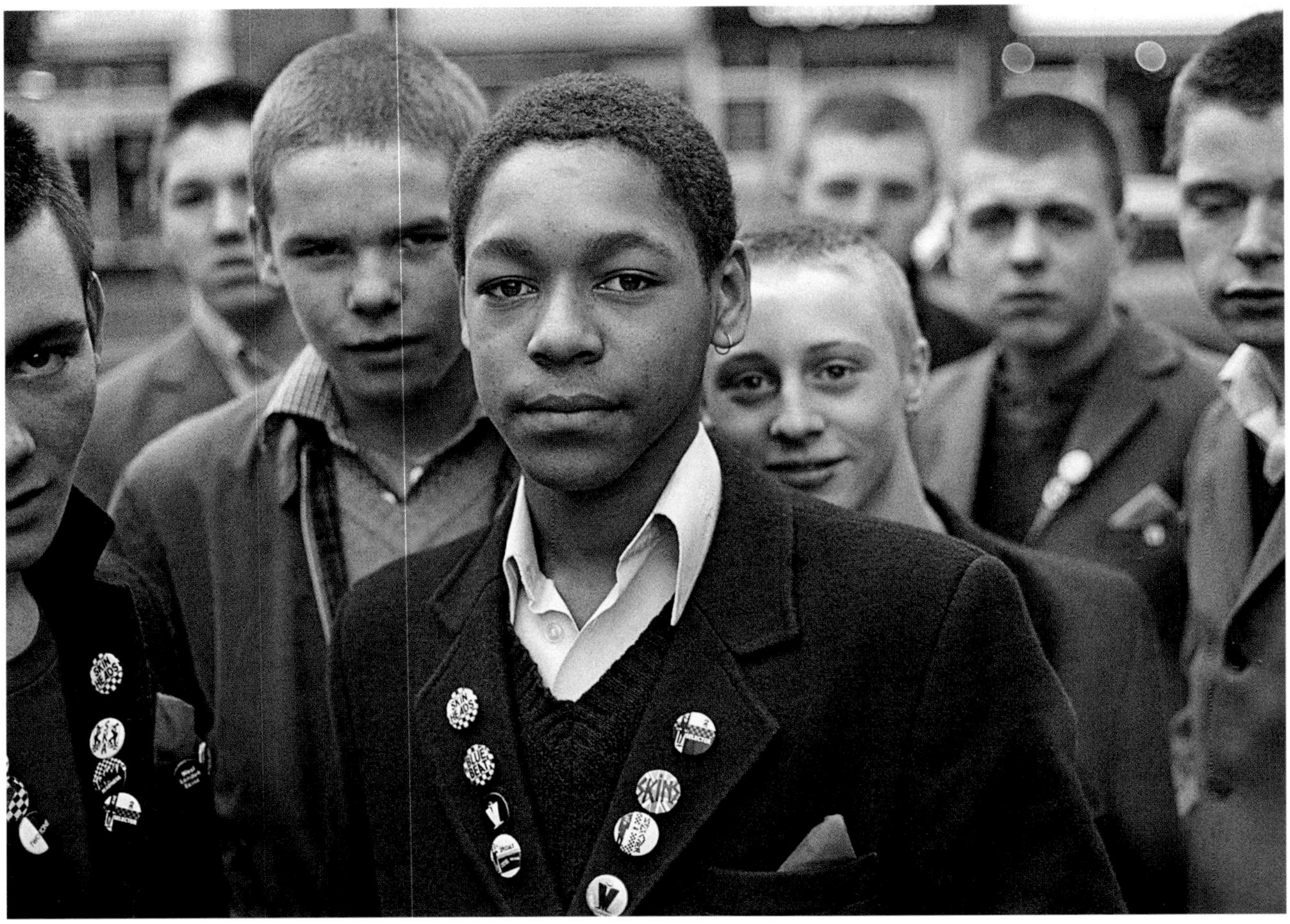

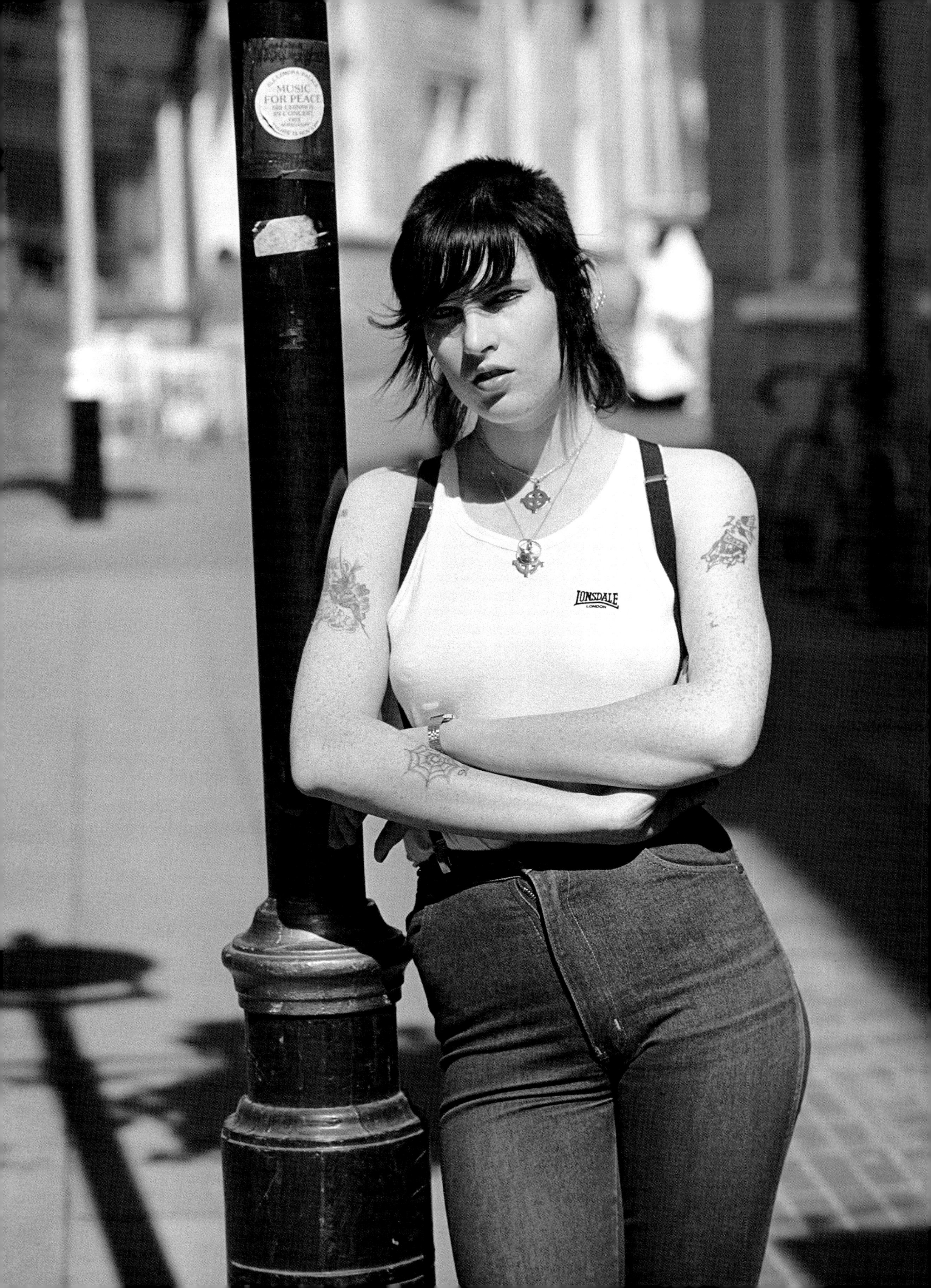
MUSIC
FOR PEACE
LONSDALE
LONDON

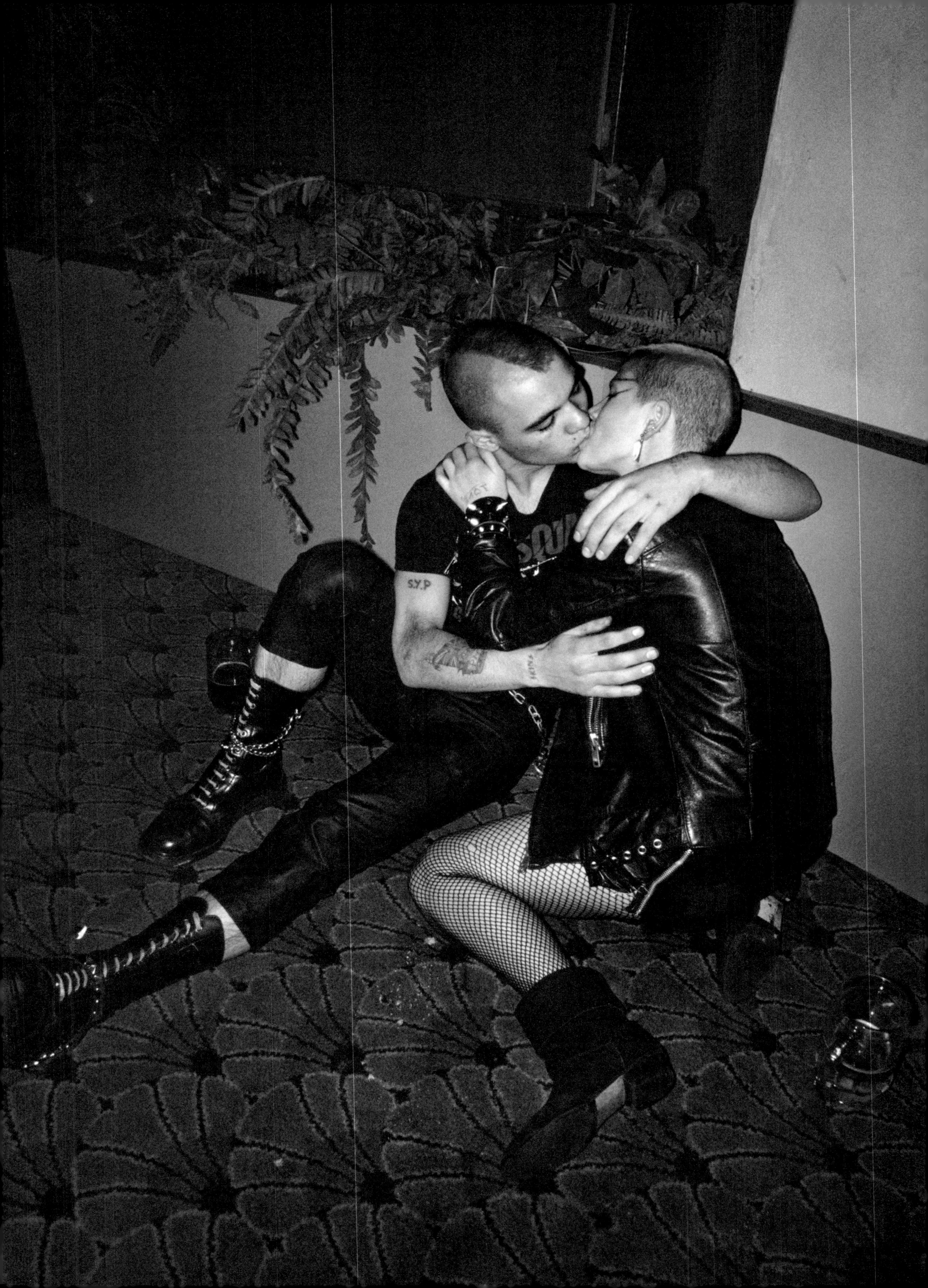
S.Y.P

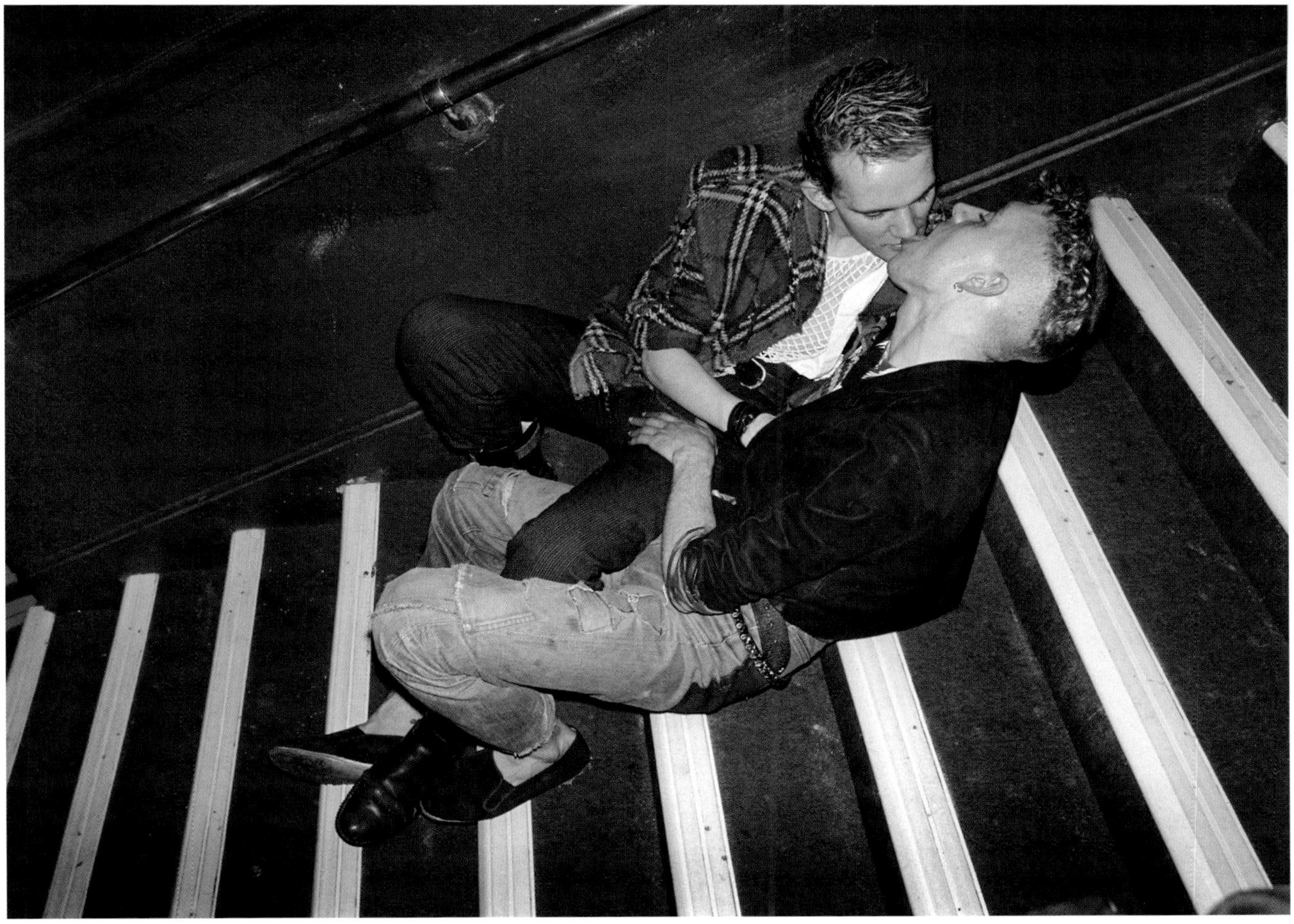

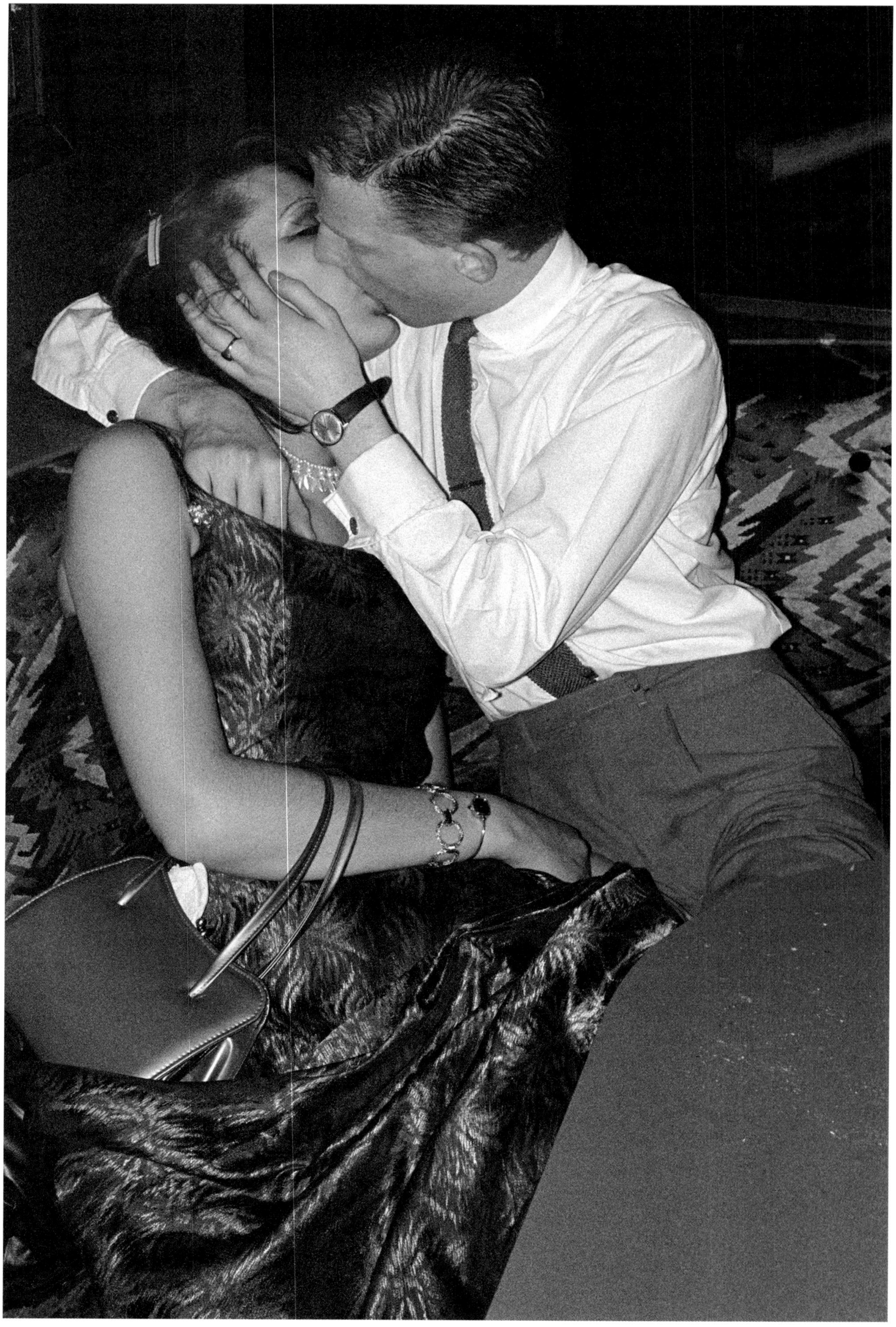

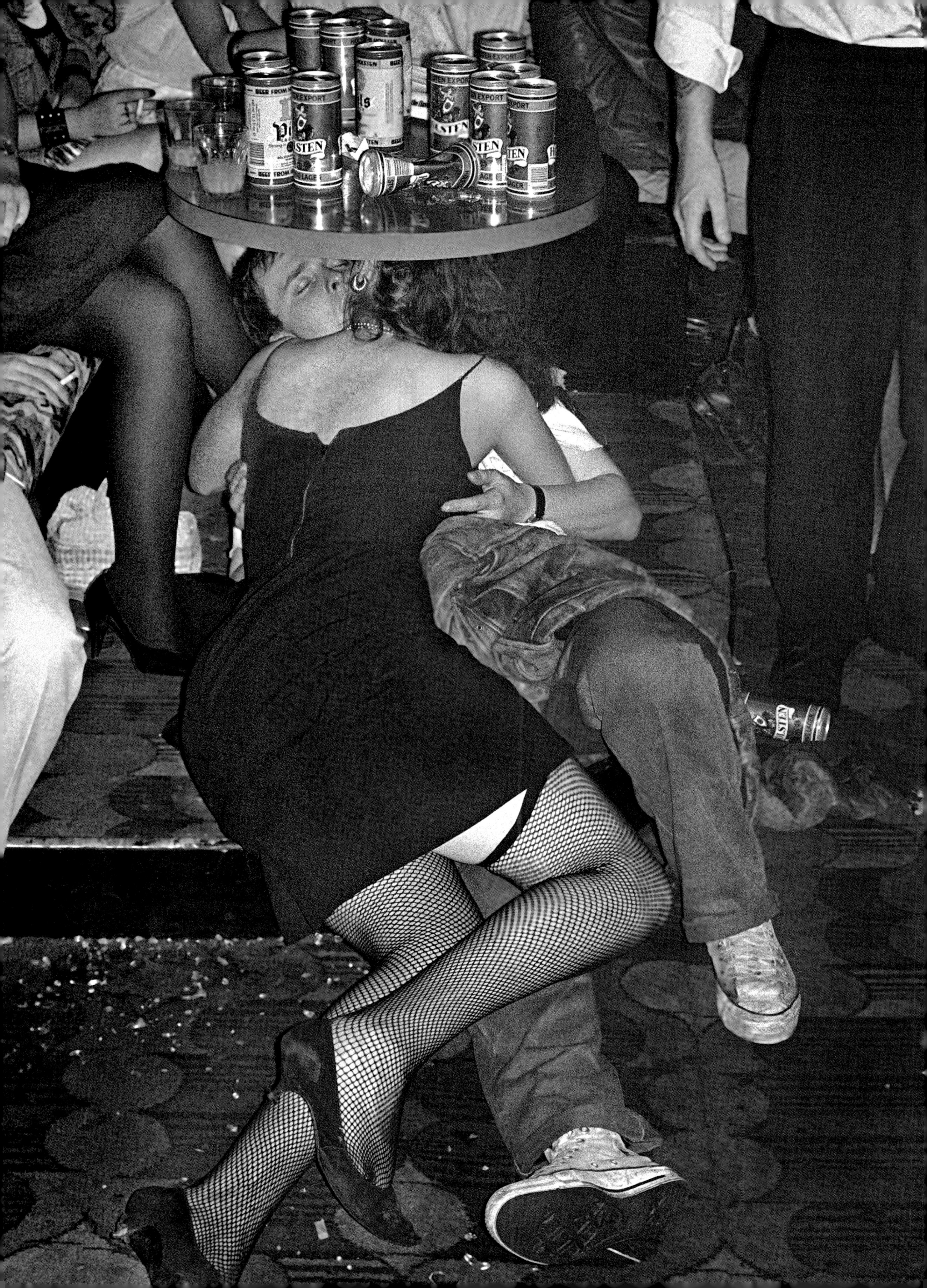
BEER FROM
EXPORT
LAGER

Cover: Sloane Square 1987.

1. Letty, Kings Road 1984.
3. At Flicks, Dartford. Febuary 1981.
9. At the Reading Festival 1989.
10. Trix, Kings Road 1984.
11. Kings Road 1984.
12. At Gay Pride, Kennington 1989.
13. At the Donnington Monsters of Rock Festival 1986.
14. At the Acid Dayze Festival, Finsbury Park 1987.
15. At the Acid Dayze Festival, Finsbury Park 1987.
16/17. Jackie, St Moritz club, Soho 1980.
18. Soho 1984.
19. Soho 1984.
20. Tooky, Portobello Road 1983.
21. Elise, Chelsea 1982.
22. Michelle, Kings Road 1983.
23. Kings Road 1985.
24. At the Acid Dayze Festival, Finsbury Park 1987.
25. At the Acid Dayze Festival, Finsbury Park 1987.
26/27. Kings Road 1984.
28. At a Psychic TV gig on the Thames 1986.
29. At Car Wash, Oxford Street 1988.
30/31. Audience at the Rocky Horror Show, Baker Street 1984.
32. At the Wag Club 1984.
33. Yargo gig at Dingwalls 1987.
34. Tank, Ladbroke Grove 1981.
35. Mark, Soho 1984.
36. Floss, Kings Road 1983.
37. Dave, Kings Road 1985.
38. Robert, Ladbroke Grove 1983.
39. Brixton 1983.
40. Brixton 1983.
41. Yasmine, Kings Road 1984.
42. Kings Road 1981.
43. Dovehouse Green, Chelsea 1982.
44. Gary, Chelsea 1983.
45. Lemmy, Chelsea 1982.
46. Glastonbury Festival 1989.
47. At the Donnington Monsters of Rock Festival 1986.
48. Helena, Chelsea 1982.
49. Nina, Sloane Square 1983.
50. At the Limelight 1987.
51. Christian and friends, Taboo 1986.
52. Suicidal Tendencies fans at Brixton Academy 1988.
53. At Fortissimo, Charing Cross Road 1987.
54/55. At the Acid Dayze Festival, Finsbury Park 1987.
56. Stace and Katy, Kings Road 1981.
57. Carnaby Street 1982.
58. At the Donnington Monsters of Rock Festival 1986.
59. At the Reading Festival 1989.
60. Ladbroke Grove 1981.
61. Robert, Kings Road 1982.
62/63. Sarah and unknown, Valbonne, Soho 1987.
64. Soho 1985
65. Alan, Kings Road 1983.
66. Lowestoft 1986.
67. Donnington Monsters of Rock Festival 1986.
68. Yar, Kings Road 1983.
69. Leicester Square 1982.
70. David, Kings Road 1982.
71. Kings Road 1983.
72. Donnington Monsters of Rock Festival 1986.
73. Donnington Monsters of Rock Festival 1986.
74. Carnaby Street 1980.
75. Alex, Hounslow 1980.
76. Lowestoft 1986.
77. Reading Festival 1989.
78. Jacinta and Chris, Brixton 1984.
79. Fiona and Paul, Chelsea 1982

80. Susie, Kings Road 1982.
81. Biba, Soho 1980.
82. Marula, Kensington 1982.
83. Stephanie, Kensington 1984.
84. Mark, Soho 1983.
85. Mark, Soho 1988.
86. Camden 1987.
87. Kings Road 1983.
88. At Le Beat Route, Soho 1980.
89. Chelsea 1981.
90. Chelsea 1982.
91. Wendy, Chelsea 1983.
92. Chelsea 1983.
93. Haystack, Portobello Road 1981.
94. At Fouberts 1984.
95. Nicola, Taboo 1986.
96. Portobello Road 1981.
97. Kings Road 1983.
98. Near Carnaby Street 1984.
99. Soho 1984.
100. Wendy, Blitz 1980.
101. Jessica, Astral Flight 1984.
102. Linzi, Subway, Leicester Square 193.
103. At Planets, Piccadilly 1982.
104. Siobhan, Wag Club 1986.
105. At the Mud Club, Soho 1987.
106. Spit, Chelsea 1982.
107. Spike, Brixton 1983.
108. Kevin, Margate 1980.
109. Margate 1980.
110/111. At the Alternative Miss World, Brixton 1985.
112. At the Hippodrome, Leicester Square 1985.
113. At a Mutoid Waste Company show, Kentish Town 1987.
114. Jacquie, Kings Road 1982.
115. Soho 1984.
116. Malcolm, Kings Road 1983.
117. Soho 1984.
118. At the Reading Festival 1988.
119. At the Reading Festival 1989.
120. At the Reading Festival 1985.
121. Brockwell Park, Brixton 1984.
122. Kings Road 1984.
123. Soho 1984.
124/125. Suicidal Tendencies fans at Brixton Academy 1988.
126. Hyde Park 1986.
127. Hyde Park 1986.
128. Caresse and Sarah, Psychic TV gig on the Thames 1986.
129. At Le Beat Route, Soho 1980.
130/131. Suicidal Tendencies fans at Brixton Academy 1988.
132. Sharon, Brixton 1983.
133. Dave Brixton 1983.
134. West Ham 1981.
135. West Ham 1981.
136/137. Kings Road 1981.
138. Clapham Common 1985.
139. At the Reading Festival 1987.
140. At Gossips 1982.
141. Rohan and friend, Fortissimo, Charing Cross Road 1987.
142. Michael at the Limelight 1988.
143. Polly at the Batcave, Soho 1982.
144. Soho 1988.
145. Battersea Park 1985.
146. Jodie, Leicester Square 1980.
147. Dave, Ladbroke Grove 1981.
148. Soho 1984.
149. Soho 1984.
150. Neal, Kings Road 1983.
151. Mandy, Sloane Square 1982.
152. Basil and friends, Hounslow Bus Garage 1980.
153. Carnaby Street 1987.
154. At the Camden Palace 1983.
155. At the Camden Palace 1982.
156. At Le Beat Route, Soho 1981.
157. At Le Beat Route, Soho 1981.
160. At Planets, Piccadilly 1981.

Back cover: Dovehouse Green, Chelsea 1981.

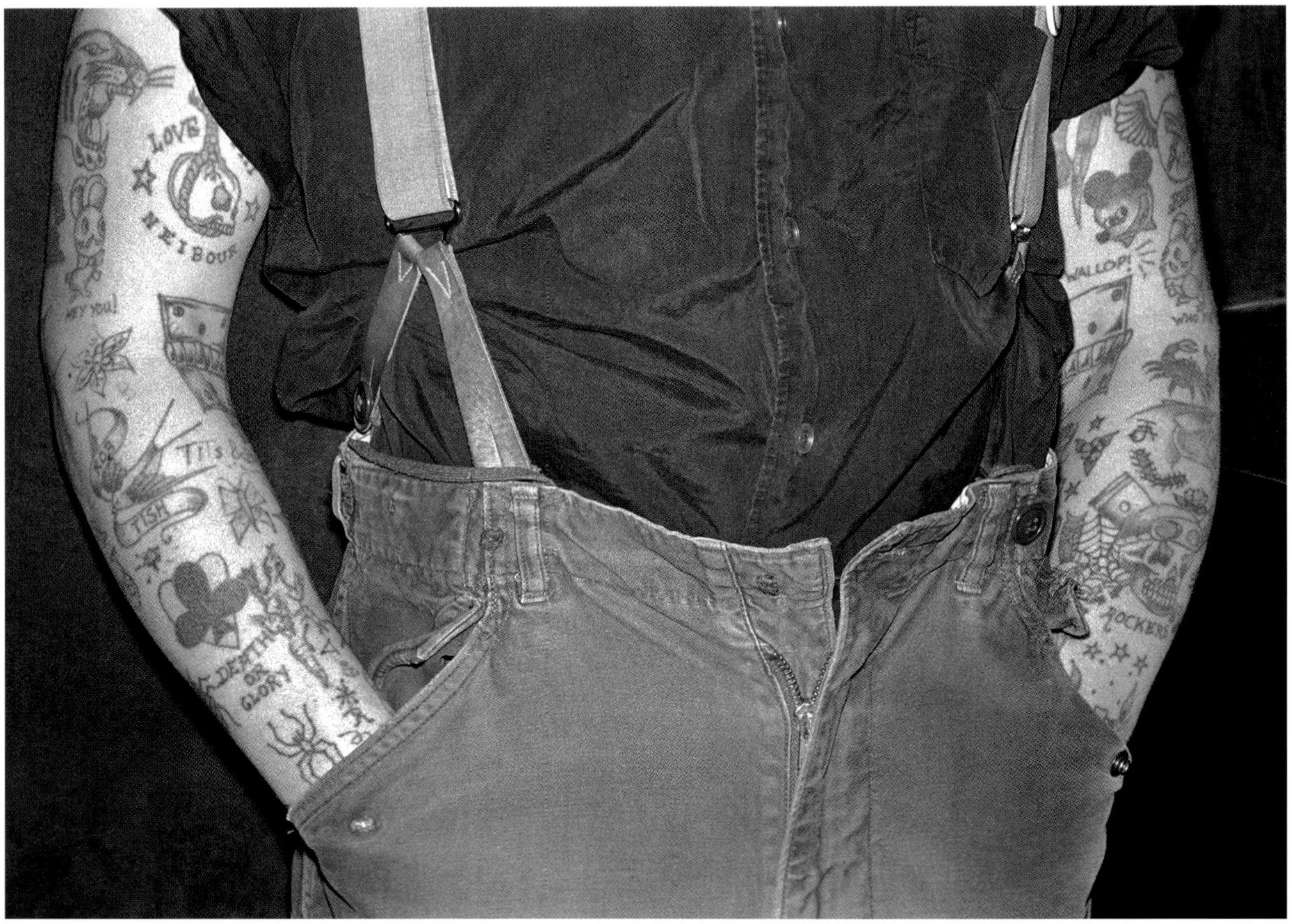

This book is dedicated to my wife Jo-Anne,
without whom it would never have been possible.

I'd also like to thank every one of my subjects for allowing me to photograph them.

Thanks also to Sarah Appelhans, Andrew Bunney, Susan Compo, Steve Davies, Marcus Georgio,
Angela Hill, David Johnson, Carrie Kania, Babette Kulik, Victoria Lukens,
Gordon MacDonald, David Owen, Gary Shove, Ava Stander and Professor Val Williams.